MISANTHROPY

ALSO AVAILABLE FROM BLOOMSBURY

MISANTHROPY

The Critique of Humanity

ANDREW GIBSON

Bloomsbury Academic
An imprint of Bloomsbury Publishing Plc

B L O O M S B U R Y
LONDON · OXFORD · NEW YORK · NEW DELHI · SYDNEY

Bloomsbury Academic

An imprint of Bloomsbury Publishing Plc

50 Bedford Square	1385 Broadway
London	New York
WC1B 3DP	NY 10018
UK	USA

www.bloomsbury.com

BLOOMSBURY and the Diana logo are trademarks of Bloomsbury Publishing Plc

First published 2017

© Andrew Gibson, 2017

British Library Cataloguing-in-Publication Data
A catalogue record for this book is available from the British Library.

ISBN: HB: 978-1-4742-9316-7
PB: 978-1-4742-9317-4
ePDF: 978-1-4742-9315-0
ePub: 978-1-4742-9318-1

Library of Congress Cataloging-in-Publication Data
A catalog record for this book is available from the Library of Congress.

Typeset by Deanta Global Publishing, Services, Chennai, India
Printed and bound in India

To all my family, friends and mentors

'I heartily love John, Peter, Thomas, and so forth. …'

And now I think you see what would become of the world if all men should be wise; to wit it were necessary we got another kind of clay and some better potter.

(ERASMUS, *In Praise of Folly*, trans. John Wilson, 1668)

Respue quod non es: tollat sua munera cerdo:
Tecum habita: noris quam sit tibi curta supellex.

Spit out what isn't you; let the cobbler take back his gifts:
Live with yourself: you will come to know how meagre are your furnishings.

(PERSIUS, Satire IV)

I just want to walk
Right out of this world,
'Cause everybody has a poison heart.

(THE RAMONES)

CONTENTS

ACKNOWLEDGEMENTS

I owe particular debts of gratitude to many relatives, friends, colleagues, students and former students, not least those who pointed me in fertile directions or pulled me up short when I was going too far or getting things wrong. They include Phil Baker, Judith Balso, Andrew Benjamin, Martin Blocksidge, Roy Booth, Jonathan Boulter, Joe Brooker, Jonathan Catherall, Warren Chernaik, Christopher Church, Sandra Clark, Ursula Clayton, Jim Cohen, Thomas Docherty, Jonathan Dollimore, Martin Dzelzainis, Bill Eason, Finn Fordham, Brian Fox, Duncan Fraser, Greg Garrard, Alan Gibson, Thomas Gibson, Harry Gilonis, Elaine Ho, Peter Johnston, Séan Kennedy, Douglas Kerr, Declan Kiberd, Karen Langhelle, Natalie Leeder, Ian Littlewood, Ruth Livesey, Pirjo Lyytikäinen, Vicki Mahaffey, Annaleen Maschelein, Beatrice Michaelis, Martin Middeke, Steven Morrison, Tytti Rantanen, Adam Roberts, Kiernan Ryan, Lenya Samanis, Sam Slote, Liisa Steinby, Yoshiki Tajiri, Jeremy Tambling, Lyn Thomas, Mark Traynor and Colin Wright.

I am especially grateful to Ahuvia Kahane for his generous help with classical sources (he is not of course responsible for any of the uses to which I have put them); and to Anthony Ossa-Richardson and Justin Wintle, who read the whole book in draft, and whose work was conscientious and immensely meticulous, helping me rectify a host of shortcomings. Many heartfelt thanks to Liza Thompson and Frankie Mace at Bloomsbury, who picked the book up and ran with it wholeheartedly, after my initial setbacks; to Ken Bruce and Grishma Fredric for all their hard editorial work; and especially to Holly Hickman, for double-checking.

I owe a serious debt and am very grateful to Bloomsbury's initial readers. One of them suggested that I bolt a politics on to the end of this book. I thought long and hard about doing this. But the book is really partly about not getting as far as a politics. Unlike so many of my contemporaries in the academy, and indeed younger academics, I see no point in taking up a political position or proposing a political theory if it is going to have no effect at all (or none beyond the academy) and cannot conceivably make a serious appeal to any constituency. The main purpose of such theoretical work all too frequently seems to be the psychic (and perhaps the moral) reassurance of the political subject him- or herself, rather than the construction of a significant and viable *praxis*. From my point of view, we might do better for the moment to meditate on what I think of as the pre-political condition, in the stark recognition, not only that it is where we are, but that it is even where we may have to stay. This condition is, objectively, a truth, but saying that by no means necessarily spells absolute disappointment, imminent disaster or feeble capitulation. In a way, my next book, *Modernity and the Political Fix* (Bloomsbury, too), will state the case all over again – but, more paradoxically, in conformity with the reader's suggestion, in clearly political terms; though it will not offer a political theory, but rather a political theology that is also a political memorandum.

I finished this book at the end of 2016, the year of Farage, Brexit and Trump. (I was making my last corrections to the copy-edited text around the time of the Trump victory). Some might feel that recent events partly bear out some of the perspectives I adopt here, but also threaten to make them look redundant. The 'new' populism, however, was always there in the contemporary culture of 'toxic positivity' I indict in my conclusion. Its emergence was a product of that culture and intricately linked to it. The early signs are that the 'new' populist drive will actually be about walling the culture of 'toxic positivity' off from those who threaten to invade and claim a share in it or to incriminate it. In any case, even if the culture goes into a mild recession for a while, that will not mean that it is defunct. Might more intellectuals at least begin honourably to defect from it? We'll see.

Except where otherwise noted, all translations are my own.

INTRODUCTION:
THE IMPOSSIBILITY
OF MISANTHROPY

Between 414 and 411 BC, in Aristophanes' *The Birds* and *Lysistrata* and Phrynicus's *The Recluse*, there are three references to a single, great, dark, misanthropic eminence: Timon. In real life, Timon was apparently an Athenian citizen who treated his friends with lavish generosity, only to have them desert him once his coffers were empty. He was reduced to labouring in the fields. There he discovered gold. His friends, agreeably, promptly returned. Timon, however, threw clods at them. As he did so, he bellowed out his misanthropy, his repudiation of the whole human race, humanity itself, *tout court*. In the late fifth century BC, he became a popular topic of conversation, not least because misanthropy seemed to chime with the mood of Athens at that time.[1] Earlier in the century, in philosophy, literature, architecture and art, Athens had reached glorious heights. It had developed advanced political and social institutions to which we still owe a debt today. But in the later 420s and the 410s, Sparta repeatedly defeated it in battle. In 415, the great Athenian military leader Alcibiades defected; then, in 412, the enemy city allied itself with the Persian Empire. For Athens, the shadows appeared to be rapidly darkening. Finally, in 411, what was in effect an army coup overthrew the rule of democracy. It is precisely at this point in time that Timon begins to loom large in the Athenian imagination. Thereafter, for the Greeks, he was a legend, the paradigmatic hater of mankind, a touchstone and focal point.

The myth of Timon had extraordinary power and tenacity. So much is apparent, for example, more or less two millennia later, in Shakespeare's decision to write a tragedy about it. *Timon of Athens* is roughly the historical tale, and, once undeceived, the fictional Timon's conviction is the same as the real one's: humankind is detestable, for it possesses 'an iron heart'.[2] Indeed, what is remarkable, coming from the pen of Coleridge's 'myriad-minded man',[3] with his exquisitely variegated, endlessly nuanced imagination, is how unrelentingly one-dimensional a character Timon is. It is as though Shakespeare were briefly experimenting with a simplicity otherwise quite foreign to him. Timon spends, with 'an untirable and continuate goodness' (TA, I.i 11, p. 4), then hates, utterly and without restraint. 'The middle of humanity thou never knewest', Apemantus says to him, 'but the extremity of both ends' (TA, IV.iii 300–1, p. 108). Timon is an absolutist: he goes just about as far as it is possible to go with the misanthropic attitude. We shall come across plenty of misanthropic men, and some women, who threatened to flee to the desert to get away from their fellow humans; a number of writers have had a lot of fun with this. But Shakespeare's Timon is Phrynicus's μονότροπος, *monotropos*: he really does flee to the desert, or at least, the wild, where, in the words of one of his former servants, he 'Walks like contempt, alone' (TA, IV.ii 15, p. 87). His misanthropy becomes all-devouring, a profound curse on the 'long sickness/Of health and living' (TA, V.i 186–7, p. 130). Timon remains consistent to the end, as his epitaph shows: '*A plague consume you, wicked caitiffs left!/Here lie I, Timon, who all living men did hate*' (TA, IV.iv 71–2, p. 140). In effect, we could regard him as a benchmark for the rest of our examples in this book.

A benchmark, perhaps, but not a type. In possibly the greatest and certainly the most famous European work on misanthropy, Molière's *Le misanthrope*, the playwright grasps a more basic feature of the misanthropic attitude than Timon can represent: its incoherence. The misanthropist declares a comprehensive rejection of the object of his or her loathing. But, though Molière's misanthropist Alceste asserts that he will 'rompre en visière à tout le genre humain',[4] that he will break violently with the whole of humankind, the complete break is necessarily implausible or unachievable; true misanthropy is finally impossible. This is the case, not least because the categorical misanthropic judgement would mean contempt for all humanity, everyone, including the individual who passes the judgement. Misanthropy, it would seem, is an intellectual attitude that is extremely difficult if not impossible to sustain. In his or her very declaration of misanthropy, the misanthropist stands self-condemned, the prisoner of a fundamental contradiction.

The logic of Alceste's position suggests that he should announce an end to human relations of every kind. In fact, he remains vitally tied to the world he affects to despise, most notably in the case of his love for coquette Celimène. So, too, a principled misanthropy should logically entail a profound self-hatred. But part of Molière's admittedly complex thesis is that Alceste's misanthropy is actually in some degree a form of self-love. This however is precisely not a recognition at which Alceste can arrive. Indeed, his critique of humanity functions on the basis of a kind of willed ignorance as to how far he is included in it and complicit with its failings: his, he thinks, is the 'merit' that should be set apart ('Je veux qu'on me distingue', LM, I.i 62–3, p. 49). Hence the irony that haunts his utterances, conceived of as emanating from a solitary voice of reason. Indeed, we might even think that there is an irony to Alceste's speaking at all. Given that, for the misanthropist, communication must be a pointless effort at connection with a worthless recipient using valueless human tools, should he or she not abjure it? Yet Molière craftily suggests that Alceste is actually charmed by the language in which he articulates himself, a language that he takes to be that of an inner man, characterized by its unique 'frankness' and 'sincerity' (LM, III.v 385–90, p. 126). As even he must concede, then, Alceste has committed himself to an incoherent position. Hence both a pathos and, again, a founding irony: he may repeatedly declare his own desire to run off to a desert. In reality, however, the roots of his needs and identity in a social life are constantly, immediately and vividly evident onstage. Thus Molière sees misanthropy as an intrinsically comic attitude. As his friend Philinte says, punning, comedy accompanies Alceste everywhere ('Partout où vous allez, donne la comédie', LM, I.i 106, p. 52).

Of course, for all Molière's laughter – a laughter he encouraged and that many have shared with him – misanthropy survived. There were also many who felt that Alceste might just be right. His most famous admirer was Jean-Jacques Rousseau. Rousseau took him to be a lover of virtue whose principled intransigence was bound to sound bitter and quarrelsome, because he was pitting himself against a general complaisance itself reflected in Molière's own willingness to pander to the crowd. In Le Philinte de Molière, ou La Suite du Misanthrope (1788), Philippe François Nazaire Fabre d'Eglantine even had a much more Timon-like Alceste, one cleansed of erotic attachments, make it to the wilderness after all, whence he graciously returns to save Philinte from the consequences of his worldliness. The persistence of serious responses to Alceste is indicative. Misanthropy turns out, for all its absurdity to some, to be oddly, wirily durable. Nonetheless, Molière clearly captured something almost irreducible about the misanthropic position, the fact that it seldom if ever quite adds up or makes sense.

There are thus several points to make about misanthropy from the outset. First, though there have certainly been more and less misanthropic philosophers, and indeed Philinte associates Alceste with a 'chagrin philosophe' (LM, I.i 97, p. 52), obviously enough, misanthropy is not a philosophy. If misanthropy is a form of thought, it is not a rigorous but an inconsistent one – inconsistent, that is, or incomplete, always trammelled in the world it pretends to escape. Indeed, in one respect, even Shakespeare's Timon finds this. So successfully does he run from the world that the world runs after him, bringing him the 'plague of company' (TA, IV.iii 353–4, p. 110). He becomes an object of fascination. Alcibiades, Apemantus, the poet and painter, others, all arrive to contemplate a man who dares to pour rude scorn on what they unreflectively assume to be the only life. The misanthropist, it would seem, sets his or her face against the truth that life is irredeemably social. So, too, Rousseau tells the story in his *Confessions* of how, the more he gained a 'reputation for misanthropy', the more he became an object of almost insatiable curiosity. ('My room was never empty of people').[5] Humanity has an uncanny way of roping one back into the fold, willy-nilly. The earliest Syriac anchorites who fled to the isolation of the Quadisha valley (in Lebanon) in the first centuries after Christ, for example, did so only to unleash a copycat phenomenon. They became sufficiently numerous to end up chatting to each other after early morning worship, and eventually forming communities. So, too, the Vietnam veterans hiding out in the wilderness as profiled in the CBS Special Report *The Wall Within* (1988) found themselves chased down by camera crews. Once again, the world they rejected refused to let go, turning the misanthropist into an object of study. Most recently of all, in November 2015, in the Maremma, mushroom pickers discovered Carlos Sanchez Ortiz de Salazar, a doctor from Seville. Ortiz had disappeared in 1995 and finally been declared dead in 2010. Though he told his benefactors he had no wish to live among people, and promptly disappeared again, his condition was soon appropriately diagnosed ('severe long-term depression') and he quickly became the subject of what, incongruously enough, was both a global media feeding frenzy and a search-and-retrieve-for-us mission. The ancient misanthropic drive has a remarkable tenacity, but so, too, does the desire to bring the dog sage to heel. The misanthropist everywhere runs up against the impossibility of a final separation from human life. Bardamu, the protagonist in *Voyage au bout de la nuit*, by one of the great twentieth-century misanthropists, Louis-Ferdinand Céline, may seem to invert what Shakespeare is telling us about Timon when he ironically observes: 'As long as you wanted to remain alive, you'd have to have the air of someone looking for the regiment'.[6] In fact, the point from a certain angle is very much the same.

However, paradoxically, the incoherence of misanthropy by no means disqualifies it from serious attention or makes it less seductive in its appeal or formidable as an object of critique, because it thrives on its very contradictions. Misanthropy is a kind of proto-philosophy or sub-philosophy, a strange form of adulterate but vital thought that may actually have a more stubborn and indomitable life and a broader hold on minds than many philosophies themselves. Hence the range of what I will include under the heading may raise a few eyebrows. Certainly, anyone who comes to this book expecting no more than a gallery of rabid, spitting oddballs will be disappointed. As an incomplete form of thought, misanthropy appears in discrete and fleeting manifestations. It can occur quite randomly and unpredictably, and individual names attach themselves to it. But misanthropy is often not comprehensively identifiable with individuals. It courses through people, cultures, societies in errant flows and fluxes, emerging here and there, rather than being, in the philosophical sense, essential to them. It is an insistence, at once an unstable theoretical formation, a fluid disposition of feeling and a construction in words. As an insistence, it may exhibit certain specific features, be determined in certain specific ways, occur in certain historical, cultural, psychosocial or psychological conditions, appear at certain times and for certain reasons and find its articulation or expression particularly in certain kinds of society or individual and not others. There are certain logics of misanthropy, even if they are partial and fitful.

Whether in people and societies, then, or in works of art and thought, misanthropy occurs as instances, in fits and starts. It may crop up quite pervasively; it seldom does so comprehensively or as the last word. It coexists with other intellectual positions, is interwoven with other emotional attitudes. This, again, is part of Molière's point about Alceste. So, too, if Shakespeare's Timon is a rare imaginative embodiment of misanthropic integrity, Shakespeare himself does not give us misanthropy in a pure form, since Timon himself is a dramatic and poetic representation, if not exactly of an idea, of a structural position within the play, and therefore within a particular configuration of thought in which Timon's misanthropy, though a powerful force, does not seem and cannot be final, since it has to be estimated alongside other positions (Apemantus's rather different kind of misanthropy, the steward's concern and compassion, Alcibiades's righteous 'spleen and fury', TA, III.v 114, p. 76). This indeed is precisely evident in the play, which concludes with Alcibiades reading out Timon's epitaph – and then, in a final brief commentary on it, refusing its implications, or in some sense 'going beyond' it.

*

It is worth emphasizing that the two works we have begun with are plays. Drama is especially well suited to the expression of a misanthropic vision – but also, because of its lack of a mediating voice (a narrator's, for instance) and its generic need for differentiation, variety of character and expression, to leavening it, qualifying its purchase, in other words, to the incompleteness of misanthropy. This is particularly evident in Elizabethan revenge drama and, above all, Jacobean tragedy. The great malcontents and revengers in these plays – Malevole, Hieronimo, Vindice, Bosola, Flamineo – are very often misanthropists or pass misanthropic judgements. Indeed, misanthropy tends at one and the same time to underwrite their cynicism and their role as moral cleansers, the lengths to which they are prepared to go in fulfilling that role. If the world is rotten, then it will necessarily corrupt or have corrupted the revenger, that is the presumption: at best, the revenger can claim that, rotten like the others, he has behaved like them for ends less rotten than theirs. Hence the sublime cheerfulness with which, having begun on the principle that 'to be honest is not to be i'the world' and murderously purged the court, Vindice in Middleton's *The Revenger's Tragedy* accepts his come-uppance. ('We die after a nest of dukes! Adieu').[7]

The misanthropic statements in revenge plays, however, are necessarily dramatic, with all that that implies for possible ironies and reversals. These may be the result of succession in time, but may also be structural. Take Hieronimo, in Kyd's *The Spanish Tragedy*:

> O world, no world, but mass of public wrongs,
> Confused and filled with murder and misdeeds! ...
> How should we term your dealings to be just,
> If you unjustly deal with those that in your justice trust![8]

At this point the effect may seem to be cumulative. Only a few minutes before, in the preceding scene, after being condemned to death, Alexandro has made a very similar pronouncement:

> But in extremes what patience shall I use?
> Nor discontents it me to leave the world,
> With whom there nothing can prevail but wrong. ...
>
>   'Tis heaven is my hope.
> As for the earth, it is too much infect
> To yield me hope of any of her mould.

(ST, III.i 12–13, 35–7, pp. 49–50)

But almost immediately, irony shreds this. The Portuguese ambassador arrives back at court with unexpected news. The vile wolf Villuppo has set Alexandro up; the Viceroy frees him at once. Not surprisingly, this improves his mood. The demonstration that misanthropy can be so dependent on circumstance reflects not only on Alexandro's but, at slightly longer range, on Hieronimo's, too. Yet in fact the irony strikes more comprehensively at Alexandro's failure to trust to fortune than it does at his misanthropy. Alexandro says what he says in circumstances poisoned by hatred, mistrust, inconstancy, betrayal and inconsequential malignity, the general atmosphere being determined by the Viceroy's melancholy. The scene appears to bear Alexandro out, although the irony does not. We might even turn our interpretation round, thinking of Hieronimo's soliloquy as confirming Alexandro's disenchantment, after the brief delusion induced by his good luck.

This is just one particularly striking instance of how far the world about which revenge drama and Jacobean tragedy tell us seems again and again to coincide with the malcontent's judgement, and indeed other characters quite often also share it, or are converted to it. De Flores's declaration, at the very end of Middleton and Rowley's *The Changeling*, that his thrillingly perverted relationship with Beatrice has been his sole and only good – 'I thank life for nothing but that pleasure'; otherwise there was only 'hell'[9] – might seem like a drastic reaction to the fact that his life is now over. But what other goods has the play made evident and given flesh to? The 'fellowship' of man is only 'a treacherous, bloody friendship' (TC, V.ii 3–4, p. 80). Change the terms a little, and, as the play repeatedly says, the same applies in sexual relations, on both sides of the gender divide. All in all, Isabella's view of Lollio's bedlam – 'Why, here's none but fools and madmen' (TC, III.ii 15–16, p. 37) – seems intended to sum up the play and, beyond it, the world it encapsulates.

In general, these plays present us with people desperately at the mercy of ferocious, ungovernable, black and destructive passions. Lust, rage, envy, unprincipled ambition, spontaneous combustions of mad violence and, above all, the imperative of wholesale and indeed extreme vengeance, these are the norms. Other values that might serve as a counterweight – family, for example; see the outbreak of fratricidal aggression and its necessary consequence, precipitate murder, in John Webster's *The White Devil*[10] – are snowflakes in the general conflagration (the consuming fire being a metaphor that recurs from play to play). The trouble is that people are changelings, in the original sense of the word, according to the OED, 'one given to change' (interestingly, it also formerly implied imbecility). The title of Middleton and Rowley's play is not a chance matter; nor is the fact that the word 'change' or 'changed' occurs nine times in the last twenty-five lines. People are categorically unworthy of trust, because they do not know and cannot understand or get to grips with what may erupt from within them. To adapt Fabritio in Middleton's *Women Beware Women*, they run mad, and 'have no reason for't for aught [one can] perceive'.[11] They are, in the full, rich sense of another repeated word, at bottom wanton. It is impossible to decree a limit to the unpredictable, dismaying havoc this may cause.

Yet this kind of vision seldom congeals into uncompromising misanthropy. Most of the relevant dramatists seek at least to pluck a brand or two from the burning. Admittedly, the rescue job may yield only modest gains: 'Our mother turned, our sister true', says Vindice (RT, V.iii 156, p. 415), providing what is in effect a final inventory, a statement of the play's moral assets, as he is borne off to speedy execution. But his own last-ditch efforts alone make the 'turning' possible when both women are tending otherwise, with the concluding bloodbath helpfully ensuring that there is no need to pursue the issue further. Indeed, given the fact that Middleton seems to have been a rather rigorous Calvinist, he quite possibly felt that he had saved as much as he decently could – certainly more than from the inferno of *Women Beware Women* – in the teeth of what was otherwise a universal damnation. Nonetheless, in revenge drama, the misanthropic circle does not often quite close. Sometimes, indeed, it closes only to open up again. In John Marston's *The Malcontent*, the snarling figure of Malevole, the deposed Duke of Genoa, surviving in disguise amidst the corrupted power of his former court, supposes that the chance of finding a man who loves 'virtue only for itself' in a 'world most vile' is one in ten million.[12] Though the sample the play provides does not run to such numbers, it comprehensively bears him out. It would seem that 'depraved nature stamps in hardest steel' (TM, II.iii 49, p. 43). Furthermore, other characters – Pietro, Mendoza – increasingly share Malevole's view. As misanthropists elsewhere have occasionally observed, misanthropy starts to spread, and even becomes epidemic. In more ways than one, as Malevole says himself, the world appears to be going to the devil. Yet the savage apocalypse that we expect is not forthcoming. As a revenger, Malevole turns out to be moderate and placable. Thanks to his new-found magnanimity and forgiveness, Pietro, Ferneze and Aurelia not only survive but are regenerated. Misanthropy, it seems, has produced a desire to get beyond, and even to disprove, it.

Some may find this rather abrupt turnabout crude and unconvincing. However, elsewhere, there is also a very special finesse to revenge drama and Jacobean tragedy. This is to a large extent a question of the extraordinary sophistication with which it thinks in terms of 'degrees of evils' (WD, IV.ii 57, p. 80). The human world is composed of devils, white devils and intermediate shades of devil. This is part of what *The White Devil* tells us. Here again the malcontent (Flamineo) casts a long shadow over the whole play, serves in part as an ironic commentary on its world, his ineffably disabused tone making a harsh worldly wisdom seem like a wholly plausible, necessary attitude and yet peremptory (not least because self-interested), throttling the possibility of believing differently from the start. In this respect, the play itself is like the 'dead bodies' to which Monticelso refers as 'begg'd at gallows/and wrought upon by surgeons, to teach man/Wherein he is imperfect' (WD, III.ii 96–8, p. 55), and begins as well as ends in deathliness. Everyone is deeply tainted and there is no escaping taint. That seems to be the premise on which the play proceeds. But there are those, notably Vittoria, who, even while sunk in their corruption, can also lift up their heads. See in particular – 'brave spirit' of a 'counterfeit jewel' (WD, III.ii 139–40, p. 57) – her compelling gravity and dignity during her arraignment, induced as it is by a mixture of guilt and a politic desire to lie about her misdeeds, not least because her accusers are so much worse and more false than she is. The scene might have been constructed specifically to drag us steadily towards misanthropy, but not let us tip over the edge.

But the superlative example of the kind of ambiguity at stake, teetering on the brink of misanthropy without succumbing to it, almost but not quite wishing that 'th'estate of the world were now undone', in Macbeth's phrase,[13] is Webster's masterwork *The Duchess of Malfi*. The complications of its characterization and plot to one side, *The Duchess of Malfi* pits the moral grandeur of the Duchess herself against that most sombre, meditative and articulate of malcontents, Bosola. We know who Bosola is at once; in Delio's words,

> The only court-gall: yet I observe his railing
> Is not for simple love of piety:
> Indeed he rails at those things which he wants,
> Would be as lecherous, covetous, or proud,
> Bloody, or envious, as any man,
> If he had means to be so.[14]

Bosola does not so much 'rail', however, as everywhere caustically observe, and he is well aware that he is himself implicated as an object of his own disgust, which, in any case, the play largely suggests that he is right to feel. Indeed, he rises above the others in his reflective attitude towards it. Yet finally Bosola is inexcusable; inexcusable because, while he can perceive the exception to the misanthropic rule, he misanthropically assumes, not only that it must be doomed, but that he must act according to that assumption. Hence he cannot take its side, but rather becomes the instrument of its persecution. He is in that respect the moral victim of his own pessimism.

The exception is the Duchess (and her steward Antonio, whom she stoops to marry, with disastrous consequences). 'In what a shadow, or deep pit of darkness', asks Bosola, 'Doth, womanish and fearful, mankind live' (DM, V.v 100–1, p. 101)? By the end of the play, the question seems appropriate enough. But 'womanish' is ironic. *The Duchess of Malfi* disproves Bosola's terms in one sole respect – the existence of a fearless woman. The Duchess's towering presence ensures that the misanthropic dimension to the play is never close to being comprehensive. Yet in another respect she actually confirms and even enhances the play's misanthropy, insofar as, like Bosola, she herself implicitly accepts a misanthropic logic according to which, even as she embarks on it, her progress will be catastrophic: 'Wish me good speed', she says to Cariola, as she determines to marry Antonio,

> For I am going into a wilderness,
> Where I shall find nor path, nor friendly clew
> To be my guide.
>
> (DM, I.ii 277–80, p. 18)

The condition of the exception can only be a cruel lostness. By the third act, the Duchess finds herself standing 'As if a mine, beneath my feet, were ready/To be blown up' (DM, III.ii 156–7, p. 48). Hence the extraordinary intimacy that develops between her and Bosola. Both believe in the absolute reality of the unregenerate world he represents and to which she, in her 'spirit of greatness, or of woman' (DM, I.ii 417, p. 23), refuses to belong ('I account this world a tedious theatre,/ For I do play a part in't, 'gainst my will', DM, IV.i 83–4, p. 66). Both therefore, in a way, conspire in her mortification. There is no appeal against her fellow humans, as she makes clear in her great speech shortly before her death; she must suffer as profoundly and hopelessly as those at the bottom of the heap, the less than or marginally human. Her terminal melancholy, furthermore, is sane:

> Th'heaven o'er my head seems made of molten brass,
> The earth of flaming sulphur, yet I am not mad.
> I am acquainted with sad misery,
> As the tann'd galley-slave is with his oar.

Necessity makes me suffer constantly,
And custom makes it easy.

(DM, IV.ii 26–30, p. 68)

From others she can expect nothing. 'Call for help', Cariola urges her, as her executioners approach, to which she replies, 'To whom, to our next neighbours? They are mad-folks' (DM, IV.ii 193–5, pp. 73–4). In the play, this is literally the case; but Webster's meaning is more than literal.

*

The opening sequence in Act III i–ii of *The Spanish Tragedy* epitomizes an ambivalent relation to misanthropy that is quite characteristic of the revenge plays. More significantly in this context, since the point is that there is a misanthropic insistence or discourse within the genre, but one that, if not cancelled out, is not quite confirmed as an all-encompassing truth either, it also captures an aporia at the very heart of misanthropy itself. Misanthropy is a flawed, uneven, partial or sporadic thought. Some of the names and titles in the book may surprise readers, and there will no doubt be disagreement with my selections. Surely Jean Rhys is not exactly misanthropic? The man who gave us Tom Sawyer, really? Certain readers may also feel that, on occasions, the book has simplified complex texts. In Plato's *Phaedo*, Socrates objects to misanthropy on the grounds that it is simple-minded where, as moral creatures, human beings are complex ('few are the good and few the evil … the great majority are in the interval between them').[15] But the argument that follows is not supposed to be at all simple, and if it has occasionally simplified particular subjects of discussion, in intention, at least, this is in the interest of a large, nuanced, complex pattern that responds to the equivocal status of misanthropy itself.

In any case, if, on the one hand, calling anyone a misanthropist is probably in some degree a simplification, on the other, in a novel, a novelist, a philosopher, a tradition and so on, misanthropy nonetheless has a regularity or structure to it, though not one that pervades or informs the whole of a thought. Its emphases are relatively homogeneous and recurrent. Misanthropy is not just the *Weltschmerz* I feel when a man in a white van cuts me up on the South Circular at 5 pm on a dreary autumn day. It may not be a philosophy, but it aspires in that direction. A grumpy mood does not. Indeed, it is possible to go further, and suggest that, in its lack of rational finality and the impossibility of its historical completion, misanthropy even indicates a path that philosophy might take rather more often. In the wake of the various recent deconstructions, we may wonder whether the rationality that underwrites Molière's perception of Alceste's contradictions as comic and ironic need be our basis for judgement. Otherwise, if there is a problem with Moliere's play, it is that, in his urbanity, he seems not to have entertained the thought that the incompleteness of misanthropy need not necessarily disqualify it, but, hypothetically at least, might rather just specify the conditions under which one is most likely to think most tellingly, those of a creature clinging to life in spite of its better knowledge.

What may be peculiarly relevant is the fact that, in consulting people about *Misanthropy*, I was struck, first by the general interest in the topic, and secondly by how frequently my interlocutors humorously suggested that I should begin with or at least include them. Both responses seemed to me partly to reflect how far, for many people, there is something oddly anomalous, familiar but unresolved, in the idea of misanthropy, something that remains to be thought through in it. This book attempts to think with, about, for and against misanthropy. It is specifically structured round a set of contras and one of pros. Thus, in particular, on the one hand, misanthropy seems open to question as repeatedly the product of anti- or undemocratic cultures (or cultures in which democracy is coming under threat, like Timon's Athens). It also tends to go together with a problematic and even diseased attitude to the body, and its generalizing discourse leaves it vulnerable to the obvious stricture that its generalizing claims are in fact historically determined. These are major objections. However, on the other hand, I also ask whether certain forms of misanthropy – the misanthropy of the terminally defeated, the misanthropy that emerges out of or along with (yet another) new set of progressivisms, like the misanthropy of modern women, and the misanthropy that doggedly opposes boosterism, 'talking up' – do not themselves enter certain reservations about any too facile assumption that we can by now consign misanthropy to the historical dustbin. Indeed, in my final chapter, I look at how the logic of my arguments against misanthropy might suggest that contemporary culture or, at least, contemporary Western culture, ought to have left misanthropy behind, declared its obsolescence; then ask in detail whether it has done so, and even has any right to see itself thus.

My omission, however, of one particular argument against misanthropy may seem disquieting and even shocking: the argument from love. The trouble is, however, that no evidence has ever been forthcoming of the possibility of a durable, universal or even wide-ranging human love of a kind that would have major historical and political consequences, thereby rendering misanthropic suspicion null and void. But otherwise love is perfectly reconcilable with misanthropy. 'I hate and detest that animal called man', wrote the greatest misanthropist of them all, Jonathan Swift, 'though I heartily love John, Peter, Thomas, and so forth'.[16] This classic statement is not an example of Swiftian derangement. It is rather a more banal reflection of how love, if sometimes a very intense form of continuing connection with humanity, can also be, perhaps quite often is, an extremely minimal one. Indeed, one might even wonder how much bourgeois love and equally the contemporary notion of 'partnership' have been more or less surreptitiously founded on precisely this double attitude.

The major sources of and influences on Western misanthropic tradition have been various. They include the Stoics, especially Seneca, and the Bible, notably the Old Testament prophets (Isaiah, Jeremiah) and St Paul, and Eastern influences like Manichaeanism. But three in particular stand out: the Cynic philosophers from Antisthenes to Bion, inventor of the diatribe, and their legacy as far as the era of the Emperor Julian, the key figure being Diogenes (412–323 BC); Roman satire, chiefly Persius and Juvenal, in the first hundred years of the Empire; and St Augustine. I shall focus the discussion on four themes that will repeatedly be present in what follows: *saeva indignatio*; total depravity (as rooted in original sin); the exception; and the *méchants* and the *complaisants*. Two pairs of terms are common in misanthropic writings. First, the world is composed of knaves and fools: gull, swindle, cozen or be the prey of those who do. That is the way of things, which means that one either plays an unappetizing role and prospers, or plays another and becomes a hapless victim. The second is less of a binary, because the opposites partly coincide: in Alceste's terms – according to Erasmus, they were in fact originally Timon's[17] – there are two types of people in the world, the *méchants* or *malfaisants*, and the *complaisants* (LM, 1.1 119–20, p. 53), those who get up to wicked tricks and those who fail to resist or are complicit with them. In misanthropic discourse at large, this equates with wealth (the 'vomit of fortune', said Diogenes),[18] power and fame on the one hand, and those who placidly go along with them or acquiesce in their operations on the other.

Misanthropy as such was not one of the most prominent themes of the Cynics. But it was a predictable consequence of other aspects of their thought (and their practice; what the Cynics did was in some ways at least as important as what they thought). In one of Diogenes's supposed letters, the philosopher declares:

> Well, I wish that everyone would turn to philosophy and be purged of stupidity. As it is, though, it may be that only people of our persuasion will die out, while the rest of the world, unconverted, will go on breeding. But if the human race were to die out, would that be any more lamentable than if wasps or flies became extinct? Such scruples only show the failure of people to see things for what they really are.[19]

The first-century Bithynian Dio Chrysostom, who adopted the Cynic regimen and is one of the best sources of information about the Cynics, is especially clear about one particular 'failure' (or irrationality) in question. Indeed, he helpfully grasps it as ironically fundamental to most human life, just as, for Molière, the irrationality of misanthropy is to misanthropy itself. The trouble with humans is that they endlessly multiply the very evils they are seeking to escape. They cannot stay still. They have just as much compulsion to proliferate, to complicate and add to things, as they do to increase, to reproduce. But that weakens as it strengthens them, continually causing problems even as it solves them; indeed, the solutions themselves breed more problems. Take medicine, for example:

> Humans ... clung desperately to life by resorting to various means of cheating death; and all the same few managed to reach old age. They lived with a host of complaints the majority of which don't even have a name. Since earth does not produce medicinal plants to cure them all they are forced to submit to cautery and the knife. Chiron, Asclepius and the sons of Asclepius, for all their powers of healing, could not offset the ill effects of their patients' pleasant vices. ... Men crowded into the cities for mutual defence against outsiders, but then turned on each other and committed the foulest crimes, as if that were their real motive for congregating. ... The fact is, all man's

ingenuity and advances in technology were at best mixed blessings in the lives of later generations. (CP, pp. 96–7)

Dio applies this kind of logic to various aspects of human life. The paradox is, he thinks, the very origin of all our disorders, as it is of all the disorder we create, of ordinary, universal human unhappiness. One should categorically distrust human beings precisely because they are thus disposed, but will not grasp the fact. It is therefore appropriate enough that, in what is almost the most famous anecdote in Cynic annals, Diogenes is patrolling the sunny streets with 'lighted lamp in hand', saying, '"I'm looking for a man"' (CP, p. 35). A real human being – the Cynics included women, notably the remarkable Hipparchia – is extremely hard if not impossible to find, since humans are almost invariably disabled by Dio Chrysostom's founding double bind.

At the heart of this line of thought lies the Cynic valuation of nature and simplicity as opposed to luxury and complication or sophistication, which 'twist everything from its natural use' (CP, p. 9). This was partly founded on a philosophical decision, a question, for the Cynics, of living in truth and, in Diogenes Laertius's phrase, of defining 'the goal of man as life in accordance with virtue' (CP, p. 12). As such, it involved a rejection of solemnly grandiose ideas and philosophical quibbling alike. Diogenes refused to take theoretical debates seriously, even showing his disrespect for Plato. But it was also political, a question of social misery and violated justice: 'Consider at what price they're acquired', says the Cynic in Lucian's dialogue 'The Cynic', of luxury and 'unnecessary complication',

> in terms of trouble, pain and danger – or rather in terms of blood, death and shattered lives, not just because many people die at sea searching for these luxury goods or ruin their health manufacturing them, but because they are the source of so much conflict among you, setting friend against friend, child against parent, even wife against husband. (CP, p. 7)

Given so much social disaster, it was important to resist its stupid obfuscation, the justifications for such a world that everyone else seemed automatically and thoughtlessly to rehearse. 'Nature [*phusis*] is mighty', says one of the letters of Diogenes, 'and, since it has been banished from life by opinion [*doxa*], it is what we restore for the salvation of mankind'.[20] Hence the Cynic motto, 'deface the currency': defile general opinion whether social, political, philosophical, religious, ethical or just as expressed in ordinary, run-of-the mill, conventional chatter.

For the Cynics, scorn of *doxa*, the everyday notions that, more or less placidly, incessantly do the rounds, what George Orwell called 'the smelly little orthodoxies which are [forever] contending for our souls',[21] was an absolute principle. This went hand in hand with 'the Cynic model of a naturally free and autonomous self'.[22] As Mikhail Bakhtin expressed the point, the Cynic refused 'to be incarnated in the flesh of existing sociohistorical categories', those by which other people organized their lives.[23] This partly involved παρρησία, *parrhesia*, freedom of speech, in a sense little known to us now, though it was one of the crucial sources of the satirical tradition (Juvenal, Lucian, Erasmus, More, Rabelais and Swift are merely some of those who refer back to it). The Cynics said what they felt it was necessary to say, irrespective of any and all social shibboleths. They were also notoriously shameless. Antisthenes declared that they 'welcomed' ignominy (CP, p. 17); theirs was a will to scandal. They behaved in public without forethought, using 'any place for any purpose',[24] and barked at their fellow human beings without forethought, too. They entertained a complete disrespect for public norms. According, at least, to his most eminent early biographer, Diogenes farted, urinated, masturbated and shat in public.[25] He refused 'the ontological basis of social conventions',[26] says Derek Krueger (if in a phrase Diogenes himself might have laughed to scorn). His body 'was out of step with the world as a whole'.[27] As A. A. Long puts the point, Cynicism was not just a philosophy but a radical practice, without which it was mere pretence.[28] This is nature, a defecating Diogenes in effect said, whereas the dirty stuff that other men get up to is not. People found Diogenes revolting, but he equally found them so. It was precisely because he or she was happy to be disgusting in public that the Cynic became known as such, κυνικός, *cynikos*, the dog sage, dog-like. For some, it meant being incapable of proper humanity. But the Cynics were calling in question what being properly human meant. As Antisthenes said, from a Cynic perspective, the 'few good men' had to fight 'all the bad ones' (CP, p. 17). Their public performances were part of how they did so.

It was no accident that the Cynics emerged when they did. The Greece they knew was a society whose increasingly affluent and luxurious culture existed at the apex of a pyramidal social structure that reflected gross and alarming social inequalities.[29] Yet the fact did not appear to disturb those who had not reached the apex. This, as much as anything else, is what charges Cynic misanthropy and aggression. On the one hand, the philosopher has to show his contempt for eminence, obscene riches, sheer power, empty fame. The classic Diogenes anecdote as related by Plutarch tells of his encounter with an almighty Alexander otherwise feted by 'statesmen and philosophers':

> But when Diogenes took not the slightest notice of him … Alexander paid the man a visit himself. There he found him lounging in the sun. … The prince greeted him and put to him the question whether there was anything that he could do for him. 'Yes', said the philosopher, 'shift a bit out of my sun'. (CP, p. 31)

The philosopher was telling Alexander that there were better, simpler things to care about than endless conquest. But equally, it was necessary to oppose all those who, simply through their inertia, underwrote the Alexanders. Hence Diogenes walked into a theatre as everyone else was coming out, and when asked why, said, 'This … is what I practise doing all my life'.[30] The determination to head in the opposite direction to everyone else was a Cynic habit: Sinope condemned Diogenes to exile. When someone mentioned it to him, he replied, 'And I them … to home-staying'.[31] As Lucian's Cynic says, Diogenes despised 'the moral coin of the masses', because they nursed 'ambitions' that were not 'worth emulating' (CP, pp. 9, 29). He 'disapproved of all that they said and did'.[32] This, the face to face with power on the one hand, and complicity on the other, the *méchants* and the *complaisants*, is integral to Cynic misanthropy.

By the time of the Roman Empire, Diogenes was another figure of almost mythical proportions, his asceticism and his shamelessness both the stuff of legend, yet Cynicism had lost some of its interest. Not surprisingly, the ways of imperial Rome sparked the Cynic tradition back to life, but in circumstances that made its existence much more precarious. Set alongside the great leviathan that was the Empire, and the extraordinary opulence that pumped into Rome from its hinterlands, the Cynic concept of the natural life was likely to seem merely negligible. Furthermore, in Imperial Rome, political circumstances were more extreme than in Diogenes's Athens, and the condition of Cynics was correspondingly riskier. This was the case, not least, because they associated themselves rather closely with aristocrats who still harboured Republican sympathies, in effect constituting a 'philosophical opposition'.[33] Whatever Diogenes's seeming indifference to Alexander's greatness, Alexander had admired him. In Satire XIV, Juvenal actually reminds us of this, as he holds Diogenes's asceticism up approvingly in contrast to the Roman *nouveaux riches*.[34] But under the Julio-Claudian dynasty (Augustus, Tiberius, Caligula, Claudius, Nero, 27 BC–68 AD) and the Flavian dynasty (from the Year of the Four Emperors through Vespasian and Titus to Domitian, 69–96 AD), the Emperors routinely banished Cynics (and Stoics). Nero drove the Cynic Demetrius from Rome. Vespasian did so a second time, after which Demetrius disappears from history. Vespasian also had Cynics flogged, and even one beheaded. Given a series of often brutal, paranoid and tyrannical rulers who presided over a world of purges, tortures, conspiracies, assassinations, arbitrary cruelties, mass executions of suspected enemies, poisonings and other suspicious deaths, sumptuous debaucheries, outlandish and barbarous practices of many descriptions, sexual and other, and a vast squandering of money and resources (under Caligula, gladiators' lives were auctioned to save Rome from bankruptcy), no sincere Roman Cynic could hope to survive very comfortably, supposing he or she survived at all. When power had assumed such monstrous and unscrupulous forms, the Cynic principle of speaking truth to it seemed irrelevant. This was hardly a world that Diogenes could have foreseen.

Thus, in Imperial Rome, misanthropy takes on a more ferocious form than the reflective and sometimes ironical modes of Greek philosophy could accommodate. It appears as wholesale and explicit moral denunciation, and its tone is that of *saeva indignatio*, the savage indignation of the satirist. The Cynics tended to be *provocateurs*. By contrast, Persius and Juvenal are lacerators of what they take to be a universal corruption. In *The History of the Decline and Fall of the Roman Empire*, without referring to them, Edward Gibbon provides a superb account of why they might have felt they had to do so:

> It is almost superfluous to enumerate the unworthy successors of Augustus. Their unparalleled vices, and the splendid theatre on which

they were acted, have saved them from oblivion. The dark unrelenting Tiberius, the furious Caligula, the feeble Claudius, the profligate and cruel Nero, the beastly Vitellius, and the timid inhuman Domitian, are condemned to everlasting infamy. During fourscore years (excepting only the short and doubtful respite of Vespasian's reign), Rome groaned beneath an unremitting tyranny, which exterminated the ancient families of the republic, and was fatal to almost every virtue, and every talent, that arose in that unhappy period.[35]

In line with the contemporary 'revisionist' tendency to help us lead untroubled lives by making our history easier to live with, recent historians have occasionally striven to make one or other of the early emperors, if not exactly cuddly, then less luridly Satanic figures, dwelling on Nero's theatrical talents and his knowledge of Roman history and mythology, or presenting Domitian as an efficient, if ruthless and despotic, administrator with very considerable managerial skills.[36] But whatever the period in question, the revisionists tend to grant only a limited weight to the relevant imaginative literature. Persius and Juvenal saw matters rather as did Gibbon, recognizing precisely a political logic 'fatal to almost every virtue, and every talent' – but homing in, above all, on the question of what a society looks like when both virtue and talent seem dead.

*

When W. H. Auden wrote, in 1939, that 'intellectual disgrace/stares from every human face',[37] he was thinking of a state of shame that was deeply moral, political and intellectual together. He was also asserting that it was not simply explainable in terms of an evil few manipulating an innocent or at least misguided many in spite of the alarm of the good. Everyone was involved, and it showed in everyone. That is how Persius, who was writing in the age of Nero, and Juvenal, who seems to have begun writing under Domitian, but only completed and certainly only published his satires during what both Machiavelli and Gibbon thought of as the 'golden age' of the Roman Empire, the century of the Nervan-Antonian dynasty that began with Nerva, Trajan and Hadrian, saw their Rome.[38] The great source of Roman satire was Lucilius, in the second century BC. Alas, only fragments of his work survive – but enough of them to show that Lucilius thought of satire as taking the whole of the human scene on board:

But as it is, from morning to night, on holiday and workday,
the whole people and the senators too all alike
bustle about in the forum and on no occasion leave it.
To one and the same pursuit and artifice all devote themselves:
to be able to cheat with cunning, to fight cleverly,
to struggle charmingly, to pretend to be a good man,
to lay a trap, as if everyone is everyone's enemies.

'Oh the cares of human beings! Oh how much emptiness there is in things! [quantum est in rebus inane]'.[39] We are not far from the world of Ecclesiastes – and Hobbes.

'Lucilius crunched the city', writes Persius.[40] Both Persius and Juvenal pay homage to Lucilius, invoke and inherit from him. Persius attacks the general decadence in Roman morals in the Neronian era. The Romans have subordinated every other value to money. Furthermore, the lust for gold joins forces with the compulsion intrinsic to the 'guilty flesh' that 'drives us to gouge pearl from shell and rip/the veins of glowing ore out of the raw slag' (Sii, 66–7, p. 144) in a quest for ever-increasing luxury, with disastrous consequences. Persius particularly dwells on what the flesh thus makes of itself. His satires drip loathing for the grotesquely indulged body. Take Natta, for example:

Vice has made *him* insensible; thick fat has surrounded his conscience; he has no feelings of guilt, no notion of loss.

Lying on the bottom, he has ceased to send any bubbles to the surface.

(Siii, 32–4, p. 145)

But virtually all will choose the sybaritic life, given half a chance, because this is what the guilty flesh urges upon us. The result, however, is that 'EVERY MAN JACK HAS AN ASS'S EARS!' (Si, 121, p. 141; Persius was clearly thinking of Midas's association with gold, as well as his punishment by Apollo).

Juvenal shares many themes with Persius, but his is a later age sunk deeper in a more profound and various moral slough, and he has an appetite for particulars that is worthy of a novelist like Joyce. He follows Persius in excoriating wholesale bribery and corruption and condemning a rotting ruling class. He shares Persius's disdain for a society besotted with money ('Of all gods it's Wealth that compels our deepest/Reverence', SSi, 112–13, p. 6). But, above all, he inherits and vastly extends Persius's contempt for social trash on the make, prospering as the tiny minority of more decent Romans do not because it understands money, but also because it is not impeded or distracted by any other considerations. It is heedless of the fact that money corrupts personal relations, and content with undifferentiated forms of pleasure. Meanwhile, the Roman slums and their abject poverty continue to spread, thugs roam the streets, illegally constructed buildings collapse and fires rage. But one can hardly expect better of Rome. The aristocracy have abandoned such virtue as it could ever muster, the people roar only for bread and circuses – and in between them come the forgers, informers, gigolos, bent lawyers, pimps, con men, malingerers, astrologers, adulterers, wheedling courtiers, greedy freeloaders, flash-git shysters and gladiators (sportspersons) favoured by power. As he walks or rather scurries apprehensively round Rome's streets, Juvenal indeed sees disgrace on every face. The decent few – the exceptions – writers, scholars, teachers, principled advocates, honourable military men, can scarcely struggle on.

It is hardly surprising, then, that Juvenal should be given to savage indignation, that an electrifying rage should pulsate through the satires (though he becomes more moderate, or at least ironical, as they progress). But what both Persius and Juvenal understand very well is that the social scene that they hold in such contempt is a manifestation of and inseparable from an arbitrary and despotic power. When Persius satirizes contemporary poets and their clichéd, thoroughly conventional box of classical tricks, he is particularly thinking of those who clustered round Nero. When, in Satire IV, Juvenal wants to expose the vacuity of Roman political structures and social life, together, he stages a discussion of the fate of a giant turbot – as held by Domitian, chilly, sadistic tyrant, with the assembled grovellers that make up his Privy Council, quailing 'beneath the Emperor's hatred', their 'drawn white faces' reflecting 'that great and perilous "friendship"' (SSiv, 73–5, p. 26; intellectual disgrace, indeed). As Persius puts matters, 'Sadistic lust with its dagger/ Dipped in fiery poison invites dictators to crime' (Siii, 35–6, p. 145). The corruption of the people is both their refuge from the horror of the regime to which they are implicitly subscribing and a token of their craven failure to resist it.

Present-day critics have complained about Juvenal's misogyny, his homophobia, anti-Semitism and racism. Indeed, they have sometimes been so embarrassed by such attitudes (as they take them to be) that they have argued he was inventing personae, as if nice Juvenal donned nasty mask in order to fulfil his principal intention, which was to satirize prejudice.[41] But they miss the point. Juvenal castigates everyone, emperors, Romans, men and heterosexuals, too. He takes aim, indiscriminately, at a social order he sees as rotten from the very top to the very bottom. The critics merely show how remote our mindset, with its liberal concern for identity politics and partial interests, is from that of the great satirists, who insist on a misanthropic critique of the whole. As Peter Green says, particularly in his early satires, Juvenal was a 'flay-all' (SS, p. xvii). So, too, was Persius, if in somewhat less specific terms.

Nor will it do to suppose that both satirists were just concerned with very particular historical cultures, and would otherwise have let people off the hook. Persius refers us to pre-Neronian times – Caligula's farcical German campaign, for example, where the Emperor avoided having his army fight, then dressed up some of his own Gauls as prisoners to persuade other people of his triumph – stretching his account of venality and frivolity back in imperial history. But it is Juvenal, above all, who thickens the historical picture, making it hard, on occasions, for us to tell in which period a satirical scene is set. He was familiar with his friend Tacitus's often scathing account of the Julio-Claudians, and illustrates what he has to say with fairly prolific allusions to the reigns of Tiberius, Caligula, Claudius, Nero, Otho and, more subversively, Julius and Augustus Caesar. Indeed, though the Nervan dynasty may have seen the beginning of a 'golden age', things certainly got better for Juvenal under it, and the tone of his satire changes accordingly, Trajan and Hadrian do not come off lightly in his hands. What seems to be praise for Hadrian at the beginning of Satire VII is carefully judged but distinctly ironic. Satire XVI attacks the much-abused privileges of the military, some of which Hadrian had conferred. As Juvenal slyly notes, Trajan and Hadrian continued with Domitian's tradition of using spies and informers against enemies and carrying out summary executions. In general, the *Satires* suggest that the social phenomena he most heartily despised remained the same under the new dynasty.

Certainly, over the *Satires* as a whole hangs Domitian, whom Juvenal recalls spending hours catching flies and stabbing them to death. The detail captures the very spirit of, or, rather, the hopelessly inane lack of spirit in, Domitian's Rome. But, as Gilbert Highet pertinently remarks, Juvenal conceived of satire as intrinsically unconfined, supposing that its purview both went back a long way beyond 'the fiendish emperor of yesterday' and looked ahead to 'perhaps another monster tomorrow'.[42] Tomorrow and tomorrow and tomorrow, Juvenal might have growled:

> To these habits of ours there's nothing more, or worse, to be added by posterity: our grandsons will share our deeds, our longings.
>
> (SSi, 147–8, p. 7)

As far as he was concerned, the Satires mocked the general way of things as it had prevailed historically, was prevailing now and would prevail in time to come:

> All human endeavours, men's prayers, fears, angers, pleasures, joys and pursuits, make up the mixed mash of my book.
>
> (SSi, 85–6, p. 5)

He toyed with the idea that, as the Sybilline prophecies of AD 19 and 64 had predicted, the story of mighty Rome was bound to end in disaster: 'Infection spread this plague,/ and will spread it further still' (SSii, 78–9, p. 11) – and indeed there was far worse to come. But if Rome, supposedly the great civilized, all-conquering power, was beyond hope, what could be hoped for from the world it ruled? Rome had blighted it. Justice had withdrawn 'to heaven' (SSvi, 19, p. 35), and,

> In all the lands that stretch far eastward from Cádiz
> to Ganges and the dawn, few indeed there are can distinguish
> true good from its opposite, or manage to dissipate
> the thick mist of error.
>
> (SSx, 1–4, p. 76)

Roman supremacy had ensured that 'there are no refuges left'.[43] But what that in turn meant was that 'the human race' had been 'condemned to a blacked-out future' (SSvi, 556, p. 51).

In the first century of the Empire, it was quite common for civilized and educated Romans to look back to the past for their moral orientation, whether to a mythical Golden Age or the Republic, its leaders and traditions (and sideways to contemporaries who were still guided by them). Thus Persius refers to Messalla and Cato (the Younger), for example, and expresses his humble gratitude to his old teacher Cornutus (whom Nero drove out). Here, again, we encounter the thought of the exception that seems so deeply written into misanthropy, as though the exception him- or herself is, in his or her strange splendour, a reason for misanthropic gloom. But, in Juvenal, even Persius's kind of austere exceptionalism (to use the philosophical term, though it is not only philosophical), insisting as it does on the rarity of the exception, tends to break down. There is a side to Juvenal that sings the praises of certain figures in the Republic, but it is hard to quell the suspicion that he at best only half means it, that he is being dutiful and knows so, that the metropolitan distruster of grandiosity in him is also surreptitiously muttering 'Oh come *off* it'. In fact, he is also capable of giving short shrift to a range of republican luminaries, from Cato (the Elder), to Rome's great moral heroine Cornelia, mother of the Gracchi, to Brutus and Cassius. This fits with his tight-jawed impatience: what is the point of dwelling nostalgically on Rome's great and noble families, Satire VIII in effect asks, if they have not themselves been able to survive, sustain themselves, foster and transmit their values? Indeed, Juvenal goes still further. Not only is he reluctant to sentimentalize the past – he can seem sceptical about the literature of the past, notably Homer, Statius and Virgil, and what he takes to be the bogus dimensions of the models they provide for us in their stories – he also debunks the mythical figures of the past, sometimes very funnily. Icarus, Jason, Achilles, Odysseus, Chiron, Hercules – these are just a few of those Juvenal sweeps up in his caustically satirical net. He tends to treat the idea of a Golden Age as a bit of a joke.[44] He treats the Gods that way, too. Athene appears to be the only one he has any time for. He seems harshly aware that, if gods are dragged in the dust, not just by money, greed and luxury but, as he and Persius both knew, by the very mediocrity of the forms of attention paid them, they may well not be revivable, whatever others suppose. Gods die. Humans turn out to be unworthy of them, and kill them.

But Juvenal does not tell us this arrogantly: that is no doubt one reason why he has inspired so many other misanthropists and satirists. His voice may be savage; it is not self-important or self-inflating. The questions that concern him get to him too intensely. His tendency is rather to be self-deprecating. He derives this partly from Persius, again. Persius's third satire, for example, presents the poet as a late lie-abed hardly worthy of his noble art or cause, not least because the world so quickly discourages him. 'What's the point of all this?' asks Satire IV (SSiv, 5, p. 150). So, too, even on the first page of his first satire, Juvenal is admitting that satire is a futile occupation (though one may as well write, since others will as surely waste the paper). Later on, he admonishes another writer for missing the prime of life when he might have become something useful, 'a sailor, soldier, farmer' (SSvii, 34–5, p. 56). Now he's stuck with an old age in which he will learn to turn in hatred on his art. Juvenal is also self-deprecating because he knows that the moralist is always too likely to drift close to or end up resembling the objects of his or her attack, indeed, that, in the end, one can only moralize about or satirize what one recognizes, and one recognizes it because it is a part of oneself. Thus, with insidious brilliance, in Satire I, he himself ends up sounding like the ever-so-exquisite, squirmy connoisseur whom he is apparently taking to task.

*

The Roman satirists were important, not least to St Augustine, who raided them for his own theological and moral purposes.[45] St Augustine is crucial to the history of Western misanthropy, for he is the major source of the Christian conviction of the fundamental, ineradicable predominance of evil in all human being. Augustine was haunted, beset by the thought of wickedness. Initially, we may see this in his *Confessions*, where the wickedness is above all individual, his own. He describes himself when young as a creature of great wilfulness and waywardness. This was the result of the vanity of life itself, which left him but a toy of the flesh, of 'a wind that passeth away, and cometh not again' (Ps. 78.39).[46] He sought pleasure not in God but in his creatures, created beings. Since he was, it would seem, a very sensual young man – he refers to his sexuality as 'insatiable' (C, p. 107) – from the 'bubbling impulses of puberty' onwards, he found himself befogged by 'clouds of muddy carnal concupiscence' (C, p. 24). A desire for 'shame for its own sake' (C, p. 29) further intensified his predicament.

Indeed, in his own terms, the young Augustine lived a life of 'total temptation' (C, p. 207). He possessed a faculty of almost delirious imagination, and the *phantasmata* or *corporales imagines*, the 'physical images' and 'unpurified notions' that it summoned up assailed the mind like swarms of insects which he was powerless to dispel (C, p. 111). The vicious drives tugged at his garments, whispered in insinuating voices, like the devils to whom, in *City of God*, he ascribes such dreadful energy (and cruel laughter). They interrupted and distracted him from his prayers. As a result he became 'to [himself] a vast problem' (C, p. 57), from which, for all his intense and indeed agonized struggles, his very serious faith and the help of others like St Ambrose, God's grace alone could save him. Mercifully, it did, chiefly in a great moment of anagnorisis in a garden in Milan: 'It was as if a light of relief from anxiety flooded my heart', he writes. 'All the shadows of doubt were dispelled' (C, p. 153). Yet even after this decisive experience, vivid sexual images continued to 'attack' him (C, p. 203). He lived, he wrote, in an 'immense jungle full of traps and dangers', and often felt 'stuck in the snares', 'pitifully captured' by 'beautiful externals' (C, pp. 210, 212). Part of what seems lovable about Augustine, as opposed to some of his flintier successors, like John Calvin and Martin Luther, is how human and vulnerable to the promptings of the world and the senses he repeatedly turns out to be.

The structure of value implicit in this narrative increasingly became the founding structure of Augustine's philosophy. Even in the *Confessions*, he is generalizing on the basis of his own experience. 'So tiny a child, so great a sinner' (C, p. 15), he says of himself. But tiny children, he tells us, are never innocent, indeed, the reverse: in their petulance, their tantrums, their incorrigibility, their crazed obsession with getting their own way, essential wickedness appears. So, too, certainly, lust is sexual, and it was as such that Augustine appears to have felt it most keenly. But others know lust differently, because it can assume many and various forms: the lust for revenge, money or applause, for superfluous knowledge or for private superiority, the lusts that make up one's personal habits, the lust for power over others and the lust to appear to good effect in their eyes. Then there is the lust for untruth, or lying. This is indeed a lust, for people positively hanker after lies, fictions, false ideas (like heresies), 'superstitions and pernicious mythologies', and are easily entranced by them (C, p. 56). Even in the very early *Against the Academicians*, Augustine is asserting that human souls, 'enveloped in the manifold darkness of error and defiled by the sordid appetites of the body', must necessarily fail to raise themselves to the highest good.[47] Lust and error are everywhere, and are the origin of all evil. Augustine quotes Ps. 130.3: 'If thou, Lord, shouldest mark iniquities, O Lord, who shall stand?' (C, p. 6; cf. Jn 8.7). God's grace alone is 'indefectible' (a key word), flawless, not subject to failure or decay. Grace and nothing but grace can melt 'the hardness of humanity' (C, p. 72).

But the truly significant turn in Augustine's thought comes about in his confrontation with Pelagius. Early in his career, Augustine had inclined towards Manichaeanism. The Manichees postulated that the world was divided between two powers, one good, one evil. There existed 'a race of darkness' that opposed itself to God. But this had to mean that there was a zone of being where God was 'open to violation and destruction', where he was nothing, where the power and reach of his goodness ceased (C, pp. 112–13). That could not be the case: God is all-loving and all-powerful. Not surprisingly, Augustine moved away from Manicheanism. But this in turn appeared to drive him towards the Pelagians. Pelagius held that God made human beings good by nature, and ordered them to do good. Humans were not intrinsically and fundamentally corrupted by sin; the lusts were not evil. Sin was not a universal imperfection, a flaw in all souls. People could attain to perfection by their own unaided efforts, and therefore had no need of divine assistance.

But to Augustine Pelagianism was extremely dangerous, because it appeared to suggest that man might aspire to the condition of God. This was overweeningly arrogant and presumptuous. Pelagianism did not accord with Augustine's thought up to the point in his life when he began to address it. But it also failed to accord with his own experience. His experience logically pointed in a Manichean direction. But he had barred himself off from Manicheanism. Thus, as a means of navigating between his Scylla and his Charybdis, in his various writings against the Pelagians (the *Work on the Proceedings of Pelagius*, the *Treatise Against Two Letters of the Pelagians*, the *Treatise on Grace and Free Will*, the *Treatise on the Predestination of the Saints*, and others),[48] to the end of his life, Augustine increasingly elaborated a moral theology based on five key concepts: total depravity, original sin, grace, election and predestination. First, we are totally depraved. Human beings are by nature *vitiata*, poisoned by sin. Their minds lie in darkness unless God purges them. Certainly, they have freedom of will, but they will to sin. They cannot but do so, for sin blinds and weakens the human will from the start. Nonetheless, humans are responsible for their sins. It is not the Devil who makes them act sinfully.[49] There could hardly be a more vivid commitment to an effectively misanthropic vision than this: in reality, humanity *in toto* constitutes what Augustine calls a *massa damnata*.

Secondly, evil begins with Adam, and is then integrally transmitted through the generations without intermission in 'the chain of original sin' by which 'in Adam all die' (C, p. 82, 1 Cor. 15.22; Augustine actually came to think that original sin was passed on by natural descent through natural generation, in and through the sexual act). Adam chose evil, and human beings can never erase the consequences of that choice from what they are by nature. Thirdly, only the unexpected, unwilled grace of God can save human beings from their depravity, in a process of *alienatio*, separation of the individual soul from common humanity and its ways of thinking and seeing. Grace comes to people, like a visitation. That is why all infants behave so wickedly, above all, before baptism (It is because they are wicked, Augustine thinks, that they wriggle to avoid it and bawl at the font). As yet, grace has not touched them. Fourthly, we return to exceptionalism: in fact, evil is really nothing, a young Augustine writes, in the *Soliloquies*, but to only the few does God grant grace to know that.[50] The later Augustine firms this idea up. The few, the saved, are God's elect, God's chosen ones. God in his mercy singles them out and prepares them for restoration to a pre-Adamic state. But, fifthly, since God is all-knowing, he must have chosen them from the start, and since he is all-powerful, he must have predestined them to salvation, though, paradoxically, it was also necessary for them to will it. We shall watch this structure, blessed few versus *massa damnata*, replicate itself again and again.

It is difficult to overestimate the importance of Augustine for Western misanthropy. His theory of evil survived the attentions of other great Christian theologians (Bede, Scotus Eriugena, Anselm, Bernard of Clairvaux, Peter Abelard, to name only the most eminent) until the thirteenth century, when it came under pressure from the new Aristotelianism (Roger Bacon and, above all, Thomas Aquinas), especially the Aristotelian insistence on formal logic. But after the Reformation, when Catholic orthodoxy had parted company with Augustinianism, ironically, Protestantism injected it with a formidable new life, particularly through Luther and Calvin, both of whom busily promulgated the doctrines of total depravity, original sin, grace, election and (in different ways) predestination, seeking to return Christianity to what Bertrand Russell called Augustine's 'gloomy sense of universal guilt',[51] the moral impotence of man and the absolute imperative of grace. In effect, as Gillian Evans says, they kept Augustine 'alive' into 'the modern world', notably in northern Europe and America.[52]

We will happen on our three traditions again, Cynic, for example, in America, indignantly satirical in eighteenth-century England, Augustinian in seventeenth-century France and America. The book will repeatedly open up differences with these forms of misanthropy, and others, but also close them. It will not stall in misanthropic griping. But neither will it meekly cede to contemporary cheerleaders. Equally, while it ranges from Timon and the Cynics to contemporary queer misanthropy and posthumanism, and there is a great deal of historical narrative in it, it does not offer a comprehensive historical account of its subject. That would take several volumes. There are obvious omissions, medieval, Victorian and German romantic misanthropy, for example, and, even more glaringly, non-Western misanthropies (alas, I have no relevant expertise). 'The Pelagians claim', writes Evans, 'that grace shines freely on all: the true light lights everyone who comes into the world'.[53] The true light lights everyone: we can be of good cheer, all is well with the world, the lusts of the flesh are a natural good. Everyone, or at least the generality (leaving aside a few terrorists and paedophiles), is basically or at least potentially virtuous, there is equality of spiritual opportunity, though true salvation comes of self-help, is born of one's own efforts and must be underwritten by law not grace (another Pelagian theme). Interestingly, in Rome, Pelagianism was a particular favourite of affluent elites, for whom it was clearly a comfortable philosophy. We live, in a loose sense, in times that, in comparison, for example, to the Cold War decades, seem more Pelagian- than Augustinian-inclined, notably in a range of public, official and, increasingly, university discourses, all of which have a certain investment in the Pelagian tone. See for example Steven Pinker (*The Better Angels of Our Nature*),[54] though Pinker actually comes somewhere between Pelagius and Pollyanna. But if cultural Pelagianism is at all dominant at the present time, it has not been so for long, is, as we shall see, only insecurely so, and may possibly not remain so for very long, either. (Pelagianism has had its moments of currency; they did not last). It is partly with such sober caveats in mind that this book proceeds.

1

MISANTHROPY AND THE OLD ORDER

It is not by chance that the most famous misanthropist in European literature appears in Paris in the middle of the seventeenth century. Molière's *Le Misanthrope* was first performed on 4 June 1666 at the Théâtre du Palais-Royal, under the sign of the Ancien Régime, by then securely lodged in place. Misanthropy was very much a part of this environment. According to Nancy Mitford, Louis XIV's Versailles was stuffed with cynics for whom human goodness was likely to seem a fantasm.[1] Molière was by no means the only writer to fasten on the figure of the misanthrope as a contemporary type. In his *Caractères*, for example, the moralist Jean de la Bruyère tells us about 'Timon, the misanthrope' (a contemporary figure). Timon is 'outwardly civil, and even ceremonious'. But he 'does not become familiar with other men', and underneath nurses 'an austere and savage mind', harbouring no 'desire to be better acquainted' with his fellow humans.[2] The writers were picking up on such strains of thought and attitude as they formed part of the culture around them. In the Louis-Quatorzian court, misanthropy was an intellectual option. Madame de Sévigné, for instance, though light of touch, recommended misanthropy as a bulwark against adverse 'strokes of love and misfortune'.[3] But why should there have been so pungent an odour of misanthropy under the Sun King? The answer involves telling a historical story.

The Renaissance monarchy in France was limited in its authority, partly held in check by the representatives of the king's subjects, the Estates General, comprising the three estates, nobility, clergy and those below both. But this system had been secured in place by Henri IV, bringer of peace, proponent of religious toleration and a skilled politician whose concern for his subjects was self-evident. Henri was assassinated in 1610. By 1614, the Estates General was in eclipse. It was not to meet again until 1789. Under Louis XIII, this paved the way for an increasingly dominant monarchy, and the rise to power of Armand-Jean de Plessis, Cardinal de Richelieu. Richelieu was intent on consolidating royal power, and displayed 'an almost sadistic attention to detail in matters of repression'.[4] For the Cardinal, the second and third estates were of no account. What mattered was chiefly control of the first estate, the nobility. The monarchy duly sought to ensure its grip on the nobles, and steadily encroached on the powers of the French *parlements*, the legislative bodies dominated by the aristocracy, of which the most eminent, in Paris, was known simply as the *Parlement*. The monarchy brought dissenting aristocrats to heel, bought or executed them. It put down revolts with summary and often extreme violence.

Richelieu was followed by Cardinal Jules Mazarin in 1642, and Louis XIII by Louis XIV in 1643. Richelieu had maintained an increasingly militarized state. Mazarin also understood that his and his royal master's power and authority were intricately bound up with waging war elsewhere. Richelieu had discovered that the French had been seriously undertaxed, and zealously set about remedying the problem, himself becoming an immensely wealthy man. Mazarin, who also accumulated a vast personal fortune, raised taxes again. Though the aristocracy was exempt from taxation, the government found ways of squeezing it, too.[5] Meanwhile the *parlements*, and especially the *Parlement*, were becoming increasingly critical of royal policy. Between 1623 and 1645, France saw various popular uprisings. By 1648, the country was ripe for major revolt.

On 26 August, the government arrested three leading parliamentarians, one of whom, Pierre Broussel, was the hero of the Parisian poor. This resulted in the 'Days of the Barricades', when, according to Jean François Paul de Gondi, Cardinal de Retz, 'cries of Republic!' were audible for the first time in France.[6] The unrest duly led to the first of the two rebellions known as the Frondes. The first Fronde crossed the boundaries between the classes, spreading to the disaffected aristocracy. Its two key themes were taxation and disempowerment. The sides signed a peace treaty in March 1649. The second Fronde, however, was far more serious, since it involved not only all the classes, but powerful princes and the leading army commanders (the Great Condé, Turenne). It was sparked off by Mazarin's arrest of Condé in January 1650. That a mere royal *créature* – and an Italian given to solecisms at that – should behave thus to a member of the ancient, chivalric *noblesse d'epée* was intolerable. The crisis became radical, then revolutionary, with republicanism much in the air. From late 1651 to late 1652, the civil war grew bloody and destructive. But Condé lost his grip on Paris, while Turenne was reconciled to the monarchy and took over command of the royal armies, finally defeating Condé in October 1652, in the Faubourg Saint-Antoine.

The monarchy definitively crushed the Frondes, but those who had been in their vanguard did not simply disappear. To understand the meaning of misanthropy during the early decades of the Ancien Régime, one has partly to imagine how far spectres from the past continued to bulk large at the court of the young Sun King, glowering resentfully, recalling the days when it was not self-evident that a stripling monarch should have such extraordinary power and wield it so arbitrarily. Condé the great warrior remained. (He was rehabilitated in 1659, though the king never entirely forgot his treason). Henri IV's bastards were moodily stalking about Louis's court as late as the 1670s. Brilliant friends of former *frondeurs*, like Madame de Sévigné and the Comtesse de Lafayette, cut significant figures at court. Memories of a France different from that of monarchical absolutism persisted. The period that runs from the Fronde to the death of Louis XIV – a period that had begun in hopes, however mixed, diverse and contradictory, of social transformation, only to see them dashed – sees the emergence of French misanthropy as a discourse. This discourse was precisely a consequence of recollections of a future curtailed.

If any single writer is associated with the Fronde, the spirit of the Fronde and the significance of its defeat, it is the beguiling figure of François, Prince de Marcillac and, from 1650, Duc de la Rochefoucauld, *le vaincu de la Fronde*, as Jean Lafond calls him.[7] The La Rochefoucaulds were an ancient and distinguished noble family close to the throne. They were deeply concerned for the honour and lustre of the family name. They had for generations been soldiers distinguished for their valour, and cherished the family tradition of gallantry, chivalric duty, fidelity to one's liege lord and fighting for the faith. They saw Richelieu as just a venal upstart, and loathed him. La Rochefoucauld *père* joined the attempt to oust the Cardinal on the so-called Day of the Dupes, and was disgraced. His son, however, remained at court, where the sets he frequented ensured him the company of people who, in large degree, shared his inherited values.

However, engagingly, Marcillac kept on joining the wrong party, to the point of becoming an outsider, even a malcontent. At Richelieu's bidding, he was briefly thrown into the Bastille. After Richelieu's death, he joined the so-called *Cabale des Importants*, who were united in their hatred of Mazarin.[8] Though, in 1648, he suppressed a minor rebellion on Mazarin's behalf, Mazarin did not reward him as he wished. He therefore broke with the Cardinal and joined a cabal against him that included Retz, the Prince de Conti, and Condé's sister and Marcillac's own lover, the Duchesse de Longueville. On that basis, according to Madame de Motteville, Marcillac 'entered gaily on the crime of lèse-majesté'[9] – punishable by death – and swiftly became one of the leading rebel officers in the first Fronde. Unsurprisingly, in the second Fronde, he allied himself with the Condés. Orders went out for his arrest. He performed prodigious feats of courage. La Rochefoucauld – as he now was – fought desperately in the Faubourg Saint-Antoine, taking a musket bullet in the face. Thereafter he would look out upon the world with damaged eyes.

By the end of the second Fronde, La Rochefoucauld was ruined, hopeless, mortally tired, his castle gutted, his aristocratic status reduced, his friends dead, fled or become turncoats. He was an unusually reflective and nuanced man, but also one possessed of what Victor Cousin called 'the elegant effrontery of the *grand seigneur*'. He was proud, contemptuous and given to 'disgust with things', but also lacked a certain worldliness.[10] He had proved incapable of bending the courtly knee or playing the game of *realpolitik*, and had therefore been fated to disenchantment in a world where king and ministry were steadily disempowering his class. La Rochefoucauld did not suppose, in modern fashion, that his melancholy was just a neurosis, or a consequence of his character. He had far too much arrogant self-belief for that: 'Much [of my melancholy] comes to me from outside sources', he wrote, and 'fills my imagination and occupies my mind'.[11] For a while, he had flared into grand, Satanic revolt against absolute power. Now, defeated, he turned to writing his memoirs, particularly dwelling on what he had come to see as the temporizations, disloyalties, deceptions, follies and failures of the *frondeurs*, their furtive but consistent prioritization of their personal interests: the tergiversations of Retz, always motivated by his own ambition (La Rochefoucauld had once trapped Retz in a door, head on one side, body on the other, and instructed his men to kill him, in vain); the self-seeking and vast greed of Condé, repeatedly willing to have the king buy him off, never satisfied with what he was offered; the inconstancy and treachery of Madame de Longueville, who deserted La Rochefoucauld for fellow-*frondeur* the Duc de Nemours; the pathetic rivalry between Nemours and his brother-in-law the Duc de Beaufort, rebels who ended up fighting each other.

The king eventually forgave La Rochefoucauld, and by 1664 he had made his peace with Mazarin and the court. He was not granted access to the court itself, however, and so lurked on its fringes. Bound from now on 'to my sulky humour', in his first published work, he 'announced his misanthropy',[12] and began to compose the *Maximes* for which he remains famous. The *Maximes* take the world to be an objective disproof of La Rochefoucauld's inherited chivalric ideals, which had come to seem like 'illusions néfastes [dangerous illusions]'.[13] The two great laws of human conduct are unrelenting self-interest, and men's refusal to acknowledge it. La Rochefoucauld became expert in tracking *amour-propre*, self-love, self-regard, through all its devious and winding ways, down to its most secret lairs, detecting its metallic insistence beneath the most virtuous and humane appearances. His was, he wrote, an endless task. 'Whatever discovery one makes in the country of self-love', he said, 'there still remain unknown territories to explore' (R, p. 43). The manifestations and modes of expression of self-love were infinite.

Everything is, at bottom, interest; interest speaks even in disinterest. Piety, honour, duty, the philosopher's superb indifference to life: all are disguised vices, tastes devised by *amour-propre*. Bounty, liberality, merit, friendship, sincerity, good sense, sound judgement must not be taken at face value. La Rochefoucauld's own sexual disposition and his sexual experience, and above all his desertion by the Duchesse de Longueville, made his view of love deeply cynical. His acuteness, subtlety, wit and grasp of paradox are unforgiving, and ruthlessly bar all ways of escape. Constancy, for example, is only secret inconstancy, a series of separate attachments to the beloved. Humility is a ruse whereby one feigns submission in order to win the submission of others. Courage is self-regarding: courage under torture, for example, springs only from the fear of envisaging death. 'Folly accompanies us through all the phases of life' (R, p. 77), and the wisdom of age is just a function of the inability to set a bad example any longer. One finds happiness when fortune justifies one's poor conduct. But pride in unhappiness is a perverted assertion of self-worth. However much one seeks to disguise one's passions, 'they will always announce themselves for what they are', that is, as the ruling powers (R, p. 43). Yet no man is sufficiently clever to know all the evil for which he is responsible, not least because the mind attaches itself to what is easy for or agreeable to it, and therefore protects itself against insight and self-knowledge. However invisible to itself, even ignorant of and stupid about itself *amour-propre* may be, 'nothing is as impetuous in its desires, as hidden in its design or as crafty in its conduct' (R, p. 129). We are naturally self-idolaters, and are therefore hardly likely to see ourselves clearly.

La Rochefoucauld's generalizations do not come without reservations and exceptions. For all that, his work of destruction is intransigent. While he never lets go of a certain conception of honesty and decency, it is clear that, in a world where self-love imperiously requires self-deception, any morality can only be precarious. Hence the dominant voice in the *Maximes* is one that refuses to surrender its elevated authority, but is in one sense also impotent. As such, it mirrors the predicament of La Rochefoucauld and his class. Yet La Rochefoucauld was destined to a still worse fate. He ended his life scarred, racked by gout, often in horrible pain and grimly disabused. Before he died, he nonetheless managed to write his *Réflexions morales*.

Commentators have sometimes sought to rescue La Rochefoucauld from the charge of a prevailing cynicism.[14] They have pointed to the variety of the *Maximes*, the extent to which they pass different kinds of judgement. Yet one might at least ask whether, in the very moments when La Rochefoucauld relaxes his vigilance, he actually confirms the second part of his thesis, that it is finally impossible to look unflinchingly at the dismaying truth. In any case, no attempt to make La Rochefoucauld sound more upbeat can withstand the *Réflexions morales*. Take for instance 'Du rapport des hommes avec les animaux' (R, pp. 179–82). Human beings are to each other, states La Rochefoucauld, as the species of animals are. There are humans who are purely ferocious, like tigers, those who dress up their ferocity in the garb of generosity, like lions, humans who are crudely and avidly ferocious, like bears, pitilessly ferocious, like wolves, and industriously and deceitfully ferocious, like foxes. Like dogs, some humans will prove noble and courageous but destroy their own kind. Others hunt for the pleasure of those who feed them or are creatures of fury, barking and biting. There are humans, like birds, commendable only for their plumage and gorgeous colours; like parrots, who gabble on and don't understand what they are saying; like monkeys, who know how to please with their manners, have a certain wit but invariably do mischief; like peacocks, who are merely beautiful, whose song displeases and who destroy their habitat; and like birds of prey, who live on rapine. Equally, there are humans who, like myriad forms of natural life, exist chiefly to nourish others.

The cats are watchful, malicious and faithless, padding on velvet paws. The vipers have venomous tongues, the poisonous toads make one shudder, while the spiders, fleas and flies are unbearably irritating. There are owls that fear the light, and animals that stay alive by hiding underground. There are horses, useful, then abandoned as soon as they have outlived their usefulness. The hares are frightened of everything, the rabbits scared and reassured in the same moment, the crocodiles weep as they kill, the hogs live in shit. There are *canards privés*, tame ducks who betray their kind, swallows always following fine weather, brainless maybugs, and cicadas who spend their lives singing. The bees respect their leader and are well regulated and industrious, while moths seek out the fire that will consume them and ants look after themselves with foresight and economy. Many animals are unaware of their own strength, notably, perhaps, the oxen, who work all day to enrich their owners.

*

With this short exercise in disillusion, the misanthropist surveys the general scene and condenses his view of it into a mere three pages. He had studied Louis's France, and learnt all he needed to know. But if La Rochefoucauld learnt from the France of the Sun King, for his part, Louis learnt a great deal from the Frondes. He would never trust Paris, the *parlements* or most of the older nobility again. With the end of the Frondes, the monarchy in France turned more and more in the direction of absolutism, and the interests of the state became increasingly separate from those of ordinary people. The Sun King declared that the state was him. A monarchical personality cult emerged. The nobility survived quite comfortably. But they had been tamed and disempowered, and were ever more clearly subordinated to the sovereign will. Meanwhile, tax demands grew ever more burdensome.

Expansionist wars, annexations and land-grabbing were the stuff of Louis XIV's reign. War was one of the Sun King's favourite pastimes, and he was happy to sacrifice other people to his passion, including the court nobility. In 1672, when the French crossed the Rhine under a hail of enemy fire, half the youth of the court were lost. But as the great playwright Jean Racine told Louis, it was predictable that he should boast that the generality of his soldiery were brave, for life in the army was so dreadful that most of them were glad to end it quickly. There were repeated outbreaks of famine and epidemics, land lay abandoned and towns became depopulated, while the impoverishment of the people was dire. France seemed increasingly describable as a conspiracy of the strong against the weak.

Hence for Archbishop François Fénelon, writing in 1694, France was 'nothing more than a great hospital, devastated and without provisions'.[15] The peasants were eating cabbage stalks and bread made from fern-roots. Unlike Henri IV, Louis XIV was indifferent to his people, did not want to listen to tales of their condition and found Christ's identification with the poor quaint if not objectionable. Thus absolutist monarchy brought greater and greater suffering and misery to the vast majority of the French. Misery indeed: 'If Paris and the court offer a prospect of wealth and pleasure', stated a Venetian ambassador in 1660, 'the provinces are a sink of indigence and misery'.[16] 'There are miseries on earth that grip the heart', wrote La Bruyère, contemplating the French peasantry, with a humanity rare in his day (CH, p. 180). No release from wretchedness was thinkable for those who suffered it, not least because the monarchy continued mercilessly to repress domestic insurrections.

Louis had broken the backs of the nobles. It was an explicit principle of his to corrupt them sufficiently to be able to govern without, but not against them, though he also resorted to terror, intimidation and casual violence. Anyone might expect a spell in the dungeons. The Duc de Nevers was imprisoned for baptizing a pig, the Comte de Bussy thrown into the Bastille for a four-line distich that suggested that the king had a 'preposterous mouth'.[17] Others were banished from the kingdom, or themselves chose exile, while punishments were frequently meted out at random and on the spot. A poor woman whose son had died during the building of the Sun King's magnificent palace at Versailles (1664–1710) shouted insults at Louis; he duly had her whipped. The Sun King made his inferiors very afraid: Madame de Sévigné recounts the story of a *maître d'hôtel*, due to entertain the king, who ran himself through with his own sword when he discovered that the sea-bass he had ordered for the king's dinner had not arrived on time.[18] At the court, spies were everywhere. When the Chevalier de Grammont made slighting reference to Mazarin, his companions blenched, since they knew the spies 'would faithfully discharge their duty toward their employer, as they accordingly did'.[19]

All of this coincided with the construction of Versailles, a testimony to the power of the king and the relative impotence of everyone else. Versailles 'imprisoned the most distinguished members of the aristocracy in a gilded cage'.[20] The byzantine atmosphere, the *luxe insolent et audacieux* of the great palace by no means concealed its more disturbing side. The braggadocio of some of the nobility was patent, if subdued. La Bruyère describes them swaggering into church, weapons at their hips, like gunmen swinging into bars in westerns: 'There was almost nobody', the moralist remarks, 'that did not have at his side the wherewithal to kill another person with one thrust' (CT, p. 11). Duels often took place. Versailles was crammed with adulterers and gamblers. More chillingly, an extraordinary criminality also lurked in the holes and corners of Louis's court. Doctors were reputed to murder children. The vogue for poisonings and devilish practices prompted chief of police Gabriel-Nicolas de la Reynie – a man conspicuous for his uncommon decency and rectitude – to declare that he had altogether lost faith in humanity: 'Men's lives are up for sale', he said, 'as a matter of everyday bargaining; murder is the only remedy when a family is in difficulties. Abominations are being practised everywhere – in Paris, in the suburbs and in the provinces'.[21] Live babies stolen from the poor were allegedly sacrificed in black masses.[22] When the police swept the underworld for the disreputable accomplices of courtly killers, they dragged up alchemists, kidnappers, counterfeiters, defrocked priests, back-alley abortionists, mountebanks and peddlers of love-philtres.

Versailles seemed to be begging for its Lewis Carroll. It was a dementedly hierarchical society that proliferated minute symbolic indicators of social rank within an extraordinarily complex system. The system covered a multitude of practices, from kissing to parking one's carriage at the Louvre. It associated certain postures with each rank; that is, it determined who could sit, kneel or stand with whom, and on what, in any given situation. The intricate rules governing the use of seating were mind-boggling. Cardinals, for example, were to stand before the king, sit on a stool when with the queen or royal children, use a chair with a back with royal grandchildren and an armchair with the princes of the blood. The system was also linguistic; remembering who was to be addressed how might have driven the fussiest practitioner of etiquette to distraction. Punctilio, however, had not the slightest bearing on conduct. The king himself was quite indiscriminately promiscuous, and once scaled a roof and clambered in through a window at Versailles in order to visit a maid of honour.[23] He had a child by a gardener. Meanwhile, his ex-mistresses were packed off to convents, sometimes to die there.

The hierarchical system was also preferential, the reverse of a meritocracy – it was only the king's friends, for example, who could hope to rise to the higher commands in the army. This, however, did not discourage court politics, but rather diversified and intensified them. The court, after all, was the place where brilliant people made careers. That there was finally only one significant source of power meant not that the court smothered ambitions, but that it focused them. 'The whole court is filled with intrigue', wrote the woman called simply Madame (a.k.a. Liselotte, the Princess Palatine of Bavaria, the king's sister-in-law).[24] Courtiers constantly sued for the Sun King's ear, or for the ears of the influential. For his part, Louis relentlessly played them off against each other. Cabals, coteries, factions, camarillas and sodalities plotted against each other, faced each other down, changed and often exchanged (or shared) their members. Splits, fissures and deadly rivalries were everywhere. Since there was no democratic system of alternation in power, everyone was caught up in a constant scrabble for its vestiges, as for prestige, money, appointments to high positions and promotions.

At this point, the logic of misanthropy under the Ancien Régime should start to become clear. Such a society was bound to generate intense, often mutual, and sometimes general loathing. As Ladurie puts it, the hierarchical structure produced a *cascade de mépris* (contempt) that flowed from top to bottom.[25] Hierarchy tended to breed misanthropy, all the way down the chain. Since the police opened letters on the king's instructions, the king's lover and later wife, Madame de Maintenon, discovered that Liselotte thought of her as a whore, a witch, an ageing ape, a repulsive horror and a pile of shit. But Louis wanted his courtiers at each other's throats. He declared for example that a special jerkin ornamented with gold stripes and braid might be worn by some courtiers but not others, in the hope, precisely, that it would create envy.[26] Envy was useful, because politically disabling, where solidarity was dangerous, a lesson that Louis had learnt from the Frondes. When Versailles' smaller cousin the Château de Marly was built, people almost literally fought for invitations. The Sun King had 'no more fervent an opponent' than the great memoirist of his court, the Duc de Saint-Simon.[27] Saint-Simon 'took the very lowest view of human nature',[28] was an inveterate loather of Versailles and most of those in circulation there. His, he thought, was an 'age of monsters'.[29] When he tartly noted that Marly had been built on a site favoured by 'snakes, carrion, toads and frogs', he also had other kinds of reptile in mind.[30]

But there was also a religious reason for misanthropy being conspicuous in Louis-Quatorzian France. If St Augustine was important for the history of Western misanthropy, he had recently provoked little discussion within the Church. But as a new interest in free will crept into learned circles, so, in opposition to it, Augustinian 'rigorism' also returned. In early seventeenth-century France, it led to an assertion of the importance of having faith guide State policy, and from this emerged Cornelius Jansen and his friend Jean Duvergier de Hauranne, (the Abbot of) Saint-Cyran. Jansen and Saint-Cyran saturated themselves in Augustine's writings. In 1634, Saint-Cyran became spiritual director of Port-Royal, an abbey for Cistercian nuns, and it flourished and grew in reputation, becoming the headquarters of Jansenism. By 1638, however, Jansen was dead and – on Richelieu's orders – the 'dangerous heretic' Saint-Cyran was in prison, to die on his release in 1643. But thanks to Antoine Arnauld, a later director of Port-Royal, and his circle, by the mid-1640s, the term 'Jansenist Party' was in use and Jansenism was spreading to male religious orders.

Jansenism sprang, again, from the Augustinian emphasis on the natural depravity of human being, which only divine grace could redeem. It comprehensively challenged the principal orientations of the Jansenists' great enemies, the Jesuits, the dominant clerical influence at court. The worldly Jesuits had refined their traditional science of casuistry to the point where it meant pandering to the powerful, rich and fashionable, since casuistry made for a seemingly endless flexibility in the salving of consciences (or so the Jansenists said). In the 1650s, Arnauld and the Jansenists attacked this Jesuit 'laxism', winning the university and even in some degree the Papacy over to their side. Jesuitry encouraged the courtly life. By contrast, Jansenism repudiated a theology that spelt involvement in the world and advocated the worldly doctrine of attrition, imperfect contrition. It tended to make people solitaries, encouraging them to flee the endemic and ineradicable corruption of the world and inclining them to misanthropy.[31]

The Jansenists were in due course to reap the whirlwind. Given their repudiation of worldliness, the character of Louis XIV's court and his absorption in it, a confrontation was certain to ensue. Furthermore, many Jansenists had originally been *frondeurs*. The king himself saw them as a Republican party inside the Church and State. They were 'the main source of discourses of resistance to royal authority articulated by the magistracy; and thus, ultimately, of the "desacralization" of [the French] monarchy'.[32] According to the Archbishop of Paris, Louis finally decided that he wanted to 'hear no more of those endless people, those Port-Royal people'.[33] He would smash this 'party of innovators'.[34] His officers invaded Port-Royal and removed all the (female) novices and boarders, dismissing its director. The royal council ordered the bishops to impose a formulary denouncing Jansenism on all their subordinates, and Arnauld went into hiding; then, like other Jansenists, fled and died in exile. The older generation of nuns struggled to keep Port-Royal going until, in 1709, Louis formally closed it down, razed it to the ground and had the bodies of its dead disinterred and dumped in a common pit.

Jansenism contributed to seventeenth-century French misanthropic discourse to a degree beyond the confines of strictly religious interests. Saint-Simon had Augustinian and Jansenist sympathies, and La Rochefoucauld was influenced by Augustinianism and increasingly overtaken by the Jansenist spirit, though, as Sainte-Beuve later noted, he had 'no use' for religion itself.[35] But here one devoutly religious figure looms particularly large. At the Jansenist Madame de Sablé's, La Rochefoucauld may have brushed shoulders with the great philosopher, theologian and mathematician Blaise Pascal.[36] Pascal turned to Jansenism in 1646, and thereafter his name and fortunes were closely connected with it. In 1654, he underwent a mystical experience that was decisive for him, and drove him still further from the claims of the world. Pascal had too painfully exquisite a mind fully to convert to any movement. But he remained an ally of the Jansenists, and they and his work formed part of the same ethos. His *Lettres Provinciales* excoriated the Jesuits and their 'laxism'. The Jesuits, however, were winning the day. As the enemies of Port-Royal forced its capitulation, one of its greatest stalwarts, Pascal's sister Jacqueline died, it was said, of a broken heart. To Pascal, who suffered very intensely at the news, nothing could seem more drastically to bear witness against the world and its party.

Pascalian misanthropy is most apparent and comprehensible in his greatest work, the *Pensées*. Its founding principle is simple: 'That nature is corrupt, proved by nature itself'.[37] For Pascal the biblical Fall of man was a historical event, and its effects had been transferred from mankind's first parents in an unbroken sequence. 'How hollow and full of ordure is the heart of man!' Pascal exclaims (P, p. 128). *'But ye are of nothing, an abomination only'* (P, p. 542).[38] Pascal gazed in disbelief at how difficult if not impossible it was for fallen man to recognize the effects of the Fall. How is it that men and women, 'the sport of every wind' (P, p. 40), weak as they can only be, are not 'astonished at their own weakness'? How can they strut about as if they know for certain 'where reason and justice lie' (P, p. 63)? How is such a wholly baseless confidence possible, given man's fickleness, his volatility, the fact that 'the crushing of a coal' can unhinge his reason (P, p. 68)? Beyond such questions lies a starker conviction of the peremptory violence of the human arrogation of the right to be, the will to persevere in one's being: 'Mine, thine. "This is my dog," said these poor children. "That is my place in the sun." There is the origin and image of the usurpation of the whole world' (P, p. 86). Everything 'tends towards itself', writes Pascal: 'That is contrary to all order' (P, p. 466). Unlike us, he was intensely convinced that original evil is inseparable from the certainty of right and rights, which must always threaten to destroy the world. The persuasion of universal merit brings only havoc in its wake. But that persuasion can always find its reasons, which means in its turn that original sin is the apparently 'unreasonable' doctrine actually more reasonable than reason (P, p. 380).

'Man's condition', announces Pascal: 'inconstancy, boredom, anxiety' (P, p. 61). In one of his best-known aphorisms, he writes that 'all man's unhappiness stems from one sole cause, which is that he does not know how to stay quietly in his room' (P, p. 121).This points to one particular theme within the misanthropic tradition, the idea that human beings should scatter and content themselves with a self-sealed, impenetrably monadic existence. Compare Pascal's near-contemporary George Herbert:

> Surely if each one saw another's heart
> There would be no commerce,
> No sale or bargain passe: all would disperse
> And live apart.[39]

Pascal's point about 'man's condition', however, is that, because they are in thrall to it, in their 'wretchedness', men and women hustle and bustle, crave pleasure and excitement, endlessly seek 'diversions' – and that 'is all that men have been able to invent by way of making themselves happy' (P, pp. 56, 59, 123). But the very concept of diversion (or entertainment) proclaims the lack at its heart. We prefer the titillation of hunting the hare to contemplating the mortal creature, alternately whip up our passions and seek objects for them. So, too, the mind flits about and 'opinions move hither and thither, succeeding one another, pro and contra, according to one's lights' (P, p. 98). Worse, man finds quarrel in a straw: 'An inch or two of cowl can put 25,000 monks up in arms' (P, p. 59). In general, folly founds the exercise of power and is its guarantee, insofar as the power of leaders themselves is rooted in the folly and the weakness of their people.

On the subject of human pretensions or hubris, Pascal was an extreme sceptic. Do not expect truth or consolation from human beings, he warns, for their reason is 'merely feeble', dwarfed by the infinity of things beyond it (P, p. 172). He famously said that 'the eternal silence of these infinite spaces terrifies me' (P, p. 95), supposing that, if others did not feel the same, they were sunk in narcotic self-deception. There is even a Pascalian theory of addiction: the addict's need is a function of an irrepressible but inadmissible terror, which is in turn a function of the 'dumbness' of the universe, the eternal refusal of infinite nature to confirm any man-made meanings. God provides no end to the infinite recession of meaning, since Pascal's God is a *deus absconditus*, hidden from human view. This leaves individuals as, like addicts, condemned to their own particular 'little dungeons' for their brief lifespans and, since 'the propensity towards self' is the source of all disorder, humans are perpetually at war: 'All men naturally hate each other' (P, pp. 88–9, 97, 466). Thus one of the *Pensées* reads: 'Contempt for our existence, dying for nothing, hatred of our existence' (P, p. 111). For Pascal, human beings can transcend themselves only through self-hatred, hatred of the merely human in them, and through faith and thought, with God aiding them through the Redeemer, miracles and proofs. But the bleak corollary of this is that 'Jesus will be in agony until the end of the world' (P, p. 575).

For obvious reasons, Pascal was not much inclined to suggest that his hatred of human existence was coloured by life in Louis XIV's France. Yet the *Pensées* repeatedly suggest that the two were inseparable, or, at least, that the court amply justified Pascal's revulsions. Politics is 'a madhouse', he writes, for which there can be no rules, and kings and emperors are madmen in it (P, p. 322). The whimsical and random distribution of power is evident enough in 'duchies, royalties and magistracies' (P, p. 409). So, too, lying and flattery are intrinsic to the relationship between the great and the Jesuits (P, p. 504). The Church is full of 'unworthy' priests (p. 347). When Pascal discusses the 'probability' of fashions – by which he means that that they are plausible only within existing cultural horizons, and otherwise absurd – his example is duelling (P, p. 262). When he discusses the fallen world, he repeatedly resorts to analogies with the king and the *Parlement*. For Pascal, there is a founding and irremediable injustice at the heart of all things, yet he never stops calling it injustice. At one very striking moment in the *Pensées*, he even becomes acutely historicizing, apparently grasping the meaning of the failure of the first Fronde: 'In 1647, grace for all; in 1650, it was rarer' (P, p. 615).

*

So, though Pascal's greatest gift was doubtless an extraordinarily fine and delicate spirituality, there is nonetheless a deep strain of contemporary misanthropy in his writings. In general, misanthropy in Louis XIV's France was less identifiable with a particular, limited set of misanthropists than it was an insistence that circulated in the society in a number of different and complex ways. Perhaps predictably, we find it in the work of Martin de Barcos, Saint-Cyran's nephew and Arnauld's friend. But the misanthropic insistence is equally traceable in François de La Mothe Le Vayer, protégé of Richelieu, critic of Jansenism and friend of Molière. It crops up (a little later) in the *Nouveaux Dialogues des Morts* by Fontenelle, in many ways a worldly and conventionally successful man (member of the Académie Française, secretary to the Académie des Sciences). According to Fontenelle's version of Guillaume de Cabestan, the Provençal troubadour, the alternatives of Reason and Folly are so only for insignificant dunces. In fact, the world is peopled with fools, all 'equally foolish'.[40] Those who are officially called fools are merely those whose folly does not fit in with that of others. But folly is necessary, for it protects men from what would otherwise be a desolate encounter with themselves. Fontenelle was getting his argument partly from La Mothe Le Vayer, who declares that those who aspire to be doctors in 'this great Hospital for the Incurable' are 'the greatest fools of all'.[41]

Nicolas Boileau-Despréaux, better known simply as Boileau, was by no means immune to the lure of misanthropy. 'The Satire of Mankind' describes man as 'the dumbest animal of all', one embarked on 'an insensate course', restlessly flitting from one thought, tenet, sentiment and style to another.[42] Their ambition, hatred and greed all make human beings more fearsome than beasts. Worse still, only human beings destroy, not merely their kind, but the earth. In their thirst for wealth and pleasure, even knowledge and learning, humans promote and hasten the devastation of the world. A harebrained Alexander 'puts Asia to the torch', and man in general is so enamoured of fame that he will be

> killed indiscreetly at the breach, to get
> his mad bravado in the next gazette.

What price, asks Boileau, the illusion of a properly civil State? Give up books and ideas, and be 'unjust, violent, faithless, two-faced, false', work in finance or in law or, best of all, become a tax collector. The men of learning will end up fawning on you, and you'll get the women, too. All in all, if the ass is 'misanthropic', it is 'with good reason', not least because humans have the temerity to call each other asses.

So much is misanthropy a discourse, and so compelling is it as such, that even improbable luminaries are caught up by it. Pierre Bayle, for example, was, from the perspective of the Louis-Quatorzian court, at least, a marginal figure, a Huguenot who (wisely) spent most of his life at a distance from Paris, an unconventionally modern rationalist and sceptic inclined to liberalism and religious doubt who advocated universal toleration. But he also stoutly believed in the doctrine of original sin, was sympathetic to Manichaeanism and adjudged that 'man is wicked and unhappy. ... History is but a collection of the crimes and misfortunes of humankind'.[43] Fénelon was a churchman, Greek scholar and liberal, pacifist and resolute opponent of Louis XIV's wars, much admired for his saintly life. Yet it is not hard to find him sounding like a misanthropist:

> Let men be men, that is to say, weak, vain, inconstant, unjust, false and presumptuous. Leave the world to be always the world. ... Leave everyone to follow their nature and habits: you will not be able to improve them: the shortest way is to leave them be, and suffer them. Accustom yourself to unreason and injustice.[44]

Fénelon's was in some ways a proto-modern mind. Yet, superficially at least, his acceptance of unalterable wrong in that last sentence hardly seems to be modern at all.

Two features of the misanthropic insistence during the Ancien Régime are worth particular emphasis, since they shed light both on the link between it and the society that bred it and on the history of misanthropy. The first is the motif of flight to the desert: in the fifth century, for misanthropists, this was quite literally a choice they might make. By contrast, it is hard to think of a convenient and nearby desert that seventeenth-century French misanthropists might have flown to (and survived in). Yet there was clearly a fad for thinking of doing so: Liselotte, for example, declared her longing for the lone wild spaces remote from the court, which for her meant 'eating cherries on a mountaintop at five in the morning'.[45] In its comic aspect, the desire for the wilderness was a ready butt of Molière's satirical humour, but it also had a serious aspect, as in the case of Pasquier Quesnel, ascetic, Jansenist, friend of Arnauld and significant influence on Saint-Simon, who recommended 'withdrawing from the world' and going into the wilderness 'in order to seek salvation'.[46] It is a testimony to the quite extraordinary power of the Augustinian mindset that what was a literal proposition in the fifth century could last through twelve centuries to become a powerful and to some extent seductive metaphor in the seventeenth.

As a metaphor, it stood for renunciation. Indeed, there were many genuine French 'renouncers', like the solitaries of Marlagne, who lived in cloistered poverty. In one of its aspects, renunciation was a religious drive. But religious renunciation was only one form of the more pervasive phenomenon of taking refuge 'from a corrupt world'.[47] Apologists for a *contemptus mundi* were legion. Not only Augustinians and Jansenists but Oratorians, Huguenots and Trappists all sought to inculcate a disdain of pride, praise, the desire for eminence and the will to dominate. The opposition between the party of renunciation and *les mondains* even stood in for a democratic politics. Logically enough, the party of renunciation was anti-Jesuit. As far as it was concerned, the Fathers who had been caught smuggling South American gold into Europe disguised as chocolate bars pretty well summed up the Society of Jesus.

The second noteworthy feature of misanthropic discourse during the Ancien Régime is the questioning of the relation between human beings and animals. We have seen this already in La Rochefoucauld. Boileau's 'Satire on Mankind' is directed partly at idle fantasies that humans are lords of creation. The notion of the great Chain of Being deriving from Plato and Aristotle passed through Neoplatonism to medieval societies, and from there to the Ancien Régime at least as far as the mid-eighteenth century, when Abbé Pluche's bestseller *Spectacle of Nature* was still placing mankind at the top of the chain, with 'the other forms of life disposed beneath it in interlinking patterns'.[48] Cartesianism, with its assertion that animals are machines and man alone is rational, provided a formidable buttress to this thought. Radical misanthropy will have no truck with this bogus order. Human beings have no ontological privilege over animality. They rather ceaselessly collapse back into it, demonstrating their difference from it only by successfully deceiving themselves about their august status. Unable to castigate the derelictions of a miserably hierarchical society without fear of dire reprisal, the misanthropically inclined could at least work to undermine its intellectual basis. Take (Jean de) La Fontaine, in the first fable of Book XII of the *Fables et épitres*, *Les compagnons d'Ulysse*. Ulysses and his companions land on Circe's isle. Circe transforms Ulysses's men into beasts, while Ulysses himself remains immune to her potions. Knowing that Circe has fallen in love with him, he demands that she restore the manhood of his men. But the lion, now a king, despises the idea of returning to mere citizenship. The bear asks Ulysses why he should think that the form of a man is any more alluring than his own. Worst of all, the wolf demands: 'If I were human, according to your faith/Would I love carnage less?' 'Scélérat pour scélérat', villain for villain, it is better to be wolf than human being. All the newly converted animals agree: they have been liberated into truth by rejecting the 'laws of acting well'.[49]

The incompleteness of misanthropy, the fact that it appears mixed with other discourses, is perhaps conspicuously evident in La Bruyère. La Bruyère is not his Timon, and does not speak with his voice. Timon is one of a range of his 'characters'. La Bruyère's task, in the fashion of the classic moralist, is partly to pick them out, describe them and thus provide a moral account of the world. This may entail 'admiring little', but it also means 'approving much' (CT, p. 86): the words do not sound misanthropic. Nor for that matter does the 'tissue of eulogies' (not least of Richelieu and the king) in La Bruyère's speech upon admission to the Académie Française (CT, p. 447). The book even includes a paean of praise to Condé. Yet La Bruyère also feared that he was spending his time to no avail: 'A philosopher wastes his life in observing men', he wrote, 'and wears his wits out in exposing vice and folly' (CT, p. 85). There is a dark counter-swell in the *Caractères* which becomes more pronounced as the book wears on. La Bruyère asks: 'If it be usual to be vividly touched by things that are rare … why are we so little touched by virtue' (CT, p. 104)? 'How difficult it is to be content with anyone!' he exclaims (CT, p. 141). He successively excoriates a range of types to the point where one wonders to whom exactly the judicious moral distinctions with which he began were supposed to apply. By the time of the chapter 'On Man', he is declaring that 'if we are not to rage against men, their callousness, ingratitude, injustice, pride, self-love and forgetfulness of others', it is only because 'they are made thus, it is their nature' (CT, p. 264). The end of 'Of the Court' effectively clinches his gloomier case:

He who despises the court after having seen it, despises the world.

The city makes one disgusted by provincial life; the court undeceives one as to the city – and cures one of the court.

A healthy mind acquires at court a taste for solitude and retirement. (CT, pp. 228–9)

Both La Bruyère's logic and his irony point to a misanthropic conclusion.

*

In the long run, the condition of France under the Ancien Régime was to engender devastating hatreds, not only of the monarchy and government but of the Catholic church. Economic crisis, poverty, starvation and tax hikes all continued until the death of Louis XIV in 1715. The power of the aristocracy, *Parlement* and towns continued to weaken. Regent Philippe d'Orléans (1715–23) was initially considerably more flexible in his policies than the Sun King had been, then retracted most of his liberal and decentralizing initiatives. The liberal Regency ceded to an authoritarian Regency. After the death of the Sun King, the country saw long periods of peace, progress and even relative plenty. However, the initially popular Louis XV (1715–74) more and more alienated his people by his persistence with high rates of taxation, his losses in wars, political incompetence and spendthrift ways, his sexual conduct and decadent court, and, most of all, his continuing despotism and indifference to the popular will. Indeed, he repeatedly, quite literally told his aristocracy to fuck off.[50] When Robert-François Damiens sought to kill the king, the extraordinary discrepancy between the 'assassin's' pathetic little weapon – a three-inch penknife – and the means of his execution – burnings, bone-breakings, flesh-tearings, dismemberment by four horses – speaks volumes.

The historian Colin Jones has demonstrated that eighteenth-century France was by no means just the sink of political iniquity and cultural backwardness it has sometimes been taken for. In particular, the Enlightenment inaugurated a thought of social improvement via human reason, and an attack on organized religion. According to Voltaire, writing in 1751, 'A revolution occurred in people's minds'.[51] Yet Louis XIV continued to cast a long shadow over his successors. The old absolutist machinery did not disappear. The monarchy was as remote from the people as ever: after 1745, Louis XV 'virtually never again ventured outside the palace circuit'.[52] Court huggermugger was still as it had been. The gulf between wealth (in 1720, the Prince de Conti needed three carts to take his converted bullion home) and poverty (in the same year, hospitals and poor-houses 'had to shut their doors')[53] was monstrous. The episcopate reached 'fabulous levels of wealth'.[54] Tax evasion continued to be 'an aristocratic point of honour'.[55] The people enjoyed no personal or religious freedoms, and the *cascade de mépris* was installed at the heart of government. The most obvious social and political grounds of seventeenth-century misanthropy had not changed. Nor did its major intellectual sources simply disappear. Jansenism had not died with Port-Royal. Figures like Antoine de Noailles, Archbishop of Paris from 1695, clung on. Indeed, the Jansenist tradition became more powerful and influential as the eighteenth century wore on, especially in the law. It even triumphed over the Jesuits along the way.

Thus misanthropy did not wane, as Jones's reassuring argument might make us imagine. Rather, its forms mutated. The scientifically minded, for instance, were now contributing to the attack on the notion of the Great Chain of Being. There was even a distinct strain of misanthropy among the *philosophes* of the Enlightenment, notably Rousseau. Perhaps the most pronounced shift in Ancien Régime misanthropy in the later eighteenth century lies in (the changes in) its relation to libertinism. In the sixteenth century, the libertines were actually a Protestant sect who believed that their own spiritual light was a sufficient guide in matters of religious faith. From there, the word came to designate persons 'who refused to accept current belief and desired to free [themselves] especially from Christian doctrine'.[56] The 'learned libertines' of the 1620s and after – La Mothe le Vayer, Gabriel Naudé, Gui Patin – were sceptics and materialists who saw themselves as disabused, their vision as clear, cured of *sottise* or rank stupidity. They thought about humanity differently, on the basis of 'a principle of incredulity'.[57]

Intellectual libertinism defined itself against the mass of people, whom the libertines took to be ignorant, superstitious, irrational and swayed by senseless passion. Political power flourished on the basis of popular idiocy; but equally, since no hope lay in the people, revolt could breed only repression and regression. The libertine *érudit* took himself to be an exception to the rule of general asininity. He was therefore quite likely to end up misanthropic. That at least was La Mothe le Vayer's conclusion, as he brooded on Democritus's melancholic view of the city of Abdera.[58] Giulio Cesare Vanini, who was soon to be burnt at the stake, asserted that humans struck the one 'discordant note' in creation.[59] Cyrano de Bergerac railed against the 'unbearable pride of human beings, which persuades them that Nature has been made for them alone'.[60] La Mothe le Vayer took humanity to be 'an impostor in nature'.[61] His *Prose chagrine* endlessly multiplies the reasons for disgust with human life.

There were also libertine poets: Théophile de Viau, François Maynard, Nicolas Vauquelin des Yveteaux, Claude de Chouvigny, Baron de Blot L'Église. When de Viau and some others jointly published their *Parnasse des poètes satyriques* (1623), the book was publicly burnt. Some of the poets almost suffered the same fate. The poets took libertine thought out into a raw, unadorned world of life lived close to the edge, a world of poverty and disease, flop-joints, taverns and whores. From this emerged a poetry that, as in the *Parnasse*, scanned the world from top to bottom, providing a social panorama and a misanthropic litany, together. 'Deliver me, Lord', writes the author of 'Quatrains contre les hommes', from vicious men, sottish men, scheming men, disloyal men, boastful, lying men, deceitful and hypocritical men, men who murder with a smile, malicious and avaricious priests, judges who side with wealth and power, ignorant philosophical disputants, irresolute and fickle, ever-changing men, men who make empty promises, men who preach false doctrines, jealous and possessive men.[62] Deliver me, Lord. Adieu (O world). I have seen (mankind and fathomed it): these are typically insistent refrains.

The libertine poets often lived loose lives, but they were not intrinsically depraved. By the mid-eighteenth century, by contrast, writers and thinkers were forging a new unity between 'licences de mœurs' and 'licences d'esprit'. *Libertinage* was becoming a science of dissipation, notably in the *roman libertin*.[63] As it did so, its misanthropic inflections changed. To the pessimism of the seventeenth century, later libertinism added an explicit and emphatic disbelief in love and marriage, and a pointed disbelief in the virtue and integrity of women. Two *eminences grises* loom large at the end of this development, Pierre Choderlos de Laclos and Donatien Alphonse François, Marquis de Sade.

In Laclos's classic epistolary novel *Les Liaisons dangereuses* (1782), two aristocratic libertines, the Vicomte de Valmont and the Marquise de Merteuil, plot Valmont's seduction of an adolescent girl, Cécile, and a judge's pious wife, the Présidente de Tourvel. The libertines are not only witty, but awesomely clever. Their plot succeeds, only for them to turn savagely on each other, with disastrous consequences for both. These few bald words, however, do nothing to convey the great web of complication that Laclos spins as the predators inch slowly towards final victory over their prey. Certainly, *Les Liaisons dangereuses* is about sex. But, above all, it is about the will to power, which it reduces to a crystalline form, a wholly ruthless and amoral manifestation. It insists on the reality of that manifestation, indeed, its typicality: Valmont and the Marquise repeatedly draw parallels between their strategies and practices and those of conquerors, generals, rulers, politicians and courtiers. Nothing, the novel suggests, can properly resist a ferocious will to power, save another such will, and then, in violent fury, they will tear each other apart.

Laclos's vision is therefore pitiless: power is inexorable, its victims foreordained. This is not just because the world is composed of knaves and dupes, and the knaves win every time. The trouble above all is that Cécile's and the Présidente's very ordinariness, their frailties, flaws and ambivalences, the fluttering vagaries of their emotions, the sensual promptings of their bodies are precisely what leave them hopelessly vulnerable to domination. Honour, piety, fidelity, romantic passion, vows of eternal love are mere straws in the fire, and the novel relentlessly empties out the language in which they are expressed. Here the rigour of Laclos's irony is terrifying. However, Laclos's misanthropically conceived world is not one like Saint-Simon's in which human monsters are everywhere, but rather a world in which there is finally no appeal against the monsters, in which the monsters alone can be sure to flourish, gloating. The basilisk will always mesmerize its victims. Indeed, the novelist himself becomes a basilisk, drawing the reader into an invidious complicity with his libertines' exquisite inventiveness, admiration for their psychological subtlety and penetration, and amused delight like theirs at their virtuoso performances. We are dishonest if we do not see this. We are obtuse if we do not see the point.

Les Liaisons dangereuses is Laclos's implacable rejoinder to the sentimental, self-deceiving presumption that the Enlightenment was busily making 'all men honest, and all women modest and reserved'.[64] The Présidente flees to a convent, where she quickly dies. Cécile retires to a convent, too. Danceny, Cécile's lover, leaves for Malta, there 'religiously to observe vows which will separate [him] from a world' that has already conveyed to him 'the idea of so many accumulated horrors' while still so young.[65] Far away, beyond all hope of consolation, in a last, mad letter, the Présidente dwells on Valmont's image. But by now it is inextricable from the idea of a demonism at large and rampant in the world. Her devil will not cease tormenting her; indeed, she cannot herself let go of him, since, however false and treacherous his appearances, they never fail to beguile. If anything encapsulates the conclusion to which Laclos wants to lead us, this letter does. The misanthropists of the Ancien Régime often started at court and ended up in solitary retirement. So, too, one of the worldliest novels ever written at length reveals itself to have been also a spiritual meditation.

Finally, in the dog-days of the misanthropic tradition, de Sade's chilling achievement is to turn libertine misanthropy around and convert it into a positive philosophy. De Sade's world is one in which Nature is ungainsayably supreme and drives us, above all, to use others for our own purposes. This means that the relatively strong will brutalize, exploit and humiliate the relatively weak and take their pleasures, however extreme, at their expense. We may as well celebrate this, thinks de Sade, since it is the principle tyrannically at work in Nature. In the 1960s, sexual radicals occasionally used to suggest that de Sade's writings were really a libertarian account of perverted drives we would all be better for recognizing and accepting.[66] But they were very remote from de Sade's historical world. Not for no reason did de Sade write a play entitled *Le Misanthrope par amour*. His insane *Cent vingts journées de Sodome* (1785) is a huge, mind-numbing catalogue of the modes of sexual use of the other which freely include extravagant torture, rape and murder. Not surprisingly, the chief users turn out to be men, especially aristocratic men, the used, women, especially women of the lower classes. If *Cent vingts journées* is not a psychosexual handbook, neither is it an archly ironic exposure of the true logic of Ancien Régime decadence.[67] Nor is it intended to shoot the ground from under itself by virtue of its very hyperbole. In *Philosophie dans le boudoir,* de Sade argues for an end to laws against murder, rape and any form of sexual misconduct (because they are 'unnatural'). The author of *Cent vingts journées* means what it says. Yet, at the same time, the possibility of irony is always latent within it. We can read *Cent vingts journées* as a sexualized allegory of the social structures of Ancien Régime France, and the horrors and miseries they produced, at a stage at which they had lasted for so long and become so fixed in place that they seemed like the misanthropic truth of human history itself.

De Sade, however, completed *Cent vingts journées* in the Bastille. A mere five years later, the prison had disappeared. The ill-fated Louis XVI (1774–92) was a well-meaning and even beneficent ruler. He abolished serfdom, torture and discriminatory taxation and promoted the toleration of Protestants and Jews. Yet the court and political power remained unhelpfully cut off from the people, a separate world. The effects of despotism had bitten too deep. New ideas became more subversive. The contemporary Church and even the Catholic religion itself came under more fire. More people were rapidly becoming more literate, and revolutionary thought disseminated itself in a range of different cultural forms. There was a widespread desire for equality, whether absolute or an equality of rights. Louis XVI supported the American Revolution, but the result was the spread of revolutionary notions like popular sovereignty, the democratic spirit, the political triumph of reason and the regeneration of society. The stage was being set for a historical event that was to transform France and indeed the world, the French Revolution. The people were about to burst on to the scene.

The Revolution killed off the misanthropic tradition, and did so brusquely. The titles of the period tell the tale: Kotzebue's *Misanthropy and Repentance* (1788), Schiller's *The Misanthrope Reconciled* (1790), Paul Emil Thieriot's *Timon All Alone* (1794). As Daniel Cottom remarks, 'in this era of the rights of man', humanity so swiftly and fully established itself that misanthropy quickly became 'all but unthinkable'.[68] The great new cause swept up the misanthropists with it. Laclos joined the revolution. So, too, more eccentrically, did de Sade. But the change is most precisely captured in the fortunes of Sébastien-Roch Nicolas, best known as Chamfort. From a humble background, Chamfort was a man of scintillating talent. He was a deeply literary and learned but also an inveterately witty man, an ingenious and fascinating conversationalist, not only a fount of *bons mots*, but a collector and recollector of the *bons mots* of others (not least, misanthropic ones). In Chamfort, if anywhere, we get a vivid sense of misanthropy as social *currency*, a talk that, to some extent, did the rounds. He gripped the attention of those who knew him. His sayings went into circulation. His misanthropy is as rooted in the conditions of the Ancien Régime as La Rochefoucauld's, and at times he echoes him. However, Chamfort's misanthropy was bred of a different experience.

Chamfort was a free spirit, for whom freedom was not only a (forlorn) political imperative, but also just his ordinary way of being Chamfort. He was heedlessly spontaneous, disinterested both by nature and by conviction. Truth as he saw it, however searing, had absolute priority over social protocols. This was not a recipe for comfortable survival in the Paris of Louis XV and Louis XVI. Chamfort lived like a republican and egalitarian. But this he did before the fact. His gifts ensured that he made the acquaintance of the great, who often greatly admired him. But Chamfort was the very opposite of the shrewd modern networker: if the key to making one's fortune was the will to '*se pousser*' (pushiness),[69] he himself was not disposed to exploit his contacts; indeed, he repeatedly declined their offers. As a young man, he scrabbled for work. To a degree beyond his comprehension, he got sucked into petty literary feuds and was abandoned by fair-weather friends. Chamfort repeatedly said that he longed to live a secluded philosophic and literary life, entirely indifferent to society. If this attracted the charge of misanthropy, then so it had to be.[70]

In short, he could reach no accommodation with the dominant idioms of his world. But it was nonetheless a world he knew very well. In a host of maxims, reflections and anecdotes, he indicted it. One should eat, he suggested, at the tree of knowledge, which induces detachment from all the usual human concerns. Society then appears as a 'factitious composition' that gets further from nature the more one ascends the social ladder (MP, p. 8). It is a giant structure of boxes into which 'no-one really fits' (MP, p. 48). Its artificiality takes many forms: a 'mania for celebrity', for example, which makes only for unhappiness and degrades 'moral character' (MP, pp. 3, 39). Yet our attachment to the artifice of social constructions is unflagging. The fool who identifies his character with his role and 'takes his importance for merit and his credit for virtue' is the very model of social life (MP, p. 50). 'Be a Charlatan', then, or expect to be pilloried (MP, p. 33). Social survival is impossible, save theatrically; authenticity is the 'rarest' of virtues (MP, p. 22). Men reduce themselves to nullities, just to fit in. Writing for such a society, Chamfort thought, merely turned him into a performing monkey. Why would one court publicity rather than shunning it, given the public's inane criteria for judgement?

Chamfort had immersed himself in 'the memoirs and monuments of the century of Louis XIV' and earlier, and was intimate with the tale of France under Louis XV (MP, pp. 47, 191). Part of him felt that he knew enough of what he took to be an age-long history to generalize assuredly on the basis of his knowledge. 'Prejudice, vanity and calculation ... govern the world', and the engine that drives society is the endless struggle between these little drives (MP, pp. 42, 57). 'Reason, truth and sentiment' have almost no place in it (MP, p. 42). The consequences of this endemic dissymmetry are best known to those charged with keeping public order, who end up 'with a horrible opinion of society' (MP, p. 66). Furthermore, men in their imbecility continually bend to tyrants. The reign of Tiberius is the norm, not an exception: history is largely 'a train of horrors' (MP, p. 122). The beginning of wisdom is therefore 'the fear of men' (MP, p. 34). Again, solitude, flight and a *contemptus mundi* turn out to be the true marks of honesty. But there is also a Chamfort who states that the evils he describes are only 'as old as the monarchy', and therefore 'not irremediable' (MP, p. 51). He thought of them as specific to certain cultures. That his France seemed to put 'all natural and moral ideas' into reverse did not discredit those ideas themselves (MP, p. 102). Thus Chamfort can argue that the misanthropist is actually a philanthropist in disguise (MP, p. 70; once more, misanthropy turns out to be incomplete). The misanthropist hates the unequal conditions under which men have to live. He despises man, because man hardly begins to measure up to what he might be. 'We must start human society all over again' (MP, p. 134).

Hence, when the Revolution arrived, it absorbed Chamfort from the start. He threw himself into it, joining revolutionary groups, listening, watching, talking, even orating. He could think of nothing else, and wrote little. He was careless of the fact that the Revolution had soon deprived him of his pension. He was, he felt, at last alive, and full of ideas and hope. For a while, he was secretary to the Jacobins. Wrenched from its moorings by a wave of change, his misanthropy abruptly came to seem irrelevant, and vanished from his thoughts. It was now clear that men could 'form a reasonable society' after all (MP, p. 138). Chamfort's progress, then, would appear to be an object lesson: as a free, just, equal, democratic republic seems close at hand, so misanthropy fades and dies. The younger Chamfort had written that 'any man who is not a misanthropist at forty has never loved human beings'.[71] Now, at fifty, what he had taken to be only the unfulfilled possibilities of human life appeared to be on the point of realization.

The story, however, has a last grim coda. As Robespierre, Marat and Danton increasingly took over the Revolution, Chamfort grew more and more critical of the Jacobins. Furthermore, he was not about to rein in his habit of speaking freely, or using his wit to devastating effect. As always, Chamfort's *bons mots* were soon on others' lips. He was arrested, imprisoned, released, then threatened with arrest again. But he was, he said, a free man, and would not tolerate any more constraint. He chose to attempt suicide, instead, but hideously botched it. He lived on for a short while, and remained avid for the latest news, though he said it merely confirmed him in the view that he had been quite right to want to kill himself. 'The horrors that I see now', he said, 'make me want to try again'.[72] He found himself livelier than ever. Too bad that he no longer cared to live. If the Ancien Régime had caused his misanthropy, the Revolution finally confirmed it in place.

But this was not the effect the Revolution had on France, or indeed on much of Europe. The misanthropic tradition of the Ancien Régime accordingly migrated, and its last flickers are visible elsewhere, in cultures indifferent or hostile to the Revolution. The most obvious heirs to La Rochefoucauld and Saint-Simon are perhaps some of Byron's great, melancholic solitaries and outcasts, filled with an aristocratic contempt for arbitrary and despotic power, a horror of senseless bloodletting and an ardent devotion to ideals of freedom and justice, but likewise with a disdain for the mass of men, for human being itself, from which their aristocratic postures leave them distant. Thus Manfred nurses 'the Promethean spark', but has 'no sympathy with breathing flesh'.[73] Cain, one of those 'Souls who dare look the Omnipotent tyrant/ In his everlasting face', is granted the 'prophetic torture', a vision of the wretchedness of man's future. But it leaves him 'unfit for mortal converse' – and spiritually equipped to kill his brother.[74] Byron's heroes are the reverse of Schiller's, for whom the struggle with power means identification with the oppressed.[75] Or take Leopardi: from the Marches in Italy, of aristocratic stock, he made plans to flee – even saw himself as about to become the very embodiment of freedom – only to be blocked by his old-school father. Thenceforth human nature would come to seem 'frale in tutto e vile', frail and base in everything, seeking 'piuttosto le tenebre che la luce', darkness rather than light.[76]

Otherwise, the discourse peters out, if grandly, in Chateaubriand, a descendant of Breton aristocrats, and Lermontov, a Muscovite of aristocratic stock. There was clearly a historical logic to this: though it would take some time to accomplish the process, modern democracy was increasingly calling the august status of the aristocracy into question, and bringing its age-long status to an end. At this point, we may grasp the full significance of what has been the most imposing European misanthropic tradition since the Renaissance. With the exception of Chamfort, it was the product of a privileged class or classes. La Rochefoucauld and Saint-Simon were scions of old aristocratic families. Pascal's father belonged to the *noblesse de robe*. La Fontaine's parentage was wealthy provincial middle class, attached to a ducal estate. La Bruyère, though middle class, had close links with the Condés. Compare these with the ancestry of some of the leading *philosophes* of the Enlightenment: Diderot's father was a master cutler, Rousseau's a watchmaker, Morellet's a papermaker, Marmontel's a tailor. Voltaire's father had been notary to Saint-Simon.

But misanthropy sprang from a complex and ambivalent set of conditions. Though La Rochefoucauld and Saint-Simon were caught up in a powerful nostalgia for a vanished aristocratic heritage, none of the authors in this chapter were apologists for the aristocracy. Indeed, to a greater or lesser extent, they were its scourge. Admittedly, they castigated an aristocracy that Louis XIV and his successors reduced to political impotence, that had fallen from grace. But that is precisely the point: misanthropy emerges from a class that continued to enjoy the fruits of its position – wealth, luxury, licence – but had also been definitively stripped of its most formidable powers. It had miserably failed in any major attempt to oppose and thwart its enemies, above all, in the case of the Frondes. Ancien Régime misanthropy proper begins with the Frondes, not just because the end of the Frondes spells defeat for the anti-monarchist cause, but because it spells disaster and moral disgrace for the aristocracy. Thereafter, again and again, aristocratic intellects, or intellects close to the aristocracy, turn on the aristocracy itself, with a sometimes gleeful scorn. The question remains, however, as to why contempt for one's own should become contempt for the human race *tout court*.

The misanthrope despises both his overlords and his peers. At moments, he may be drawn to the cause of the suffering classes, and even, fleetingly, to that of social transformation. La Bruyère had his moments of compassion for the poor. The peasantry, he suggested, should not be in need of the bread for which they sowed the seed when they were sparing others the trouble of sowing themselves. Saint-Simon, too, was capable of generosity to the poor and took a genuine interest in their welfare. He worked to improve the condition of those who laboured on his estates. He could recognize that social problems had political and economic causes, and even blamed the starvation of the people on a conspiracy (the 'famine pact').[77] From time to time, Pascal is wistfully aware that the social evils he anathematizes may not after all be the inevitable consequence of fallen nature, but stem from the historical particularity of an autocratic regime. Somewhere struggling desperately at the back of his mind, like a tiny, almost asphyxiated creature, there is even an undimmed notion of a 'brilliant flaring of true equity' that would enthral 'all peoples'.[78]

Yet none of this is finally material. For La Bruyère, the peasantry belonged to a world entirely apart – in effect, subhuman:

> Certain wild animals, male and female, spread throughout the country, dark, livid and burned by the sun, are bound to the earth they are always digging and turning up and down with an invincible obstinacy; they have something resembling an articulate voice, and when they stand up they display a human face, and in effect are men. At night they retire to their burrows, where they live on black bread, water and roots. (CT, p. 300)

Similarly, Saint-Simon's good works in no way mitigated his *hauteur* or *esprit de caste*. It was the disempowerment of the aristocracy that had doomed French society from Mazarin on, and that alone.[79] Saint-Simon hated most of the court, but anyone outside the nobility was merely a specimen of the *lie du peuple*, the dregs of the populace, and probably a crook or a scoundrel. Below a certain (elevated) point in the social hierarchy his *Mémoires* never deign to descend.

In effect, for the misanthropically inclined, France was populated with distinct life-forms. The misanthropes could not begin properly to acknowledge the existence of the people or take account of their circumstances. In this they remained thoroughly a part of Ancien Régime culture as a whole. There is good reason for Marie Antoinette being remembered for having suggested that those without bread should eat cake. La Bruyère and Saint-Simon were operating in a very narrow space. Indeed, though it would have been a conspicuously brave person who ridiculed Saint-Simon, he was very much caught up in exactly the kind of inconsistency that Molière mocked in Alceste, denouncing the world while failing to renounce it. It begins to look as though misanthropic discourse did not so much take issue with Ancien Régime culture as radicalize its assumptions, turning the aversion it felt for the French people upon its own representatives and the court.

Indeed, more disquietingly still, in some degree, misanthropy conformed to, even was, State policy. Richelieu was very influenced by contemporary Augustinianism, founding the new state itself on an Augustinian premise: men were incapable of knowing what was best for them. He would therefore serve as an authority on the subject. To some extent, too, the misanthropy of the courtier was a question of just getting out while the going was good, cutting one's losses, having one's cake and eating it too. There were many prudent characters who, like the wit and poet Isaac de Benserade, protégé of Richelieu and friend and confidant of the Sun King, finally cultivated a 'disgust with the court and the world' when virtually satiated with their pleasures. (De Benserade went off to translate the *Psalms*).[80] In this respect, misanthropy could sometimes just be worldly wisdom. Even the accomplished schemer and factionist Madame de Maintenon, whose ascent through the court to the side of the Sun King was apparently so inexorable, claimed to hate humanity: 'I am filled with sadness and horror at the very sight of Versailles', she declared. 'That is what is called the World; that is where all passions are at work: love of money, envy, ambition, dissipation. How happy are those who have put the World behind them!'[81] That 'the World' and 'Versailles' are equivalents, here, is in one respect beside the point. For Madame de Maintenon, no other world was worth attention.

The Ancien Régime was a society given over to dire oppression, inequality and injustice. Above all, perhaps, it was a society that granted no one save the king the right to live according to one's lights. True, the freedoms at stake were not those that tend to preoccupy today's democracies. Homosexuality was accepted, commonplace, indulged, even paraded at Louis XIV's court. Surprising as it may seem today, this made not a whit of difference to the general level of political virtue. The best people at court were women: subtle, intellectual, literary women like de Sévigné and de Lafayette, or saintly types like Louise de la Vallière. But odious and unscrupulous women like Maintenon and Madame de Montespan were also among the most powerful figures at the Sun King's side. It was in a different sense to the postmodern one that, for the American as well as the French Revolution, the Ancien Régime would serve as the paradigm of liberty foreclosed, of a world gone wrong.

Its misanthropic discourses are comprehensible, then, not as a recognition of what humankind in itself is and can only be, but as a reflection of what it, the Régime, had made of humans, accepted, connived in, fashioned as human being, a life that for most was often little better than that of beasts. In a sense, the misanthropists in this culture saw straight, but what they saw straight was a historical culture, as other misanthropists have repeatedly despaired – 'O tempora! O mores!' – of other historical cultures. We might wonder, too, whether, at some level, the culture did not owe its misanthropy to an obscure sense of shame or self-disgust, a secret knowledge of its own degradation. That the misanthropic tradition did not long survive the Revolution suggests, by a seemingly incontrovertible logic, that, as the modern democratic spirit becomes a reality, as the people assert their claims, as the multitude declares itself to be unignorable and makes itself so, so misanthropy is bound to look increasingly like a historical phenomenon, past its sell-by date. There would seem to be a contradiction in terms between popular democracy and misanthropy. How can the people affirm itself, assert itself as arbiter and authority, and at the same time write itself off? As we shall at length see, however, the form of that question is altogether too simple. It may even be quite the wrong question to ask.

2
MISANTHROPISTS AND THE BODY

There are certain perhaps rather obvious objections to misanthropy, of which three stand out at this point. One of these seems to me to be much more convincing than the other two. First, misanthropy is essentially self-preening. The misanthropist is contemptuous, arrogant, aloof. He or she keeps an exorbitant ego inflated by peering down disdainfully at his or her fellows. This is in some degree Molière's critique of Alceste. But if, certainly, we will encounter misanthropists who are not exactly immune to this charge, they will probably be in the minority. As we shall repeatedly see, misanthropy is actually quite frequently born of care, disquiet, an intense (some might say, hypersensitive) response to the seeming ineradicability of human misery, radical injustice, the flagrant and irremediable evils of the world. Such misanthropists may evidently be preening themselves on a superior quality of sensibility or soul. But Swift and Tobias Smollett, who will feature in this chapter, stand as examples to the contrary, and there are plenty of others. The misanthropist also has a specific sense of proportion, in that, for him or her, abiding evils tend to have priority over any supposed counterweight or antidote to or mitigation of them. Equally, while the misanthropist may be almost overenthusiastic for reform or good works, he or she also seems persuaded of their futility and inefficacy in the larger scheme of things, and obstinate in a refusal to entertain any (more or less pious) consolations. The misanthropist tends towards a moral absolutism that has less to do with simplification, the resort to crude, oppositional categories, than with the assumption that the intractable self-interest is always in fact on the other side, that of the 'reasonable view'. Far from being snooty Olympians, misanthropists often appear to have lived in, at best, psychic discomfort, at worst, moral grief or dreadful torment.

Furthermore, if misanthropists are sometimes unpalatably harsh and serious-minded, they also quite often have not only very amusing but distinctly ironical minds (as in the cases of Smollett and Swift). Grimly, stoically, they face up to their own implication in what they attack. But above all, imagine the tones of a gruff, pragmatic critic of misanthropy, harping on the vanity and egotism of the misanthropist, and then read the following:

> While in the camp almost all my comrades thought, as I did, that if ever God allowed us to leave the camp alive, we would not live in towns, or even in villages, but somewhere in the depth of the forest. We would find work as foresters, rangers, or, failing that, as herdsmen, and stay as far away as we could from people, politics, and all the snares and delusions of the world.[1]

This is V. V. Pospelov, survivor of the Gulag Archipelago. He and the common-sense critic do not belong to the same world. The Russian would no doubt have thought the critic quite as remote from reality as armchair misanthropists are for the critic who scorns them. Pospelov speaks with the authority of extreme experience. Of course, there is no immediate reason why we should privilege extreme experience over other kinds – as experience. But the more important question here is what kinds of experience might matter for thought. What can be said in favour of a human world in which it was possible for Pospelov to say what he says? It is not unimportant that Pospelov asserts that his views were those of almost everyone who shared his tribulations. How would it conceivably be possible to show them all that they were wrong?

The second objection is less commonsensical than humanistic: what about the great human achievements, in the sciences, the arts and humanities, literature, philosophy? What of Wilberforce, Gandhi, Mother Teresa, Martin Luther King, Mandela? We shouldn't limit the evidence to big names: what of the countless instances of humble, ordinary, unassuming inventiveness and goodness? The trouble with this argument is one whose terms we will come across at intervals, but repeatedly. History furnishes no evidence of any prevalence, let alone triumph of the good, other than very fleetingly. The good, it would seem, is an exception, and, like other exceptions, merely goes to prove the rule. As we have already seen, misanthropy and exceptionalism (to introduce the philosophical term, though it is not only philosophical) are by no means incompatible. Given the fundamental incoherence and incompleteness of the misanthropic case, this is surely logical enough: the misanthropic position will necessarily include a space for the exception. From time to time, some figure or instance lifts him-, her- or itself out of the general ruck. But the very fact that we recognize how very remarkable he, she or it is only reinforces one's sense of the general quality of the ruck itself.

The most powerful of the three arguments against misanthropy mentioned above is rooted in something both more subtle and simpler than the other two, but weightier, though even this argument is not wholly immune to question. However compelling the arguments for renouncing humanity might seem on, say, intellectual, moral or political grounds, placed in one particular context, they are merely trifling. They are reasons for misanthropy – but only reasons.[2] They do not survive delight, the seductiveness if not the thrill of human beauty: the sparkle in the eye of a beautiful woman, the glow on the flesh of a beautiful man, a child's tenderness, the pathos of the old that Rembrandt captured. The true misanthropist must surely at the very least have difficulties with organic life, the (sometimes mesmeric) physical charm of people, their vivid appeal to the senses, to the affections, most obviously parental and sexual ones. In other words, the misanthropist has trouble with the body, and in this is likely to seem an aberration or a pathological case. Persius's and Juvenal's satire sometimes reeks of physical revulsion. Pascal actually censured his sister Gilberte for caressing her children. Everything 'which drives us to become attached to creatures is bad', he states. 'I have never been able to form such attachments'.[3] Note the implication: his alienation from human feeling came first, the bleak edifice of his thought second. Or take Saint-Simon: he seems given over to a disgust-obsession. He returns compulsively to descriptions of Versailles as full of filthy, shitting beasts, devoting great tracts of the *Mémoires* to commodes, enemas and purgatives and dwelling appalled (for example) on Richelieu's way of defecating (he would 'walk around for three hours and then, wherever he happened to be, unburden himself so copiously that the bowl could scarcely hold it all').[4] Piss and shit were much in evidence at Versailles – indeed, on open display. But to extrapolate from such details to a vision of Paris as 'the sewer which gathered in all the spawn of all Europe's sensuality',[5] however justified it might be morally, is to take side against the senses from the start, as though the sewer is where they belong. Here as much as anywhere else we encounter the Saint-Simon who was drawn to Jansenist asceticism.

However, the misanthropic tradition that perhaps most clearly poses the question of misanthropy and the body is English and Anglo-Irish and eighteenth-century, if for reasons beyond my scope here. In *Not in Timon's Manner: Feeling, Misanthropy and Satire in Eighteenth-Century England*, Thomas Preston has described this tradition, and I shall take one or two of my bearings from his work. But he does not raise the issue of attitudes to the body, still less how far they might compromise the power of the tradition. I will focus on three key instances in Preston's book, the order in which they appear being decided not by chronology but by the development of my argument: Johnson, Smollett and Swift.

*

Samuel Johnson cast himself as an observer of the world, remarking that whoever surveys it 'must see many things that give him pain'.[6] This could end in a 'horror at life in general'.[7] Preston immediately directs us to *The Rambler* no. 175, and its initial quotation, from Bias of Priene, makes the reason self-evident: 'οἱ πλέονες κακοί, the majority are wicked'.[8] Johnson says that it is impossible to ignore this:

> The depravity of mankind is so easily discoverable, that nothing but the desert or the cell can exclude it from notice. The knowledge of crimes intrudes uncalled and undesired. They whom their abstraction from common occurrences hinders from seeing iniquity, will quickly have their attention awakened by feeling it. Even he who ventures not into the world, may learn its corruption in his closet. For what are treatises of morality, but persuasives to the practice of duties, for which no arguments would be necessary, but that we are continually tempted to violate or neglect them? What are all the records of history, but narratives of successive villanies, of treasons and usurpations, massacres and wars? (R 175, vol. v, p. 160)

Where the truth of original sin is concerned, he declared, 'the inquiry is not necessary; for whatever is the cause of human corruption, men are evidently and confessedly so corrupt, that all the laws of heaven and earth are insufficient to restrain them from their crimes' (LJ, p. 1160).

Johnson's certainty about this was cast-iron, and it fixed him in some fairly merciless attitudes. His politics were by no means as unvaryingly, stuffily conservative as some take them to be. He was ferociously anti-slavery, for example, appalled by the (discriminatory, anti-Catholic) Penal laws in Ireland, and enraged by British warmongering over the Falkland Islands. But such responses did not stem from a liberal disposition. Johnson had far too dark a mind to tend in the liberal direction. Men are fit to govern neither themselves nor each other, he states, and liberty is a juvenile passion, a 'love' appropriate only for '*boys*' (LJ, p. 1017). He regarded the liberalisms as mere cant, a 'whining pretension to goodness',[9] an affectation of a virtue unmerited because sentimental and self-deceiving. It is the saints and sufferers who are likely to see things right: thus, for example, with Floretta in *The Fountains*, finally crushed by human folly. Johnson's play *Irene* sacrifices its doughtily independent-minded heroine to a tyrannical social order founded on a universal docility that, in Demetrius's phrase, ensures a 'gen'ral fraud from day to day'.[10] In *The Vision of Theodore: The Hermit of Teneriffe*, Theodore himself, though once 'a groveller on earth' who 'purchased the assistance of men by the toleration of their follies', subsequently chooses solitude, and then has a vision of the true nature of the 'Mountain of Existence'.[11]

Hardly the Johnson, it would seem, who famously declared that 'when a man is tired of London, he is tired of life' (LJ, p. 859). However, Johnson specifically said only that this would be the case with 'any man, *at all intellectual*' (my italics) – in other words, London was the best place for intellectual life; equally, for intellectuals to observe life – and, at any rate, the remark says nothing about any supposed value to the human life in question. Indeed, Johnson's (admittedly much earlier) Juvenalian satire 'London: A Poem' might make one suspect the seeming enthusiast for London of ironic craft. There Johnson, not a fan of the Scots, nonetheless asks who could conceivably leave 'unbrib'd, Hibernia's land/Or change the rocks of Scotland for the Strand?' In the city that holds and represents all life, where 'all are slaves to gold,/ Where looks are merchandise and smiles are sold' and 'malice, rapine, accident conspire/And now a rabble rages, now a fire', you should 'prepare for death, if here at night you roam,/And sign your will before you sup from hoam'. Even at home, however, you will hardly be safe, since 'the midnight murd'rer' may always burst 'the faithless bar'. At all events, within London's 'curst walls, devote to vice and gain', 'rebellious virtue' is 'quite o'erthrown'.[12]

It is possible to make Johnson sound a little like Pascal. (The resemblance in general is greater than one might suspect). According to Mrs Thrale, he 'never could endure' his father's caresses.[13] Boswell tells us that not only did he never want a child. He also thought he could not have had 'much fondness' for one (LJ, p. 737). However, it would be quite mistaken to develop the parallel very far. Certainly, Johnson conceived of himself as a solitary – life was essentially an affair of solitude. Samuel Beckett later remarked that 'there can hardly have been many so completely at sea in his solitude as he was or more horrifiedly aware of it'.[14] But he was also an immensely gregarious and convivial man, and had a huge acquaintance drawn from all ranks in society, which he clearly genuinely enjoyed – indeed, needed. As the biographies make clear, he not only treated his many friends very warmly, but was seriously generous and charitable. At the very least, then, it would seem that he shared Swift's recognition that the misanthropic attitude could not be wholehearted. No doubt, in Johnson's case, this was partly a question of impulse. But *Rambler* no. 79, for example, also makes a theoretical case for benevolence, and does so with particular clarity: a categorical mistrust of others is itself 'an enemy of virtue', since it corrupts, and probably stems in any case from the mistruster's knowledge of his or her own character. It is therefore 'happier to be sometimes cheated than not to trust' (R 79, vol. iv, pp. 53, 55). Johnson's writings make it abundantly clear that he did not stop believing in goodness and its limited efficacy. He can make the limits sound drastic: if our sole hope of achieving 'the conquest of the world and of ourselves', he asserts, 'lies in the cultivation of piety and reason along with virtue as our reigning ideas' (R 203, vol. v, p. 319), finally, only God can underwrite that hope. But this hardly makes of Johnson a La Rochefoucauld or a Saint-Simon.

Preston quite rightly argues that Johnson falls into a specific category, that of the religious and benevolent misanthropist.[15] His distinctive misanthropy shares neither the profound contempt of La Rochefoucauld nor the unappeasable rage of Saint-Simon. Its sources are different in kind, apparently more philosophical. One might argue, here, that one need go no further than Johnson's greatest work, *Rasselas*, and its wistful, haunting, lapidary first lines:

> Ye who listen with credulity to the whispers of fancy, and pursue with eagerness the phantoms of hope; who expect that age will perform the promises of youth, and that the deficiencies of the present day will be supplied by the morrow; attend to the history of Rasselas prince of Abissinia.[16]

In the beginning of *Rasselas* lies its irrefragable end: what the story itself will do is lay bare the mechanisms, the logic that leads to the inevitable conclusion. As *Rambler* 203 puts matters, 'It is not therefore from this world, that any comfort can proceed ... that hope only is rational, of which we are certain that it cannot deceive us' (R 203, vol. v, p. 295), by which Johnson means religious hope. Both *Rasselas* and his great poem *The Vanity of Human Wishes* are intended as objective, even exhaustive demonstrations of the inexorable structure of deception and undeception. The second title makes the whole point clear. As Boswell said, the poem comprises a string of 'instances of variety of disappointment' (LJ, p. 139).

In effect, Johnson sets out from the Pindaric apopthegm, 'wrapt in error is the human mind' (R 151, vol. v. p. 37). But he was thinking of a specific kind of error, the error produced by the ceaseless demand of desire. For 'we desire, we pursue, we obtain, we are satiated; we desire something else, and begin a new pursuit' (R 6, vol. iii, p. 35). 'The mind of man is never satisfied with the objects immediately before it' (*Rambler* 2, vol. iii, p. 9). After satisfaction, desire is resurgent in a different form. Thus we hasten on from experience to yet another hope or expectation. The object of desire, once attained, is insufficient, and the fulfilment of desire invariably breeds an ensuing disappointment. Since the satisfaction of desire turns to dust between the fingers, life becomes 'a progress from want to want, not from enjoyment to enjoyment' (LJ, p. 754). We can see, then, why, in Johnson's view, to 'repress the swellings of vain hope' should be the immemorial task of the moralist (R 29, vol. iii, p. 160). 'Every desire is a viper in the bosom' (LJ, p. 336). But why should this view necessarily make for misanthropy? First, intellectual powers are no proof against the 'swellings', which are imperious. Arriving at a knowledge of the structure of experience does not mean that one no longer falls prey to it. Secondly, the structure is in fact intrinsic to morality itself. Even morally, we 'see more than we can attain': moralists cannot live up to their precepts, 'and those who raise admiration by their books, disgust by their company' (*Rambler* 14, vol. iii, pp. 76, 78–9). In any case, as *Rambler* 87 insists, no one can bear to listen to moral advice, because of the strain in their desire that can only be satisfied by a belief in their own superiority. Thirdly, in general, the vanity of human wishes breeds envy, affectation and dissimulation, fallacies and impostures, and delusions about oneself and others. Everyone envies everyone else, in the belief that others are getting more satisfaction than they are (see *Rambler* 128). This is the circle we are doomed to tread, and it means that the world remains unchanged and, it seems, unchangeable. Indeed, the desire to alleviate misery is caught up in the same structure of hope and disappointment, and only breeds more misery in its turn. But fourthly, and most tellingly, according to 'The Young Author', hopes are illusory because the person who hopes trusts his fate 'to human kind,/more false, more cruel than seas or wind'.[17] It is human beings themselves who invariably fail to live up to what they seem to promise.

The quintessential human folly, then, is the refusal of 'immediate ease for distant pleasures' (R 2, vol. iii, p. 99). The natural flight of the human mind is not from pleasure to pleasure, but from hope to hope. This might sound likely to lead to an attitude of *Carpe diem*. But that is not remotely Johnson's bent. Quite the reverse: he remained committed to 'the severest and most abstracted philosophy' (R 18, vol. iii, p. 99). If any 'ease' is to be found, it is religious (naturally, since the logic is that of Kierkegaard's Either/Or). The present spells displeasure. One is ceaselessly driven to hope, Johnson wrote, precisely because the present moment is 'irksome' (quoted LJ, p. 263). Those who give up on the hopelessness of hope and 'look no further than the present life' are misguided, for it is one only of 'vanity and vexation of spirit'.[18] In general, any compliance with the motion of 'life merely sensual' is a downward descent, and 'every source of pleasure is polluted' (*Rambler* 7, vol. iii, p. 38; 203, vol. v, p. 293). This chilly disdain for the senses fed into Johnson's style. Boswell asserted that 'his example has given a general elevation to the language of his country' (LJ, p. 159), and 'elevation' was indeed the Johnsonian manner. He cast his knowledge and experience into great, weighty, marmoreal, abstract concepts, seldom if ever making any sensuous appeal to his readers. Significantly, when he tries to evoke a terrestrial paradise, as in *Rambler* 33, the language is stock, clichéd, dead, inert. It is also significant that, while a select few loved *The Rambler*, it had only a limited readership, because of its unrelenting gravity, the absence from it of ordinariness, the life of the senses, any attachment to the visible, material world, Johnson's lack of interest in what bluestocking Catherine Talbot called 'the living manners of the times'.[19] He hankered after a 'disembodied state', supposing that it meant that one would be able to see 'with more extent' (LJ, p. 544). It is this 'larger vision' that he appears to aspire to in his prose.

Johnson fiercely and insistently rebutted any notion that the 'state of the body' might at all determine the 'faculties of mind' (R 117, vol. iv, pp. 262–3). The whole of *Rambler* 117 is devoted to mocking the idea. Yet he had good reason to ignore the behaviour of his own body, if only through the resources of language and thought. Boswell supposed that Johnson's judgement stood at the centre of his being like a gladiator in an arena, with wild beasts assailing him that he knew he must drive back to their den. Mrs Thrale possessed fetters and padlocks that she asserted after his death had been for Johnson. It is far less likely that they played a part in any sexual practices than that they were the result of his fear of onsets of uncontrollable insanity. (Johnson would have associated them in the first instance with lunatic asylums).[20] He was afraid he might need forcible restraint. He himself said that he wanted protection against 'lust', 'pollutions', 'wickedness', 'sinful habits', 'sensuality in thought' and 'vain longings of affection'.[21] He stopped drinking precisely because he knew that otherwise he might not stop drinking – at all. Though he had as little faith that relations between the sexes generally worked out as, later, did Jacques Lacan,[22] his amorous inclinations were 'uncommonly strong and impetuous' (LJ, p. 1375). He was a man of immense, indeed, Boswell thought, gargantuan appetites. But they were unlikely to be satisfied, as Johnson well knew, and as he made clear in 'To a Young Lady on her Birthday': 'With his own form acquaint the forward fool,/Shewn in the faithful glass of ridicule' (P, p. 36). He was writing, of course, of himself.

In other ways, too, Johnson's body was for him increasingly an extraordinary and finally a tragic burden; this is partly why we continue to find him so arresting. He told others that he was born almost dead, and immediately developed a lesion on the buttock. It was a tiny harbinger of things to come. The young Johnson was 'much afflicted with the scrophula, or king's evil', a tubercular infection of the lymph glands, which disfigured 'a countenance naturally well formed' and permanently affected his hearing (LJ, p. 31). He was also blind in one eye, which left him very near-sighted. He particularly suffered from 'a vile melancholy … which has made me mad all my life, at least not sober'.[23] Boswell thought that his melancholy disposed him to a poor view of physical life. But it was equally his body that disposed him to melancholy. If he was subject to 'a dejection, gloom, and despair, which made existence misery', it was inseparable from overwhelming physical symptoms, 'an horrible hypochondria, with perpetual irritation, fretfulness, and impatience'. The 'baleful influence' of this 'dismal malady' persisted throughout his life, and 'all his enjoyments' were but 'temporary interruptions' of it (LJ, p. 47). He had frequent cramps, and endured protracted bouts of prostration or sheer sloth. He fell victim at various times to gout, palsy, asthma, emphysema and chronic dropsy, especially in his later years. Sleep was a major problem. 'I pass restless and uneasy nights', he said, 'harassed with convulsions of my breast, and flatulencies at my stomach' (LJ, p. 890). This was quite typical. He was bled from early childhood, and subsequently underwent a lifetime of phlebotomy, including inept and distressing attempts to bleed himself. Towards the end, he was bleeding himself so clumsily and inordinately that he needed friends to patch him up (while also subjecting himself to an 'increasingly ghastly, farcical drama of drugs').[24]

In addition, his body behaved in very peculiar ways. 'Such was the heat and irritability of his blood', wrote Boswell, 'that not only did he pare his nails to the quick; but scraped the joints of his fingers with a pen-knife, till they seemed quite red and raw' (LJ, p. 121). He was frequently overtaken by involuntary tics and mannerisms, 'convulsive starts and odd gesticulations' (LJ, p. 68), and emitted the oddest noises. When he laughed, his companions thought he was having a fit. ('He laughs like a rhinoceros', said Tom Davis, LJ, p. 637). He had a peculiar, untidy way of dressing, with numerous 'slovenly particularities' (LJ, p. 281). People remarked on his bizarre carriage: 'When he walked the streets, what with the constant roll of his head, and the concomitant motion of his body, he appeared to make his way by that motion, independent of his feet'.[25] It 'was like the struggling gait of one in fetters', said Boswell, adding that 'when he rode, he had no command of his horse, but was carried as if in a balloon' (LJ, p. 1398). Those who did not know him and had not spoken to him sometimes 'concluded that he was an ideot' when they first met him (LJ, p. 107). He was easily made fun of: the schoolboys at Johnson's private academy at Edial used to peep through a keyhole at the 'awkward and tumultuous fondness' of his sexual approaches to Mrs Johnson (LJ, p. 71). David Garrick, at that time a pupil, was later given to mimicking a pre-coital Johnson running round the bed: '"I'm coming, my Tetsie, I'm coming, my Tetsie! Ph! Ph!" (blowing in his manner)'.[26] Alexander Pope thought that his body made of Johnson a 'sad spectacle'.[27] For his own part, he wrote of his 'constitutional unhappiness' (LJ, p. 233), and said 'I am often, very often, ill' (LJ, p. 150).

It is not hard, then, to understand why Boswell saw Johnson's spirit as 'grievously clogged by its material tegument' (LJ, p. 571). Thought and writing were his means of escaping the body, but the flight from the body also bred misanthropy. His own body being so obviously unendurable – or so the anti-misanthropic case might run – Johnson took the only means at his disposal to transcend it. However affected we might be by his ordeals, we can nonetheless see quite clearly what is problematic in his misanthropy. The logic of Johnson's philosophy is epicurean: give up on unrealistic hopes, will o'the wisp notions, and cultivate the moment, in a modest knowledge of its and one's own limitations, and the limits to desire. In contemporary terms, enjoy. But Johnson's body did not make that possibility available to him. Indeed, to settle for the moment was the ultimate nightmare, for it would have meant accepting the lumpish, uncoordinated, trouble-ridden thing he carted round with him as all there was, his only truth. So Johnson chose religion and misanthropy together. But, though his predicament may move, even awe us, it need not incline us to share his austere logic, or the conclusions to which it leads him.

*

Smollett is a different case. His is above all a picaresque misanthropy, a misanthropy towards which the picaresque novel from its Spanish origins (*Lazarillo de Tormes*, Quevedo's *The Swindler*, Alemán's *Guzmán de Alfarache*), through Grimmelshausen's *Simplicissimus* and Lesage's *Gil Blas* to Defoe and Smollett himself, repeatedly tends, particularly in three of its recurrent features: the experience of a range of different social strata; an emphasis on the worldly education provided by travel or the journey along the road; and, most pungently of all, the idea of 'the school of hard knocks'. In the picaresque, truth and reality are literally beaten into the hero. In Smollett's greatest achievement in the genre, *Roderick Random*, Roderick journeys from Smollett's native Scotland to London, to the West Indies (thanks to the navy), to France, to Germany (thanks to the French army), then to Flanders, and so back to London. Along the way, he runs the full social gamut: beaux and belles, smugglers and soldiers, bluestockings, prudes and whores, country squires and Scots villagers, homosexual noblemen with ministerial influence, naval officers, surgeons and ordinary seamen, footmen, highwaymen, little businessmen and 'fine gentlemen' (or coxcombs)[28] – and, to round it all off, a destitute writer, who tells him the dismal truth about the world of hacks, authors, booksellers and publishers. The lesson Roderick must at length learn is that treachery, knavery, artifice, fraudulence, cowardice, resentment, vengefulness, faithlessness, heartlessness, skulduggery, false witness, rank injustice, want of charity and peremptory and reasonless hostility are prevalent everywhere. The simple and 'milky disposition' cannot but live at their mercy (RR, p. 390).

In this fashion, *Roderick Random* seeks 'to animate the reader against the sordid and vicious disposition of the world', and 'to represent modest merit struggling with every difficulty to which a friendless orphan is exposed, from his own want of experience, as well as from the selfishness, envy, malice, and base indifference of mankind' (RR, p. 5). Scoundrels rise to the top, by infamous practices, while merit is almost never rewarded. The emotional perversions – wanton ingratitude, the enmity of ill-doers, pleasure in inflicting quite unnecessary suffering, the desire to be superfluously cruel to those one has already casually or involuntarily wounded – insistently seize hold of people. Senseless and sometimes fatal violence flares routinely. Roderick's world is one of casual slap, slash, smash and bang where people cannot but do each other damage. When Roderick's confederate Bragwell goes randomly kicking hungry, down-and-out whores in London early one morning, he merely affords a rather extreme example. Seldom does anyone care about the pain inflicted on anyone else. Rather, from the start of the novel, innocence and candour fall 'miserable victims to rigour [hard-heartedness] and inhumanity' (RR, p. 10). When, as a bleeding, destitute victim of a robbery, Roderick finds himself in a strange village, none of the inhabitants has kindness enough 'to administer the least relief' (RR, p. 214). But Roderick himself is not exempt from his own strictures. Smollett cunningly and increasingly makes this clear in his protagonist's treatment of his quondam schoolmate, companion, benefactor and valet, Strap, whom he not only ruthlessly exploits, but whose ear, for instance, he may twist so violently that Strap 'roar[s] hideously with the pain', sending Roderick into 'an immoderate fit of laughter' (RR, p. 352). The reasons why Roderick arrives at the familiar misanthropic desire to retire 'to woods and deserts, far from the hospitable haunts of man' (RR, p. 243) are clearly multiple. By the end of the novel, they are sufficiently strong for him to opt, if not for the desert, at least, for pastoral retirement.

In *Roderick Random*, the progress through the classes and across the nations and the immersion in brutality seem intended to lend the protagonist's manifold, profound and various disgusts a certain authority. The same is true of Smollett's much later *Travels Through France and Italy*. The book is made up of letters about the novelist's own trip abroad. But it also makes clear how far, for him, the picaresque was not just a literary genre, but his way of understanding and imagining the world at large. Critics have seen the *Travels* as prejudiced, and the more slighting passages about the French and Italians obviously seem to bear this out. National vanity is above all what characterizes the French.[29] They are slothful, volatile, affected and prattling, natural lightweights who have at best been preposterously educated. But they are also insidiously corrupt. The licentious gallantry of the Niçois, for example, is mere *porcheria*, piggishness. Indeed, France is so bad as to be 'the general reservoir from which all the absurdities of false taste, luxury, and extravagance have overflowed the different kingdoms and states of Europe' (TFI, p. 52). Anyone travelling there will be 'imposed on'. But this is hardly surprising, since poverty has reduced 'all the common people' to 'thieves and beggars' (TFI, p. 174).

The Italians fare no better at Smollett's hands. They punish transgressions against the church, he says, but pardon flagrant crimes. They have a 'jealous and vindictive temper' (TFI, p. 230) and are 'treacherous and cruel' in revenge, which they take all too seriously (TFI, p. 244). They, too, impose on visitors. Frenchwomen get off comparatively lightly in the *Travels*, at least insofar as they are slightly less 'ridiculous and insignificant' than Frenchmen (TFI, p. 90). But Italian women are 'the most haughty, insolent, capricious, and revengeful females on the face of the earth' (TFI, p. 231). There are also occasional sideswipes at other nationalities. Smollett tells us, for example, that 'the German genius lies more in the back than the brain' (TFI, p. 240). To make of the Smollett of the *Travels* merely a good old British Euro-hater, however, is to ignore the account of the abominable England he quits. London, the Dover road, Kent Street, Southwark, the 'beggarly and ruinous' suburbs (ibid.): the capital and its environs are in many respects as bad as the worst of Europe. Thus, when, in perhaps the most arrestingly nauseous passage in the book, in Letter V, Smollett lists disgusting habits around the world, he equally includes English derelictions along with the rest. The English abroad repeatedly turn out to be as repulsive as the locals. Smollett is not partial. This is the travelogue not of a xenophobe, but of a misanthropic picaro.

Preston suggests that Smollett is a benevolent misanthropist (like Johnson) and a 'risible' one (unlike him). The benevolence appears, for example, in the fact that, at heart, Roderick is really something of an indignant 'man of feeling', given to a 'natural tenderness' he is all too ruefully aware the world will everywhere bruise, and indeed warp.[30] This seems to square with what we know of Smollett himself. Friends and contemporaries like John Anderson testified to his being 'a man of upright principles, and great and extensive benevolence'.[31] Others repeatedly noted that he seemed exceptionally thin-skinned, a man with too much sensibility for his own peace of mind. It was as though the world could all too promptly break through to his innards and turn the knife there. What Preston might mean by Smollett's 'risibility' is perhaps a little trickier to grasp. But he is conscious (as was Smollett)[32] that, in the eighteenth century, the word had at least two senses, ludicrous (as today), and inclined or disposed to laughter. Like Molière, Smollett was certainly able to see the absurd side of the misanthropic position. At his very best, however, more subtly, he was also able to turn misanthropy inside out, wresting playfulness and even geniality from its very contradictions. This is the case, above all, with *Humphry Clinker*.

In *Humphry Clinker*, Smollett takes a misanthropist, Matthew Bramble, and plays his misanthropy off against both other points of view and its own internal fissures. The epistolary form of the novel – it is composed of letters written by divers hands – allows for a shrewd awareness of how far 'prejudice and passion' may be 'falsifying mediums' (HC, p. 374). This perspectivism tends to leaven Bramble's grumbles and makes them seem relative. Thus Smollett follows and counters Bramble's evocation of London as an 'immense wilderness' where only the worthless, trashy and specious flourish (HC, pp. 118–20), as exemplified above all in the pleasure gardens of Ranelagh and Vauxhall, with a letter from his niece Lydia, who is 'utterly unacquainted with the characters of mankind' (HC, p. 43). She therefore has the capacity to imagine Ranelagh as like 'the inchanted palace of a genie' (HC, p. 123), a perception the more persuasive for its recognizing while containing the fact of metropolitan rowdiness. True, there are others in the novel, like Dr Linden and Lismahago, who at least sporadically coincide with Bramble in his crustiness, and indeed Lydia herself gets much closer to his position as the story wears on. But Bramble himself also keeps on warming to human life. His blood rises at every instance of insolence, cruelty and thanklessness, Smollett tells us, and he can seem as generous, kind-hearted and forgiving as the average philanthropist. It would seem that, as Bramble's nephew Jery says, his uncle 'affects misanthropy, in order to conceal the sensibility of a heart, which is tender, even to a degree of weakness' (HC, p. 45).

But there is also a more unusual aspect to Bramble. The novel repeatedly stresses his originality, what Jery calls his 'oddity' as a 'humorist' (HC, p. 36). This is evident, perhaps above all, in that he is a man possessed of a knowledge he persistently refuses to indulge to the full. Peculiarly and paradoxically, in *Humphry Clinker*, misanthropy looks increasingly like, at one and the same time, an extravagant position, a logical one, and an attitude that should be held at bay, handled with a certain ironical levity. This does not so much cast a doubtful light on the generalities on which misanthropy depends as it underlines the gulf that yawns between the vast panorama of humanity written off by the misanthropist, and the littleness of any particular life, including his or hers. The point is not that the little life is hardly sufficient basis for the big judgement. Rather, the tininess of a life raises the question of whether it is ever worth making any such judgement the centre of one's view of things. Hence what is often Bramble's decidedly wry and spirited tone, which has less to do with common sense than his commitment to his own short span, which is best not eaten up with detestations: preferable to remain of good temper, and try to escape noticing the world around one too much. The rural English idyll that Smollett's virtuous few seem set to enjoy at the end of the novel is helpful in both respects.

But the trouble with this conclusion is that Smollett's physical imagination undercuts it, as it tends to undercut resistances to misanthropy throughout his work. The point about Bramble's loathing of the miscellaneous, swarming crowds of Bath and London ('without respect of rank, station, or quality, all those of both sexes', HC, p. 66), their habits, attitudes and opinions, manners and relationships, is that it is very effectively underwritten by bodily loathing. This is notably the case in his great, repulsive vision of the waters of Bath, thick with the matter of scrofulous ulcers and other 'scourings of the bathers', 'the straining of rotten bones and carcasses', 'sweat, dirt, and dandriff' and 'abominable discharges of all kinds'. The vision was clearly Smollett's own. His *Essay on Water* sinks quite as deeply into such noisome matters. Bramble's Bath is rife with contagion and infection, which for him is commensurate with 'the folly and the fraud' of its denizens, its character as a 'sink of profligacy and extortion'. 'But what have I to do with the human species?' asks Bramble (HC, pp. 74–7). Smollett is clearly of the view that, at the very least, it is better to have nothing to do with any fluid that the species has bathed in. Note, too, Dr Linden's virtuoso meditation on 'the nature of stink', chiefly that of faeces. It includes an account of his own habit of raising his spirits by 'hanging over the stale contents of a close-stool, while his servants stirred it about under his nose'. It also contains details of 'the last Grand Duke of Tuscany, of the *Medicis* family, who caused the essence of ordure to be extracted, and used it as a most delicious perfume' (HC, pp. 43–6). Bramble will later expand on it in his catalogue of the '*villainous smells*' of Bath ('putrid gums, imposthumated lungs, sour flatulencies, rank armpits, sweating feet, running sores and issues', etc., HC, p. 96). Alongside the huge imaginative energy that Smollett invests in such passages, their stomach-churning verve and gusto, the sweetness, decency and order of the rural idyll look pallid and insipid.

For all his geniality, Smollett's misanthropy can seem fundamental to him and irreducible. It is inseparable from three pathological syndromes (pathological in that they appear everywhere in his work): his fascination with pain and torment, if not what his biographer Jeremy Lewis calls his 'sadistic relish' for them;[33] his sustained focus on squalor and the ugliness of bodies; and his endless preoccupation with the insides of bodies finishing up outside them, most egregiously in the case of his scatology (preoccupation with excrements) and his descriptions of casualties in battle. Where the first is concerned, Smollett clearly had a seriously violent side, as in the case of his assault on luckless hack Peter Gordon.[34] He transferred his sadism most completely to Peregrine Pickle, particularly in the early part of the novel of that name. But one might equally cite, among many such instances, the account in *Roderick Random* of the scourging of O'Donnell (with nettles), dwelling on its after-effects; the almost lascivious description of the whipping of Roderick's schoolmaster (which Lewis points out was an entirely invented and strictly unwarranted addition to autobiographical fact); and the extraordinary, protracted account of the American Indians torturing Murphy in *Humphry Clinker* (HC, p. 228). Such passages often seem caught up in an appalled if somewhat obscure revulsion from both tormentor and victim which may leave room for laughter, but none for kind thoughts.

There is certainly an abundance of ugliness in Smollett. People colour up vilely (red, orange, green) or go sooty with putrefaction. They have monstrous mouths and noses and grotesque chins, and bear scars, blemishes and pockmarks. Skin and flesh sag and hang down, or dry up and corrugate into numberless wrinkles. Of teeth there are often few (and rotting) or none. Expressions of emotion have extravagant and deforming rather than endearing effects, as when Lavement 'grins like the head of a bass viol' when he hears that his wife is (he supposes) unfaithful (RR, p. 106). But what strikes one most is what Lewis calls Smollett's 'lavatorial imagination'[35] and, more largely, his obsession with secretions, excretions, exudations, protrusions, extrusions, eviscerations and amputations. People squirt (sometimes tobacco-tinctured) spittle, ooze 'froth and slaver' and weep gummy or tearful slubber (RR, p. 20). They belch gin-soaked reproaches, and piss or pour chamberpots on each other. They are 'stinkards' (RR, p. 198): they smell horribly of shit, farts, decay, stale sweat or just booze and cheese. In battle, body parts are shot off or out and then bounce around or disintegrate, spraying others.

All part of eighteenth-century life, my gruff pragmatist might snort, and a lot of it certainly was. We should also note Smollett's training and work as a surgeon, particularly his experience, as a surgeon's mate, of the harshness and cruelty of eighteenth-century British naval life. In the eighteenth century, moralists repeatedly harnessed bodily disgust to satirical ends (not least where armies and navies were concerned), as Hogarth and other contemporary artists amply testify. The titles of prints like *The Festival of the Golden Rump* and *The Evacuation, or the Shitten Condition of the King of Prussia* are indicative. But if Smollett's most scathingly satirical work, *The History and Adventures of an Atom*, is also his most scatological, from the very start, when the Atom begins its textual life 'discharged' in a Dutch's mariner's 'scorbutic dysentery' at the Cape of Good Hope, the scatology takes on a life of its own and has its own independent *raison d'être*.[36] This is typical.

Furthermore, though the eighteenth-century realist in Smollett makes plentiful reference to sexual encounters, unlike his scatological passages, his descriptions of them are invariably matter of fact. Sex has to happen, it seems, but Smollett conveys no sense of any possible excitement or pleasure involved. Indeed, he seldom has any language for the physical beauty of men and women, save the conventional, hackneyed and vaporous. His evocation of the grotesque appearance of the bluestocking who takes Roderick on as her valet, with her 'chin peaked like a shoemaker's paring-knife', her upper lip exhibiting 'a large quantity of plain Spanish', her habit of spitting in her snuff-box and wiping her nose with her cap and her decision to retain her urine so she can put out the 'general conflagration' when it comes (RR, pp. 218–19, 222), has power and vitality. By contrast, the descriptions of the bluestocking's supposedly entrancing niece, Narcissa, whom Roderick will finally and quite improbably wed, are notably lacking in both. Narcissa's body tends to disappear into clusters of abstract nouns. Smollett the moralist and man of sensibility wanted his novels to have a certain impact. He really did think that literature ought 'to inculcate sentiments of virtue and honour' and 'inspire a horror of vice and immorality'.[37] His attempts at such inculcation are sometimes so implausible as to seem almost self-mocking, as in the case of the transformation of the aristocratic, amoral, eponymous hero of *The Adventures of Ferdinand, Count Fathom* into an obscure, retiring, pious Yorkshire doctor. But it is the sheer vividness of Smollett's bodily imagination that, by generating effects quite apart from positive moral ones, most comprehensively overpowers his official messages. It ensures that his misanthropy continues to prevail to a greater extent than he might finally have wished.

*

The Anglo-Irish Swift is perhaps the misanthropist who looms largest in this book. He was a writer of great learning, wit and imagination and a scintillating ironic gift. He was also a man of rare conscience, acute sensibility and extraordinary penetration in moral and political affairs, though these qualities often drove him to despair. Furthermore, he was given to the kind of reckless, quicksilver, speculative audacity that one usually associates with later, more modern minds, like Nietzsche. Though he was a churchman for much of his life, his world sometimes seems closer to shelving into modern philosophical nihilism than finding a buttress in religious belief. Indeed, others continually questioned his faith. John Sharp, Archbishop of York under Queen Anne, understandably supposed that the man who wrote *A Tale of a Tub* had to be an atheist at heart, and Thomas Smedley's verses after Swift's death said more or less the same:

And now, where'er his deanship dies,
Upon his tomb be graven:
'A man of God here buried lies,
Who never thought of Heaven'.[38]

Swift's *Argument Against Abolishing Christianity* turns a beautifully toned, exquisite scorn on those whose religious commitment is fundamentally 'safe' and 'prudent', worldly and pragmatic. It is nonetheless evident that neither the argument nor the ironic perspective it implies refers us to any spiritual values, though we are told that they existed 'in primitive times' now superseded.[39] Indeed, Swift's writings and particularly his sermons and correspondence suggest that, unlike Pascal or Johnson, he was not a spiritual man. In effect if not in theory, the terrestrial appears to have been substantially his only world. This underwrote his immense rage against humanity, an aggrandizement of Juvenalian *saeva indignatio* quite foreign to the French philosopher and English sage. It helped make Swift's specific form of misanthropy what it was.

Swift's *saeva indignatio* is devastating partly because he refuses to take at face value even the subtlest ruses by which people escape noticing the monstrosity of their own conduct, or the conduct in which they are implicated, rather cruelly laying both monstrosity and ruses bare. Paradoxically, the means by which he expresses but channels and controls his indignation also enhance and intensify it. There has hardly been a greater master of the ironical mimicry of a cogent but finally specious logic, a logic so plausible that it cannot but seem to coincide, not only with the way of the world, but also with a moral decision which, if imperfect, must surely be the best in the circumstances, and which we therefore cannot but make. The refined and civilized manner, the wise nod of the urbane and even (as far as is sensible) benevolent realist, the poised, equable, judicious, reasonable tone, the seemingly incontrovertible claim to the unquestionably superior, common-sense position: Swift not only grasps them with extraordinary accuracy, but takes them to a point where they reveal the moral inadequacy they have previously concealed, their failure to acknowledge the moral sum of their conditions. He thus repeatedly raises the shocking question of how far good sense may not also be moral madness. Indeed, making it sound mad is integral to his purposes.

This is precisely the point with *A Modest Proposal for Preventing the Children of Ireland From Being a Burden to Their Parents or Country*. Swift's Anglo-Irish speaker argues a case for a demented political economy. The Irish Catholic poor are having too many children and are unable to support them. This not infrequently leads mothers to the shameful crimes of infanticide and abortion. The repercussions of this situation are a grievance to the Kingdom. The solution to the problem is to recognize that 'a young healthy Child well Nursed is at a year Old a most delicious nourishing and wholesome Food, whether Stewed, Roasted, Baked or Boiled', and to treat such children accordingly.[40] Swift was exposing what he himself took to be an implicitly cannibalistic social system, as he slyly makes clear when he has his speaker suggest that the flesh of children will be particularly suitable to the diet of the landlord class, 'as they have already devoured most of the Parents' (MP, p. 24). But the great *tour de force* of the *Modest Proposal* is the passage in which the speaker decides that, on balance, it would be better not to extend his proposal to using under-14s to supply 'the Want of Venison'. He well-nigh squirms with anxiety over so delicate an issue, concluding in the end that 'it is not improbable that some scrupulous People might be apt to Censure such a Practice, (although indeed very unjustly) as a little bordering upon Cruelty', and the extension would therefore be ill-advised (MP, pp. 25–6). The supposedly 'scrupulous People' represent a point of misgiving beyond which, even if one does not share their doubts, it is better not to proceed. Swift exactly captures the moment at which, by setting a limit to moral or political evil, a practical decision ends up making those indefinitely preceding it and bound by no such limit look not only prudent, shrewd and indeed just necessary, but also moderate as far as it was possible to be so, and even virtuous. This is doublethink and doublespeak in action. It is the task of irony to expose it as such. Hence Swift's biographer David Nokes calls him 'a hypocrite reversed'.[41] His misanthropy is a reversal, above all, of our most intimate hypocrisies.

Swift's art is profoundly unnerving, since it suggests that there is an absolutely imperious human will to comfort above all things. On the one hand, it reveals itself as a will to prosper, a desire for the good life however defined, intentness on promoting one's own interests. On the other, it takes the form of incessant self-justification. This reflects an imperative need to believe in one's pardonability, if not innocence, that will always ensure that one shrinks from any serious confrontation with moral truth. Here Swift partly follows La Rochefoucauld, who he asserted was his favourite author, finding his 'whole character' in him.[42] Certainly, one can emerge from reading Swift only finally to shrug one's shoulders again, and stay firmly on the side of good sense. One is perhaps almost bound to. Part of his aim, however, is to show us that the more this becomes a choice, the more obscene it looks. Yet he also tells us that such obscenity is the very stuff of humanity. This, if you like, is what the structure of our DNA *actually* looks like. So much is clear from another superb passage in *A Modest Proposal*:

> Therefore let no man talk to me of other Expedients [than eating children]: Of taxing our Absentees at five Shillings a Pound: Of using neither Cloaths, nor Household Furniture, except what is of our own Growth and Manufacture: Of utterly rejecting the Materials and Instruments that promote Foreign Luxury: Of curing the Expensiveness of Pride, Vanity, Idleness, and Gaming in our Women: of introducing a Vein of Parsimony, Prudence and Temperance ... Of being a little cautious not to sell our Country or our Consciences for nothing: of teaching Landlords to have at least one Degree of Mercy towards their Tenants. (MP, pp. 29–30)

'Expedients', or children's lives? The Ireland of the time was never going to take even a selected few of such policies on board. The passage was (and is) characteristic of a certain political realism, one that insists on political impossibility. Nowhere in this book will a certain defining condition of misanthropy be more evident. Swift's whole enterprise is to exhibit to us what he takes to be the true meaning of political 'realism', rather than the meaning we would like and commonly believe it to have, but without suggesting that we can get beyond it. In effect, too, he dares us to defy him, whatever our historical situation. For Swift, contemporary 'ethical', philanthropic and humanitarian voices that present us with clever, 'creative', 'innovative' but 'economically realistic' plans to address the consequences of the colossal imbalances in wealth and power in a globalizing world, to harmonize a seemingly insatiable drive to enjoyment on the one side and immense panoramas of global desolation on the other, would no doubt seem to work chiefly to erase an insupportable truth. The tone in which they do so bears quite a close family resemblance to that of Swift's projectors, who are often benevolists.

A Modest Proposal might seem more concerned with a misanthropic logic than with misanthropy itself. But fleeting touches make it clear that Swift thought that the logic in question might equally be found among the Chinese, Americans, Jews, English and other Europeans – in effect, generally. This is certainly the case with Gulliver's Travels, even if the focus (hardly surprising at that time) is European. The tiny Lilliputians in Part I in some degree function as a scathingly parodic reductio ad absurdum of the vainglory of the imperial European powers, the rhetoric by which they keep it inflated, the irrationality, self-serving pettiness and arbitrary authoritarianism of their rulers, the trivial quarrels ('intestine Disquiets') of their parties or factions.[43] The deliberately silly names throughout Part I make Swift's point clear: considered from an exterior perspective, whether historical or geographical, any political or social system looks similarly footling. But, typically, Swift also turns the structure round. He fancifully endows the Lilliputians with certain enlightened, democratic and indeed morally admirable political and judicial practices. Once again, however, the main point to Gulliver's describing them is to put their real counterparts to shame.

In Part II, Swift reverses his structure in a different way. Gulliver himself now becomes the representative of ordinary humanity. The giant Brobdingnagians are at best genially, humorously incredulous at what Gulliver tells them about human life, its 'Manners, Religion, Laws, Government'. To them, however indulgently they view him, Gulliver appears chiefly to be an ardent defender of ridiculous folly. The king particularly observes 'how contemptible a thing was human grandeur. ... And yet, said he, I dare engage, these Creatures have their Titles and Distinctions of Honour; they contrive their little Nests and Burrows, that they call Houses and Cities; they make a figure in Dress and Equipage; they love, they fight, they dispute, they cheat, they betray' (GT, p. 100). Finally, however, when Gulliver gives him a 'historical account ... of our Affairs during the last Century', the king protests that 'it was only a heap of Conspiracies, Rebellions, Murders, Massacres, Revolutions, Banishments, the very worst effects that Avarice, Faction, Hypocrisy, Perfidiousness, Cruelty, Rage, Madness, Hatred, Envy, Lust, Malice, or Ambition could produce'. 'I cannot but conclude', he adds, 'the Bulk of your Natives, to be the most pernicious Race of little odious vermin that Nature ever suffered to crawl upon the Surface of the Earth' (GT, p. 123). The irony in the chapter works very much in the king's favour and against Gulliver. Above all, when Gulliver offers some routine defences of the human appetite for destruction ('in so familiar a manner as to appear wholly unmoved', GT, p. 125), the king is left merely aghast. Far from being the very pinnacle of nature, humankind begins to look like a *lusus naturae*, a freak in nature, a trick played by nature – at nature's own expense.

What underlies all this? Perhaps, as much as anything else, what Swift takes to be the human penchant for 'vapouring',[44] (coming up with vain or pretentious notions, though sometimes it seems as if he just means thinking). Swiftian misanthropy is the very opposite of the contemporary notion that the more opinions on any subject there are flying about, the better. He thought people got bees in their bonnets whose often disturbing if not shattering consequences were proportional to their lack of any truth-value. His satirical treatment of this theme appears, for instance, in his descriptions of the inventors and projectors who feature in *Gulliver's Travels* Part III. His truly extraordinary treatment of 'vapouring', however, comes in his most extravagantly, dizzyingly ironical work, *A Tale of a Tub*.

A Tale of a Tub is ostensibly a satirical history of the Christian church which promotes Anglicanism as the true faith. It is also an assault on the 'moderns' (Richard Bentley, William Wotton), who asserted that the modern age had by now progressed beyond the confined thought of the classical world. Swift takes the side of the 'ancients', like William Temple, who stoutly maintained its pre-eminence. Such a bald little summary suggests what some might think of as a double commitment to fuddy-duddy orthodoxy. But this is to ignore the actual writing of *A Tale of a Tub*, its elaborate digressions (including a digression on digression), its reversals and non-sequiturs, the variety and ambiguity of the voices we hear in it, our persistent uncertainty as to where they are coming from, where Swift is really coming from. Again and again, he seems dangerously close to identifying with the objects of his attacks, with modernity itself. All this turns the *Tale* into a vertiginous work whose orthodoxy seems constantly thrown into question. This is not, however, to make of Swift a 'radical' or a postmodernist *avant la lettre*: Swift's vital concerns are not fundamentally epistemological but ontological and misanthropic together, a dissection of 'the Carcass of *Humane Nature*' to the point where 'it *smelt* so strong, I could preserve it no longer' (TT, p. 123). His targets are legion: alchemists, occultists, gnostics and many others. But what underlies his scepticism regarding them all is not just his war on absurd credulity, but his persuasion that the '*Forma informans* of Man' itself, which others dignify as '*Spiritus, Animus, Afflatus* or *Anima*', may be just Wind (TT, p. 151). For it is clear enough that, while Humanity as a whole is fond of 'bright Ideas', it is also given 'to furnishing every bright Idea with its reverse' (TT, p. 158). Swift is superbly, brilliantly ready, as very few are, to confront something that the form and discourse of *A Tale of a Tub* themselves reflect, the infinite recession of all thought, the fact that it has no final purchase anywhere at all. Hence the great Digression on Madness tells us that reason and madness may be indissociable. How can we not fear so, when the world regards the lunatic terrorism of Louis XIV so placidly? Reason may very well turn out to be mad. When Swift sedulously matches forms of human behaviour in the great, sane world to the forms of madness in Bedlam, his point is clear.

The crumbling of the base, the founding instability repeatedly evident in much of Swift's greatest writing, prevents his misanthropy from seeming either simply conservative in tendency or a product of ego. This fits with friends' and cronies' awareness that, during his time as a member of and an important influence on the inner circle of Tory government under Harley and Bolingbroke, he promoted others' careers and interests but notably failed to promote his own. Swift poses as the man who sees through the man he is posing as. He uses rules to confute rules. Those he defends become those he attacks. He hates the mob and appeals to a shared common sense. The Irish patriot dwells on his contempt for the Irish. In a way, we might accept Richard Steele's presentation of Swift as 'nothing but an Irish clown'. But we should only do so if we also accept that Swift's willingness to sink himself in profound contradiction is the very measure of his incalculable superiority to the worldly nimbleness of mind, the political skill with which the English Steele hangs him out to dry, thereby achieving his little victory.[45] Swift disdained the pointless, unreasonable use of mere reason against insanity. He was incessantly blown about by great gusts of rage at men and women not so much for their evil as for their moral shallowness, a rage that his sublime irony seeks to manage. The misanthropic self swirls into a black hole at the centre of his turbulent discourse. Self-deprecation, self-annihilation, self-evacuation – *le mot juste* – are integral to Swift's misanthropy.

No misanthropist has ever been more strangely, more stunningly inventive than Swift. Yet for all that, it is hard not to harbour a major reservation about the sources of his loathing, and this has to do, again, with the body. Swift suffers from a compulsive hatred of the body and bodily functions, what he takes to be the manifold deformities and blemishes of bodies. He nurses a dark, demented, if highly imaginative fixation on the repulsiveness of organic human life which keeps on exploding into his writings, sometimes in the weirdest and most unexpected ways. He is creatively gripped by excretion and excrements, physical punishments, mutilation and other forms of physical cruelty. He is obsessed with bodily stains and discolorations, physical dirt, 'nastiness' and its corollary, the imperative of 'cleanliness'.[46] Also diseases, not least venereal ones, and unpleasant smells: it would not be too extreme to suggest that, at the most fundamental level, man, for Swift, is the animal that both reasons and stinks. There is little or no countervailing sense in his work of the possibility of physical rapture. In effect, he seems to have been dead to it. His Pascalian resolve, as a young man, 'not to be fond of children, or let them come near me hardly', seems to reflect that.[47]

The objective demonstration of the point lies in the extent to which satire allows Swift to launch himself into mephitic fancies that he cannot finally altogether haul back and harness to merely satirical purposes. In this he resembles Smollett. But Swift has a scatological imagination far more richly filthy than Smollett's, and produces flesh-hating extravaganzas that quite outstrip the Scotsman's. This is most conspicuously the case in his treatment of women. Swift was capable of his own peculiar forms of attachment to women, notably in the famous cases of 'Stella' (Esther Johnson), whom he may well have secretly married, and 'Vanessa' (Esther Vanhomrigh), with whom he partly simultaneously maintained a queasily playful intimacy. But he seems never to have had a sexual relation with either of them, or with any other woman – not surprisingly, since he was troubled almost to paroxysm by women's flesh. It is in the case of women that the excess of Swift's physical horror over and above his moral disgust is most obvious. In *A Modest Proposal*, for example, he abruptly extends the projector's notion that the bodies of the young might serve as 'prime dainties':

> Neither indeed can I deny, that if the same Use were made of several plump young Girls in this Town, who, without one single Groat to their Fortunes, cannot stir abroad without a Chair, and appear at a Play-house, and Assemblies in Foreign fineries, which they never will pay for; the Kingdom would not be the worse. (MP, p. 26)

These groatless adolescent girls are not infants. Nor is their supposedly culpable vanity the innocence of babes and sucklings. The passage is strictly beyond the satirical and ironic remit of the *Proposal*. In suggesting that there might be a warped aspect to its imaginative mode, it threatens to unbalance it.

The poem 'The Lady's Dressing Room' seems similarly peculiarly twisted. Young swain Strephon discovers that, beneath her cosmetic exterior, Celia is in fact a dirty, sweaty, scabby, snotty, spitting, spewing, malodorous, 'begummed, besmattered and beslimed' creature. She even has worms in her nose.[48] Can we really take this catalogue of physical evils as the basis for any insight into womanhood, as Swift appears to want us to? We might object, too, that, if Celia is so deplorably ugly, it seems not only mean but perverse to fasten on her ugliness, rather than the skill with which she disguises it, and the resulting 'goddess' who, at length, issues forth to greet the world. But Swift and Strephon drive forward inexorably towards their notorious conclusion:

Thus finishing his grand survey,
Disgusted Strephon stole away
Repeating in his amorous fits,
Oh! Celia, Celia, Celia shits![49]

Yes, we respond, but she presumably does other things too. If you happen to find her shitting distasteful, why not dwell on them instead?

The same issue keeps on cropping up when we read Swift's works. In Part II of *Gulliver's Travels*, for example, Gulliver has a 'near sight' of a giant, naked breast, remarking that 'the Nipple was about half the Bigness of my Head, and the Hue both of that and the Dug so varified with Spots, Pimples and Freckles, that nothing could appear more nauseous'. As a piece of 'fantastic realism', this is powerful writing. But when Gulliver also tells us that it made him 'reflect on the Skins of our *English* Ladies, who appear so beautiful to us, only because they are of our own size, and their Defects not to be seen but through a Magnifying Glass' (GT, p. 87), he sounds deranged. Who would seriously argue the moral imperative of assuming that the truth about women's bodies, human bodies, emerges from this kind of microscopic inspection? Outside a scientific or medical context, the perspective is unnatural. But *Gulliver's Travels* as a whole does not correct it. There is no counterbalancing sense of human beauty, especially women's beauty, in the book.

No one has better insisted than Swift that human beings do not know what they do and do not want to know what they do, with morally disastrous consequences, while himself floating quite free of the charge of undue self-regard. The trouble is that he is also quite immune to the reasons for others' being unmisanthropic. He has no antennae for the commonplace but absorbing, indeed irresistible, human seductions that make them so. This turns out to be often the case with misanthropists: they seem, in more senses than one, to have taken leave of their senses, producing a diseased phantasmagoria of the body. Alongside them, and particularly alongside Swift, we might place Wilhelm, in Chapter 15 of Goethe's *Wilhelm Meisters Lehrjahre*, in love enough to be placidly at ease with Mariana's cast-off towels and her lavatory habits. This kind of relaxed acceptance of the flesh in all its aspects seems intrinsic both to Wilhelm's doctrine of cheerfulness and to Goethe's robustness. It also just seems sane. By contrast, whether pathological or not, misanthropy seems to have missed a trick, one not the less but rather the more valuable insofar as it is very much a part of ordinary, mundane experience.

3

MISANTHROPY AND HISTORY: A FEW PHILOSOPHERS

This chapter is about the vulnerability of grandly misanthropic attitudes to historical explanation – and where better to demonstrate it than in the case of philosophical abstraction. Initially, however, there are difficulties with this: as we have seen, misanthropy is not a philosophy as such, nor a tradition within philosophy. Its philosophical manifestations are too diffuse, variegated and compromised for that. But there is another reason, too, why we should not think of misanthropy as philosophical: the positivity of philosophy itself. As Nietzsche 'philosophizes with [his] hammer', for example, he may seem to be not only the prophet of modern nihilism – 'Nihilism stands at the door: whence comes this uncanniest of all guests?'[1] – but its representative. Yet both the Nietzschean work of destruction and his confrontation with nihilism are preludes to a possible *Umwertung alle Werte*, the 'transvaluation of all values', which for Nietzsche would mean salvation. Indeed, Nietzsche turns out to be 'the ultimate yes-sayer'.[2] As Alain Badiou puts matters, for Nietzsche, philosophy can only be 'integrally affirmative'.[3]

Nietzsche, however, is just one peculiarly vivid instance. The affirmative tendency is deeply written into philosophy itself, and is unlikely to shade into misanthropic negativity. In its very abstraction, its turning away from grubby, footling particulars, from mere observation, philosophy inclines to the affirmative mode. Take the Kantian concept of the categorical imperative. It clearly involves an affirmation. As opposed to a crafty, worldly little hypothetical imperative, which always includes an 'if' – if I want to be rewarded with A, then I must B – the categorical imperative unconditionally, absolutely, thunderously asserts that I must do A whatever the circumstances, that A, the good, is an end in itself. The idea that we can think like this is clearly, in principle, inspiring – and yet it does not take much for the concept of the categorical imperative to begin to slide in a misanthropic direction. Sceptics have wondered exactly what reality it addresses, Guy Lardreau even suggesting that there is no significant Kantian morality, that Kant himself thought that 'Kantianism … was of no use' and that 'a truly moral act could not be found'.[4] For Kant, any serious morality always fails to understand this world; indeed, 'not understanding' is the very condition of morality.[5] Thus the Kantian affirmation of the categorical imperative requires a prior gesture that brackets the world off. The question of what it might mean for ordinary people who are not philosophers need have no bearing on it. The Idea is its own *raison d'être*.

This holds true for a practically unlimited number of philosophical concepts and systems, whether or not they are as immediately affirmative as Kant's and Nietzsche's. It does not matter if they do not apply: that is even their splendour. Of course, not every philosopher has accepted that philosophical affirmation need break with the human world. This is notably the case with Marx. But if Marx wants to bridge the gap, as Jacques Rancière has shown, in the very struggle to do so, he ends up falling straight back into it. Marx famously affirms the proletariat while setting actual workers at naught. For the proletarian is not a worker, but a subject of a new historical science. Real workers in Marx appear as the brute, recidivist, troglodytic French peasantry of *The Eighteenth Brumaire* and *The Class Struggles in France*, or the unredeemed and unregenerate *vulgus*, 'the whole indefinite, disintegrated mass' that Marx thinks of as the *lumpenproletariat*.[6] Thus Marx at once affirms the proletariat and rejects the people, people at large. Under Marxist bullishness, there is a strain of misanthropy. Marx imagines his ideal proletariat in contradistinction to working people, who are not only not good enough, but not really much good at all.

This is a version of a founding philosophical procedure that goes back as far as Parmenides. In asserting that the world of appearances was deceitful, Parmenides made a singularly audacious claim. The world is not really what it looks like. That conviction powered another, both Platonic and Aristotelian, that philosophy 'begins in wonder',[7] in a profound estrangement from the familiar. It repeatedly sets out by bracketing the world off. Thus, in his *Meditations on First Philosophy*, Descartes postulates a *malin génie*, the evil demon who presents the illusion of the existence of an external and bodily world, who must be kept at bay if philosophy is to proceed. So, too, in Husserlian phenomenology, the speculative moment of the *epoché* suspends the world of prior consciousness, ideas, images, a man-made world, in the interest of a direct, naive encounter with materiality itself.

Philosophers never tire of repeating that philosophy begins with a wondering question. But the intense, even rapt perplexity of the founding philosophical attitude, the sheer surprise at the fact that the world exists at all, or is as it is, can also from time to time translate into bafflement at men being as they are. Schopenhauer, too, declares that 'philosophy has the peculiarity of presupposing absolutely nothing as known; everything to it is equally strange and a problem'.[8] As we shall amply see, however, by this point in the history of philosophy, the implications of the philosophical procedure have become apparent: it is precisely humanity itself that is in some measure 'problematic'. If philosophy repeatedly sets out by bracketing the world off, then, in doing so, it brackets off human beings as they exist outside the door, in the next room, round every corner. See for example Rawls's *A Theory of Justice*, in which he explicitly demands that all human particulars be left to one side. In *The Philosopher and his Poor*, Rancière shows us how far, in screening out the familiar world, philosophers also screened out the world of the people; this was deeply inscribed within the philosophical tradition. The Marx so contemptuous of the French peasantry is in fact resorting to an ancient philosophical trope, the people as 'the motley crowd of the Platonic *polloi*'.[9] The philosophical tradition is not misanthropic in itself, but the possibility of misanthropy is rooted in it.

It is therefore logical enough that at least a few philosophers should sound explicitly misanthropically inclined. I shall look at three, not in chronological order, again. For the Thomas Hobbes of *De Cive* (*On the Citizen*, 1642) and *Leviathan* (1651), *homo homini lupus est*, man is a wolf to man. The state of nature is a *bellum omnium contra omnes*, 'a perpetual war' in which 'every man to every man ... is an enemy'.[10] For Hobbes, what lies at the root of this war is equality, which is a law of nature. Nature grants 'a full and absolute liberty in every particular man'; in nature, '*every man has right to every thing*' (L, p. 163). But that means that, in nature, there is no property, 'no *mine* and *thine* distinct, but only that to be every man's, that he can get: and for so long, as he can keep it' (L, p. 101). Under these conditions, there can be 'no security to any man' except insofar as he retains 'the natural and necessary appetite of his own conservation, the right of protecting himself by his own private strength' (L, pp. 103, 138).

The consequences of living by natural law must therefore be lawless disorder, internecine violence, 'horrible calamities' (L, p. 140). The *bellum omnium contra omnes* suspends all notions of right and wrong, justice and injustice. There is no common power, and therefore men hold no values in common save force and fraud. Man's life is 'solitary, poor, nasty, brutish and short', and he 'lives in continual fear, and danger of violent death' (L, p. 100). Fear is the great motive force in Hobbes's philosophy. He was born in 1588, just a few months before the defeat of the Spanish Armada, at a time when England was running scared of Spain. His mother bore twins, he wrote, 'me and together with me fear'.[11] Hobbesian fear is above all fear of other people. Most men, he writes, 'are of evil character, bent on securing their own interest by fair means or foul',[12] and one should distrust them accordingly.

However, Hobbes does not merely think of the state of nature as a savage universal anarchy. All human passions have to do with power, but power may stem from different sources and manifest itself in different forms. The one that most preoccupies Hobbes is *inanis gloria*, vainglory, the pleasure that individual persons take in contemplating their own 'virtue, force, knowledge, beauty, friends, wealth', intellect, or any other quality that flatters them with a sense of their own eminence (OC, p. 177). This is what men most treasure, 'their own glory', not society. For 'all the heart's joy lies in being able to compare oneself favourably with others and form a high opinion of oneself' (OC, pp. 22, 26). Human beings are insatiably bent on self-advancement, self-promotion and self-justification and are determined to maintain their own authority, be it political or intellectual. For they inveterately want '*to believe themselves wise and appear so to others*', and find '*culpable evil*' in others' achievements (OC, pp. 81, 162). They do not naturally value other men, but tend 'to exasperate each other' (OC, p. 29), from which hatred and contempt naturally spring.

But there is worse to follow. Because men invest so massively in their self-image, they also invest massively in their own ideas, and deplore or are incredulous about those of others. Hence they fall into interminable disputes over 'what is conformable, or disagreeable to reason' (L, p. 123). The passions – those 'notable multiplying glasses' – make ideological differences heated, which in turn leads inexorably to violence (L, p. 141). It is not selfishness or aggression in themselves, nor even the will to defend oneself and one's property against others, that most drives men to fight each other. They fight above all when *inanis gloria* turns beliefs into causes for quarrels.

Where present-day culture at least claims to value difference, for Hobbes it is a nightmare from the state of nature, and not to be allowed free rein. The mere act of disagreement is offensive, and differences in ideas, judgements, tastes, opinions, temperaments and habits all result in conflict. Intellectuals are among the worst, for they not only pride themselves on their clever ideas, but have clever ideas about change, which clash. Furthermore, they have a way with words. Hobbes is singularly afraid of the power of language. Intellectuals are troublesome because they use words to heighten their own and others' passions, often with disastrous effects: it is intellectual dissension that 'causes the worst conflicts' and the 'bitterest wars' (OC, p. 26). If Hobbes distrusts the power of rhetoric, however, he equally distrusts the slipperiness of language. People's judgements are shifting and unreliable, and what they call good and evil are 'nothing simply and absolutely so' (L, p. 48). This leads to the creation of absurd ambiguities and to senseless disputes over true meaning. So, too, words are always coloured by 'the nature, disposition, and interest of the speaker'. One man 'calleth *wisdom*, what another calleth *fear*; and one *cruelty*, what another *justice*; one *prodigality*, what another *magnanimity*; and one *gravity*, what another *stupidity*, &c' (L, p. 40). By the same token, language is perfidiously disposed to accommodate paradox and evasion, which means that men routinely use words like 'rapacity' of others but refuse to apply them to themselves, though they are up to exactly the same kind of business. They see '*their own actions reflected in others as in a mirror*' (OC, p. 4), but do not see those actions as they are.

Hobbes's violence- and fear-soaked but grippingly cerebral and astringent vision of the state of nature might indeed seem misanthropic. However, the label only stretches so far, for human beings are not compelled to remain within the world of natural law: they are also intent on transcending it. Indeed, 'as soon as they recognize [the] misery' of the hateful state of nature, they want to escape it (OC, p. 12). We should not ignore the strain of pure thought or idealism in humans. Here fear again is 'the passion to be reckoned upon' (L, p. 111). So, too, another fear, fear of death, inclines people to search for peace. Unfortunately, while they willingly accept that 'man is a wolf to man', they do so as though they themselves were exempt from the general ferocity. But if they cannot bear to look straight at their own implication in the universal madness, at the obnoxiousness of their own 'impetuous desires' (L, p. 256), they may at least grow more aware of how far those desires drive them to hurt, not only each other, but themselves. This also takes them beyond natural law, and encourages them to pay attention to the question of order.

Humankind can rescue itself from itself through its capacity for particular forms of social organization, the origin of which lies not in mutual benevolence but, again, in a fear of an instability that only authority can finally resist. Hobbes resolves the war of all against all via a theory of civil contracts, which he calls covenants. To create an order beyond the disorder of natural law, a democratic act is first required in which the people contracts itself off the scene, agreeing to the sway of a superior power, necessarily so, because otherwise we remain in the world of equality, which is always anarchic. Each man 'obligates himself, by an Agreement with each of the rest, not to resist the *will* of the *man* or *Assembly* to which he has submitted himself' (OC, p. 72); that is, he transfers his own force and power to an authority and its *jus imperandi*, thereby giving up his right to resist.

The covenant is the means whereby the people decides to surrender its own anarchic world to government or sovereign power, whether monarchical, aristocratic or democratic – Hobbes preferred the monarchical – the power that will be eminent among the people and rule it for the good of the commonwealth. When mere private men claim authority for themselves, 'they are aspiring to be as Kings' (ibid.). When by contrast they covenant among themselves to establish their sovereign, they surrender their will and their natural right to rule, and sovereign power supervenes upon natural law, regulating difference in coming up 'with rules or measures that will be common to all', and publishing them openly (OC, p. 79). Indeed, sovereign power can 'decide which opinions and doctrines are inimical to peace ... and forbid them being taught' (OC, p. 80). This, too, is necessary to the security of the commonwealth, in which '*the safety of the people is the supreme law*' (OC, p. 143).

Hobbes's concept of sovereignty may sound severe, autocratic and even dismal, but it might nonetheless seem to protect him from any charge of misanthropy. Yet so philosophical is the concept that one must wonder whether it really involves man as such. If for example one reads Hobbes on the myriad variety of religious beliefs – human beings can worship 'an onion, a leek … their own privy member' (L, p. 91) – one can hardly doubt that he thought people were dolts. If human beings can redeem themselves, it is by virtue of a philosophical disposition or power of abstraction. Hobbes identifies this power with mathematics. In 1630, he underwent a conversion to geometry, aiming thereafter to transfer the form of geometrical demonstration to the natural and moral sciences. This aspiration is abundantly evident in his political philosophy. For Hobbes, '*whatever distinguishes the modern world from the barbarity of the past, is almost wholly the gift of* Geometry' (OC, p. 4). The final aim of a commonwealth is 'a geometer's peace'.[13]

The capacity for abstraction is for Hobbes a power of artifice. Man is the animal that saves itself insofar as it is afraid of itself, and consequently 'abridges' and 'restrains' its own humanity (L, p. 200), making something other of itself through artifice. For 'the attaining of peace, and conservation of themselves', human beings make 'artificial chains, called civil laws' (L, p. 160). This produces 'the great LEVIATHAN called a COMMONWEALTH, or STATE', a kind of 'artificial man', as the *persona civitatis* is the artificial person of the Commonwealth (L, pp. 19, 160). The thesis, however, leaves the Hobbes so wary of paradox in a paradoxical position himself, a position that looks more or less misanthropic depending on which way we turn the glass. Man releases himself from his own dreadful nature only by becoming more, or other, than human. Yet the capacity for that transformation of human being is itself human. The position becomes even more equivocal once we consider just how precarious Hobbes took Leviathan to be. The establishment of a commonwealth, he states, is a rarity, an event (OC, p. 22). But even this rare event is imperilled, since without the help of sublime political architects, the people are likely to end up with a 'crazy building' that is all too likely to collapse, not least on the heads of posterity (L, p. 237; an observation, we might think, repeatedly borne out by history, and that some fear will be borne out yet again later this century). In any case, most men secretly hate sovereign authority and are wilfully inclined to desire novelty, so they are all too likely to upend their own best and stablest constructions. Moreover, as Bertrand Russell smartly pointed out, the Hobbesian *Aufhebung* via civil law has the paradoxical effect of merely re-establishing the state of nature at a different level, since its logical consequence is an 'international anarchy' in which the war of all against all is translated into that of States.[14] Hobbes himself knew this, envisaging commonwealths as perpetually 'upon the confines of battle, with their frontiers armed, and cannons planted against their neighbours round about' (L, p. 162). This hardly seems like the ideal antidote to fear.

In truth, Hobbes's conception of the State under civil law was finally only a speculative venture, a 'thought experiment'.[15] It could hardly have been more than that, since he was distinctly sceptical about the strength and durability of such a State: 'No great popular commonwealth', he writes, 'was ever kept up, but either by a foreign enemy that united them; or by the reputation of some eminent man amongst them; or by the secret counsel of a few; or by the mutual fear of eminent factions'. As for 'very little commonwealths', there is 'no human wisdom can uphold them, longer than the jealousy lasteth of their more potent neighbours' (L, p. 197). The Hobbesian State, so intent on security, cannot be securely founded. Men may always be laying 'the foundations of their houses on the sand'. All Hobbes can add, by way of reassurance, is that 'it could not thence be inferred, that so it ought to be' (L, p. 158).

Thus Hobbes's arguments might appear finally to bend back towards misanthropy. But as misanthropic arguments, they are obviously produced in a specific set of circumstances. Scholars once tended to ignore this. Hobbes was a philosopher. To see him as addressing his own historical context was to risk treating philosophy in all its extra-historical grandeur as ideology, and the philosopher as having a *parti pris*.[16] Increasingly, however, others have argued that it is only by historicizing Hobbes that we can properly understand him.[17] He was born in 1588, died in 1679, and lived in the midst of a peculiarly turbulent, indeed catastrophic, age in Europe, the period of the Wars of Religion consequent upon the Reformation and Counter-Reformation. In particular, between 1618 and 1648, the years of Hobbes's intellectual development, Europe was overtaken by the unprecedented anarchy and havoc of the Thirty Years' War. Hobbes passed a lot of time in places arterially linked to the war and with people concerned with it, and knew a great deal about the European disaster.[18] He translated a work of Austrian propaganda, *Altera secretissimus instructio*, which helped steep him in the contemporary European war of political ideas.[19] Here, in what was going on around him, he witnessed the very proliferation of intellectual differences and their translation into violent disputes that he so feared, taking place on a continental scale.

But above all, Hobbes's major writings are overwhelmingly conditioned by an England increasingly riven by political divisions and religious schisms so ferocious that they ended in a collapse of social order, and eventually civil war and regicide. In a late work, *Behemoth, Or an Epitome of the Civil Wars of England, from 1640 to 1660*, he asserted of the period that 'he that should have ... observed the Actions of Men, especially in England, might have had a prospect of all kinds of Injustice, and of all kinds of Folly that the world could afford, and how they were produced by their Hypocrisy and Self-conceit'.[20] No doubt the times did indeed give good reason for a dim view of human beings, but for the Hobbes of *Behemoth*, the reasons were immediate. Charles I had not exercised his sovereign power appropriately, and had had to confront 'Perfidy upon Perfidy' in his opponents, the 'corruption' of the people and the anarchic influence of a 'great number of Sects' that the feebleness of sovereign authority had allowed to flourish.[21] *Behemoth* says what *Leviathan* says, but within a historical narrative, not a philosophical disquisition, thus laying bare the historical roots of Hobbesian philosophy itself. Hobbes lived in a foundering world that only extreme authority, he felt, could successfully resist. His philosophical position everywhere reflects this. Insofar as his conclusions are misanthropic, he reaches them by generalizing out of a particular historical experience that might have seemed to justify them at the time, but hardly amounted to the 'state of nature' in itself.

One might say something rather similar of Schopenhauer, though his philosophy is less immediately readable as a commentary on a historical world. Some preliminary basics first: for Schopenhauer, there is the Kantian *mundus phaenomenon*, a world of appearances structured by forms, those of space, time and cause and effect. Certain laws determine these forms (causality, succession, position). The laws are those of the empirical world, and are governed by the principle of sufficient reason, which provides a 'ground' for phenomena (WW1,

p. 163). The 'ground' founds explanation, will always answer the question why. However, the laws of the phenomenal world apply only in consciousness (WW2, p. 46). They possess no unconditional validity or 'veritas aeterna' (WW1, p. 32).

This means that the forms of knowledge are representations, as *The World as Will and Representation* states: 'The world is my representation. This is a truth valid with reference to every living and knowing being' (WW1, p. 3). Schopenhauer accepted the Kantian view that we cannot know the world in itself. When we represent something, we represent its appearance, the phenomenon only, doing so according to the principle of sufficient reason. There is no access to the object outside the subject. We cannot arrive at a representation of the 'innermost being' or 'kernel' of either the object or the world, the *Ding an Sich* (thing-in-itself, WW1, p. 31). If a fabulously gifted alien from another planet with such a superior capacity landed on earth, we would find what she was saying utterly incomprehensible (see WW2, p. 185).

Hence relations are unimportant. Things perceived in their relations are not seen 'in their absolute essence and existence' (WW1, p. 11). This is the limit of the principle of sufficient reason: it can never present us with more 'than the relation of one representation to another' (WW1, p. 28). Thus all its forms are 'empty and unreal as any dream' (WW1, p. 7). Relations are valid only within certain horizons, and it is only on earth and for men that such forms of representation are binding (WW1, p. 6). The philosopher must look beyond them and 'apprehend the universal in beings' (WW2, p. 372). This is the task of philosophical reason.

So far, the argument hardly seems to portend anything grimmer than an advanced if idiosyncratic form of Kantianism. Yet in fact we are at the top of a slippery slope. For the 'universal' that Schopenhauer apprehends in beings is will. The world is will, and only will. Will exists beyond the principle of sufficient reason and 'may therefore in this respect be called *groundless*' (WW1, p. 101), and hence is 'completely and fundamentally different from ... representation', the forms and laws of which 'are wholly foreign to it' (WW1, p. 99). It exists within the subject doing the representation, but also in the world itself, and appears as such not only in animal but also 'in inorganic and vegetable nature' (WW1, p. 275).

Will, then, is not just or even principally human. Nor is it energy or vital force, as in the vitalisms (Nietzsche, Bergson, Deleuze). Schopenhauer is explicit about this. He thought people needed metaphysics, not radical materialisms, and therefore aimed to provide a metaphysics of will. In the long run, Schopenhauer takes will for Being. When he tells us that it would be better not to exist (WW2, p. 605), the gloomy snarl also involves an ontological assertion. It is clear that 'this world's non-existence is just as possible as its existence' (WW2, p. 171). But what determines, then, that the one should prevail over the other? The answer is will. Will is what ensures that there is not nothing. Indeed, conceived of more subtly, the will is even 'an expression of ... nothingness' (WW1, p. 149); they are the two sides of a single coin. If the will is finally terrible, that is because nothing is its most intimate companion.

The will strives for existence, and that is all it does. We can be only as will, and will is simply intent on asserting existence, whether that of a prime minister, a billionaire or a lump of mud. It is inexorable, the larger impersonality that encompasses our personality, so the condition of the subject is total unfreedom. But the will itself is not free either. Like 'the young spider which has no idea of the prey for which it spins a web', it is mere 'blind activity' (WW1, p. 114). It springs forth lustily from death, to which it is indifferent, like a dark moth from a cocoon, proclaiming with Goethe, '"A new day beckons to a newer shore!"' (WW2, p. 501). The irony to Schopenhauer's quotation is unmissable. The will does this quite meaninglessly and to no good end, save that the universe may continue to have being. We should stress that it is the universe that is at stake: the will is never principally concerned with the survival of the individual entity. In living beings, at least, the concern manifests itself above all in the imperative of continuing the species, of self-preservation, nourishment – and propagation. This is notably the case with humans, as is obvious in the primacy of the sex drive, which is practically an outrageous trick of the will, since, as 'cool reflection' suggests, sex is actually repugnant and even disgusting (WW2, p. 569). Schopenhauer himself actually had quite a bit of it, but then, he made no claims to have outsmarted the will.

Here the grounds for Schopenhauer's disbelief in humanity become clear. For Descartes, the reason of the *cogito* confers unity on the world, but Schopenhauer brutally undermines the Cartesian consolation. It is will that serves as the unifying force. Unconsciousness, not reason, is 'the original and natural condition of all things' (WW2, pp. 141–2). This decisively closes the gap between human and non-human. The essence of man has nothing to do with reason or 'the so-called soul', but is the same as the essence of the polyp or slug (WW2, pp. 205–6). Indeed, 'the will proclaims itself' no more 'in the action of man' than 'in the fall of a stone' (WW2, p. 299). Thought, knowledge, representation, the principle of sufficient reason are all parasitic on the will, functions of it, the means to sheer persistence. Will is the core of the person, and no particular value attaches to his or her humanity.

Of course, the will endlessly achieves its simple purpose. But as the drive is quenched, so it at once begins afresh. Satisfied desires can only give birth to new ones. This means that 'the phenomena in which the will objectifies itself' are involved in an 'endless and implacable struggle' with each other (WW1, p. 153). All creatures compete for the air of being, as if in an infinite jungle crammed with feuding forms. The will buries its teeth in its own flesh: life forms eliminate each other. Admittedly, the human race is exceptionally good at this, regarding nature as manufactured for its own use, subduing all the other species and 'necessarily devastating its world' in the process (WW1, p. 147). But the will also feasts on itself within humanity. As, according to Schopenhauer, La Rochefoucauld supremely knew, the individual is ready to annihilate the world in order to maintain his or her own self. This is how we get Hobbes's *bellum omnium contra omnes*. Everyone 'wants everything for himself, wants to possess, or at least control, everything, and would like to destroy whatever opposes him' (WW1, p. 332). Moreover, in yet another turn of the screw, the naked will-to-live in animals is clothed, in man, by 'the capacity for dissimulation' (WW1, p. 156). In the end, refer to Dante's hell: it is a magisterial portrait of the actual world, and Luther was right to suggest, in his *Commentary on Galatians*, that the devil is 'prince and lord' of the world, and we are all subject to him (WW2, p. 580). Optimisms are pervasive, but they are peculiarly fatuous if not pernicious manifestations of the will. The only good thing about Leibniz's *Theodicy* is that it provoked Voltaire's *Candide*.

The conduct of men towards one another is determined by the general struggle, which stems from an irreducible 'want or deficiency, from dissatisfaction' (WW1, pp. 308–9). The 'ultimate constituents' of human experience are trouble, anxiety, craving, 'pain and boredom', 'the terrible envy that dwells in all'. We are weighed down by 'the heavy earthly atmosphere of need', the definitive lack that generates endless longing and rage (WW1, p. 313, WW2, pp. 388, 578). Yet these are the very whips 'that keep the top spinning' (WW2, p. 359). Human life 'presents itself as a continual deception, in small matters as well as in great. If it has promised, it does not keep its word, unless to show how little desirable the desired object was' (WW2, p. 573). What Schopenhauer calls 'the in-itself of life' is therefore 'a constant suffering' (WW1, p. 267). The great tragedians have the profoundest grasp of this, because they know such suffering for what it is, the immitigable consequence of the hellishness of the will, the ferocious combat of the phenomena (WW1, p. 253). But the will is 'so closely concealed behind [its] masks' that it can usually not recognize itself (WW2, p. 318). Thus, for example, humans turn a blind eye to the meaning of their indifference to others' sufferings. They cannot bear to see themselves as they are, that is, as mere functions of will. Schopenhauer explicitly filters Kant through the seventeenth-century French occasionalist Nicolas Malebranche, with very un-Kantian results. For Malebranche, human beings paste illusions of freedom and autonomy over a condition of definitive enslavement. Even the slightest movement of my little finger is the 'occasion' of other activity, caused by a *volonté*, a will beyond me which is the sole cause of all. True, for Malebranche, the *volonté* is God's: God is the direct occasion of my actions, rather than just making me the kind of person disposed to perform certain kinds of action. But Schopenhauer has no interest in this line of thought. He keeps Malebranche's concept of the occasion, but thereby turns man into a figure who stalks through the world like a sleepwalker, a regulated automaton, a puppet 'set in motion by an internal clockwork' (WW2, p. 358).

Furthermore, if human beings can only live in a world determined by the principle of sufficient reason, in which everything becomes their representation, they also unwarrantably extend the principle of sufficient reason far beyond its sole province, beyond the empirical, given, immediately historical world. By virtue of doing so, they think they know far more than they do, when in fact they are condemning themselves to live in error, illusion, *maya*, a preposterous synecdoche. We can therefore understand how ideas 'can reign' over mankind 'for thousands of years' without having the slightest purchase on anything real or true (as in the case of the religions). 'The ignorant and dull mob' never escape error, or even bother to try (WW1, pp. 35, 47). Human beings in general are infinitely impressionable. The Chiliasts who, in

1818, moved from Würtemberg to Ararat because they thought the kingdom of God was imminent were typical if extreme cases of a total imbecility.

So we are playthings in a senseless game. The true 'being-in-itself' of every living thing 'lies primarily in its species' (WW2, p. 510). But if the purpose for which individuals exist is clear, for what purpose does the species itself exist? This is a question to which nature makes no reply. The drive to life is not a measure or result 'of any objective *knowledge* of the value of life'; indeed, 'life is a business whose returns are far from covering the cost' (WW2, p. 352), and 'no one has the remotest idea why the whole tragi-comedy exists' (WW2, p. 357). One can finally take only the objective view of the will to live, which is that it is a folly, or the subjective one, which commits one to a delusion (WW2, p. 357). Thus Schopenhauer is ambiguous about whether the species should survive or not. He will not preach annihilation, but he thinks that, for our own sake, we should admit that it would be better for both us and the world if we were not to be. 'Our existence is happiest when we perceive it least; from this it follows that it would be better not to have it' (WW2, p. 575). This leads him to the arresting view that 'it is quite superfluous to dispute whether there is more good or evil in the world; *for the mere existence of evil decides the matter*, since evil can never be wiped off, and consequently can never be balanced, by the good that exists along with or after it' (WW2, p. 576, my italics). Evil has a vivid moral reality that good does not. For evil is felt positively, while good, like happiness and pleasure, is the mere negation of evil. Everything that surrounds us bears the traces of the moral reality of evil, 'just as in hell everything smells of sulphur' (WW2, p. 577). One should therefore admire Lessing's son, who 'absolutely declined to come into the world', had to be 'forcibly dragged' out into the world by forceps (WW2, p. 579), and died very soon thereafter. Schopenhauer even has his own distinctive consolation for the dying: 'You are ceasing to be something which you would have done better never to become' (WW2, p. 501).

Not surprisingly, then, he is often brusquely dismissive of the supposedly most precious or significant aspects of human experience. Love, for example, does not survive his 'gross realism' (WW2, p. 535): 'All amorousness is rooted in the sexual impulse alone' (WW2, p. 533), and therefore in the will within the species, its drive to continuation. Men seldom feel sympathy or compassion; the more human response to others' sufferings is *Schadenfreude*. Individuality and liberty are meaningless counters. We are tied to what we have to be by character, which is a splinter of will. As for politics, the State springs from egoism, and exists merely to serve it by managing it. Religion is bred of boredom and emptiness, with man creating gods, demons and spirit-worlds in his own image (WW1, pp. 322–3). Morality is futile, because it does not motivate us. Only self-love does that, but 'what springs from it has no moral worth' (WW1, p. 367). The intellect is incapable of governing the will, and 'no system of ethics which would mould and improve' the will is possible (WW2, p. 223). The struggles of conscience are therefore a waste of time and effort: the emotions are bound to break loose and rage. Eminence is rooted in self-delight, an 'arrogant, triumphant vanity, a proud, scornful, contemptuous disdain of others' (WW2, p. 233). Indeed, human projects themselves are of trifling importance, for they are just expressions of will, and any serious commitment to them is merely a way of giving oneself airs. In general, all our judgements and preferences, our concepts of what is 'fair, just and reasonable', 'the prejudices of social position, rank, profession, nationality, sect, and religion', are hollow, for they are all determined by interest, by 'the deceptions of inclination and liking' (WW2, pp. 217–18).

But there are also two features of the Schopenhauerian vision that tend to lighten the gloom, his affirmations of art and asceticism. These alone can liberate a subject from servitude to the will. If representation is limited by its being of the phenomenon only, we can also abstract from our representations and represent them all over again, as Ideas. The object passes 'out of all relation to something outside it', so that 'what is thus known is no longer the individual thing as such'. For its part, the abstracting subject passes 'out of all relation to the will', and becomes the pure '*subject of knowledge*' (WW1, p. 179). This act of abstraction is the basis of every work of art, and the state of 'pure objectivity of perception' in which the subject also becomes 'the pure subject of knowing' is a fundamental constituent of aesthetic enjoyment (WW2, p. 371). In art, the will turns on itself, displaying itself for what it is.

This is as close as we can come to the only true purity conceivable, that of being beyond or outside will – with one exception. For the saint or ascetic can cure his or her heart of 'the passion for enjoying and indeed for living' (WW2, p. 635). Saintly knowledge brings about 'the Sabbath of the penal servitude of willing; the wheel of Ixion stands still'

(WW1, p. 196). The will no longer 'affirms its own inner nature', but rather experiences a horror of it, which 'proceeds from the immediate and *intuitive* knowledge of the metaphysical identity of all beings' (WW1, p. 380, WW2, p. 601). Furthermore, because the original sin is the affirmation of the will-to-live, the saint also comes to understand the 'heavy guilt' the human race incurs simply '*through its existence itself*' (WW2, p. 604, italics mine). But such understanding is constant pain, a 'hairy garment that causes its owner constant hardship' (WW2, p. 607). This pain can only be allayed by a denial of the will in oneself. Yet that at last leads to the better wisdom. One sees that the apparently 'exceedingly desirable benefits' of life are in fact 'chimeras', and acknowledges 'the true end of life' as 'a euthanasia of the will' (WW2, pp. 635, 637).

Schopenhauer's thought is therefore another form of the exceptionalism we have occasionally remarked on. As voluntary suppressions of the will, art and asceticism are exceptions to the rule. Schopenhauer quotes Spinoza's *Ethics*: 'All that is excellent and eminent is as difficult as it is rare' (WW1, p. 384). The genius of the artist, in particular, is 'something foreign to the will', to the ego proper. Since the will is ubiquitous, genius is always added 'from outside so to speak', and is therefore uncustomary, and even unnatural (WW2, pp. 377–8). Indeed, genius only rarely takes possession of its subjects. By these very tokens, it is a sealed book 'to the dull majority of men' (WW1, p. 234). So, too, goodness, beauty, nobility, saintly asceticism and wisdom appear but scantly. For the will itself closes the mediocre mind to genius, and insists that it must contest and depreciate it.

Like Hobbes, then, Schopenhauer works from a misanthropic presumption, yet also scrapes value together on the basis and in the teeth of it. Schopenhauer contends that, on rare occasions, the will may turn against itself (WW1, p. 146). Yet this can happen only as a kind of abnegation of life, if it suffers a kind of hypertrophic growth that introduces a glitch into an otherwise altogether normative system, since, in the end, art and asceticism are ways of not living. Schopenhauer is a quietist, a philosopher who finally recommends disinterest, the wisdom of letting go of the world. He agrees wholeheartedly, or perhaps faint-heartedly, with Artabatus in Herodotus: there has never been a man who did not wish he did not have to live through the following day.[22] That one's life is likely to be short is one of the very few things to be said in its favour.

'Only with me', wrote Schopenhauer, 'are the evils of the world honestly admitted in all their magnitude' (WW2, p. 643). One obvious source of this conviction is his emphatic repudiation of historical thought. Schopenhauer loathed Hegel, and the reasons are not far to seek. Hegel thought historically, even supposing that there was a unity to history. 'The Hegelian pseudo-philosophy', Schopenhauer writes, 'that is everywhere so pernicious and stupefying to the mind', comprehends 'the history of the world as a planned whole' (WW2, p. 442). But no plan has ever existed. Hegelians nourish a fantasy about 'inexistents', entities that, historically, do not exist and have never existed. On the basis of their assumed plan of the world, according to which everything is managed for the best, they believe that an inexistent like justice or the Good 'is supposed to come into existence' (WW2, p. 443). In fact, no inexistents pass into existence at all. The only unity to history is ahistorical, the *nunc stans*, 'an endless present' (WW2, 479).

But the polarity on which Schopenhauer's thought depends at this point – the static permanence of the will versus historicism and progressivism together – is not self-evident. As Michel Foucault understood, historicism need not imply faith in progress. Given this, it is worth asking, again, what in Schopenhauer's own historical context might have led to his philosophy taking on the complexion that it did. Schopenhauer was born in 1788, in Danzig, which from the fourteenth century had been a member of the Hanseatic League. It had been a free city, was proud of its commercial independence, and its *Volk* shared a robust sense of being *leidensgeprüft*, much 'tried by suffering', not least because Danzig had long been surrounded by menacing, powerful neighbours. As an 'aspiring and self-confident *Rechtstadt*', it was conscious of sharing in a Baltic tradition of cosmopolitan, mercantile life and culture.[23] Schopenhauer's merchant father possessed many of these qualities, and the city shaped the character of young Arthur (or so he thought). But in 1793, when Schopenhauer was only five, his family were forced to flee. Russia and Prussia were starting to carve up Polish territory, and Danzig was a mere pawn in the game. Prussia abruptly grabbed it. (The aldermen laid aside their official costume and dressed in Schopenhauerian black, in mourning for centuries of history).[24] After this particular experience of the ferocity of the will, Danzig's illusion of sturdy autonomy was abruptly snuffed out. As for its greatest philosopher, in his own words, he 'never acquired a new home'.[25]

The family moved to Hamburg, another city conscious of its Hanseatic past, where, again, they joined the mercantile elite, only further reinforcing Schopenhauer's rooted sense of Hanseatic superiority to most Germans. Then Russia and Prussia formed an alliance against Napoleon and, in 1806, Prussia declared war on France. Schopenhauer left Hamburg in 1807, after his mother had gone to Weimar, where, having joined forces with Prussia, Karl August of Saxony assembled an army. But Napoleon routed the Prussian and Saxon troops at Jena and Auerstedt, and Schopenhauer was left alternately dodging the fighting and reading his mother's stories (in letters) of French depradations in Weimar: sacking, rape, looting, soldiers running amok.

Napoleon's 1806–7 campaign took him north and eastwards, to the most noteworthy sites of the young Schopenhauer's biography: Danzig, Gotha, Weimar, Jena, Berlin, Göttingen, Dresden. The features of the world in which the philosopher scrabbled for survival were comprehensively determined by invasion, devastation and humiliation. That he was not only close to this world but much troubled by it was partly what pitted him so violently against Hegel. Hegel saw the Napoleon triumphantly entering Jena in 1806 as a world-historical figure doing the bidding of spirit and furthering the ends of historical progress. For Schopenhauer, by contrast, plausibly enough, he represented the two faces of the will, malice and misery, as they appeared fresh from the killing fields. If the Hegelian refuge in progressivism was trivial and derisory, that was because Hegel took sides, singled out what he decided was a justified cause according to a logic of sufficient reason, and then committed himself to a system of representation, in wilful indifference to the will that governed it.

The two faces of the will that were abundantly evident in northern Germany in 1806–7 were still more gruesomely present in 1812–13. In 1811–12, Napoleon assembled a new version of his Grand Armée, around half a million men. It massed in northern and eastern Germany and Poland. Prussia had no alternative but meekly to submit to 'being ground under the wheels of great-power politics'.[26] As a good revolutionary army, Napoleon's men despised non-revolutionary Germany, and therefore looted and extorted freely throughout the country.[27] Napoleon drove his victorious troops as far as Moscow, but then was forced to retreat as the fearsome Russian winter set in. The soldiers of the Grand Armée died pathetically, like flies, often in ways and circumstances that defied belief. Schopenhauer's northern Germany witnessed the funeral procession of the will in defeat, as the surviving stragglers came back ragged, maddened, famished, frostbitten, purulent, gangrenous, thick with vermin, typhus- and fever-ridden. The men had crossed an 'empire of death' where all manner of horrors had been possible.[28] If the French had formerly ransacked Prussia, the Prussians and other Germans now had their turn, gleefully setting upon, dispatching and on occasions massacring the wretched remnants of Napoleon's vast military machine.[29] Russia duly succeeded France as the great continental power in Europe.

Just a few months before the Grand Armée passed through Berlin on its way to war, Schopenhauer had gone to the University of Berlin to study philosophy. He was still there when the ruined ghosts of men started appearing.[30] The University had hardly remained untouched by events. Students had gone to fight and, while Schopenhauer was listening disapprovingly to Fichte's lectures, Fichte's wife was nursing wounded soldiers. It was during this period that Schopenhauer came up with his first sketches of the three great cornerstones of his philosophical system. According to Cartwright's biography, it was in 1812 that Schopenhauer alighted on the idea of the 'better consciousness', a mind that holds itself at an 'ultimate distance from the world', as in art and asceticism.[31] He did this precisely when he was ducking and diving to avoid 'the troops of Hegel's horse-riding world-spirit', and the general mayhem that followed in their wake.[32] In order to grasp 'better consciousness' more clearly, however, it was important to know the law that governed ordinary consciousness. Thus as Napoleon was seeking desperately to save himself from total defeat, Schopenhauer was beginning his *On the Fourfold Root of the Principle of Sufficient Reason*. Furthermore, as early as his *Notebooks* of 1813, he was already toying with an avatar of the will, the idea of a universal power that runs eternally through all things, is within oneself as it is in the world, and is not to be set aside or vanquished.[33] Exception, sufficient reason, will – all three came to mind in 1812–13. True, Schopenhauer would reorder them in *The World as Will and Representation*, in that there we understand the logic of sufficient reason in order to understand the limits of particular historical worlds, grasp the elemental thing that lies behind all and then seek a consolatory ethics of the exception. There is nonetheless a degree to which *The World as Will and Representation*, though published some years afterwards in a much developed form and later revised, is a text of 1812–13.

Indeed, within it, there is a sombre philosophical poem on the Napoleonic Wars. More than at any time before the twentieth century, the world had become 'a battlefield of all the phenomena' (WW1, p. 265), absorbed in a will-driven 'war of extermination' (WW1, p. 161). In 1812–13, northern Europe seemed an objective demonstration of the inner self-variance of the will and the truth of '*homo homini lupus*' (WW1, p. 147; Schopenhauer himself quotes Hobbes). The strife of the will, and the suffering it causes, were apparent everywhere. Equally, the Napoleonic Wars provided eloquent testimony to the structure of need, satisfaction and need revived that Schopenhauer thought the will imposed. Nor did he have to look very far to suppose that the will to live constantly 'objectifies itself' in 'scenes of horror', or that men are led by the nose, 'today by one braggart tomorrow by another' (WW1, p. 173, WW2, p. 35). In the *mundus phaenomenon* of 1812–13, to a Hanseatic snob and hater of Prussian weakness like Schopenhauer, the *canaille* were all too likely to seem brain-dead machines. His dream of a 'better consciousness' is comprehensible in this light. So, too, a philosopher on the run from armies, and stubbornly avoiding all summons whether military or maternal, might seem more likely to write of a 'desire for non-relation' than some others.

So historicism appears to have the edge on misanthropy again, casting doubt on its plausibility if not its power. Rousseau is another intriguing case, not least because his successors have more often conceived of him as one of the great sources of revolutionary, romantic and progressive strains in modern thought than as a man-hater. Like Hobbes's, Rousseau's thought hinges on a structure that opposes a 'state of Nature' to civil society.[34] But he also inverts that structure, asserting that civil society tends to corrupt all that is best in 'natural man'. Such a belief may seem dismissive of a rather awesome range of human activity. It is not for all that misanthropic. Indeed, Rousseau explicitly enjoins us not to 'dishonour man' (E, p. 510).

Yet during his lifetime, as he himself repeatedly underlines,[35] others often called him a misanthropist, and his justification for seeming one – that 'a disposition apparently so sombre and misanthropic' in fact arose 'from my too affectionate, too loving, too tender heart', which found 'no living creatures resembling it'[36] – hardly changes the point.

Rousseau became 'a solitary', 'living little among men' and preferring plants (E, p. 348, RPS, pp. 1066ff.). He hated men for 'the miseries into which they have plunged me', believing that he alone qualified as 'wise and enlightened among mortals' (RPS, pp. 1011, 1020). In an obviously misanthropic work, the late *Reveries of a Solitary Walker*, he tells us that he was happiest living in almost total isolation on an island in the middle of a lake.

So Rousseau, it would seem, is an anti-misanthropic misanthropist. We can make quite a lot of this contradiction. For Rousseau, everything is good in nature. One of his best-known creations, the Savoyard Vicar in *Emile*, presents the 'order of beings' as a 'picture of nature' in which, universally, there is 'only harmony and proportion'. However, it turns out that this picture does not include man at all: indeed, in stark contrast to it, 'Mankind presents me with only confusion, disorder', says the Vicar, 'evil on earth' (E, p. 583). Everything 'is good as it leaves the hands of the Author of things. Everything degenerates in the hands of man' (E, p. 246). If man would respond 'only to what nature demands of him', then he would 'do nothing but good' (E, p. 322). But he is, 'from the first steps', outside nature (E, p. 259). He is in thrall to 'prejudices, authority, necessity, example', and spinelessly conforms to social institutions (E, p. 246). He therefore mixes and deforms things, produces confusion and monstrosity, and surrenders to the perversities and vices.

Institutions corrupt: Rousseau's *Confessions* is perhaps the first great modern tale of the growth to adulthood as a process of corruption. Rousseau promotes the supreme value of natural simplicity over civilized complexity, and this determines the character of his thought as a great structure of antitheses. He lauds the peasantry over city folk and the senses over the intellect. He treasures sincerity, spontaneity, impetuosity, enthusiasm, honesty, frankness, sensitivity, heart and ardour, all of which are works of nature and associated with integrity, honour and disinterest, over moderation, forethought, circumspection, concealment, diplomacy, dissimulation, wit, superficiality, affectation and style, all of which are soiled by worldliness. He seems himself to have been temperamentally incapable of cautious speech or the politic view. He hates luxuries, thinking of them as 'useless and pernicious affectations' (E, p. 292): according to the *Confessions*, he sold his watch, and gave up gold lace, white stockings and his sword. He distrusts fables, myths, histories and even books (the 'instruments' of 'the greatest misery' of childhood, E, p. 357). Like Hobbes, he is suspicious of language. There is, he feels, far too much talk and chatter in the world. Like Hobbes, again, he hates 'ténèbres', ambiguities, mysteries and uncertainties (RPS, p. 1007), finding it impossible to distinguish between them and duplicity and prevarication. It was for him an 'inviolable maxim, with my friends, to show myself to their eyes exactly as I am' (CO, p. 663): there is no reason, he thinks, why one should not be perfectly candid at all times. He is perhaps the great inaugurator of modern earnestness.

Rousseau's logic leads to his famous declaration: 'Man is born free; and everywhere he is in chains'.[37] Many have heard this as a great liberal apopthegm or a revolutionary call to arms. But matters are not quite so clear. First, there was a side to Rousseau that felt that the chains were unbreakable. It is always too easy for that which 'favours the malignity of man' to 'establish itself' (CO, p. 588), as law, for example, 'will always favour the strong against the weak'. Justice and 'subordination' are mere 'specious names' for the 'arms of iniquity' and 'will always serve as instruments of violence' (E, p. 524). Secondly, the chains are not necessarily those of gross inequalities in wealth and power, though Rousseau's *Discourse on Inequality* might lead one to think so. They are partly the twining fetters of sheer complication, with which Rousseau was impatient. Thus, while *Emile* begins with a version of the familiar case regarding nature, in Book II, a more startling argument appears. Rousseau asserts that man is good by nature but bad by association, that social involvement *of any kind* is dangerous; or, as he puts it himself, more pungently, 'Man's breath is deadly to his kind' (E, p. 277). It is not just mediocre societies that breed evil, but the social instinct itself. 'The precept of never hurting another' therefore 'carries with it that of being attached to human society as little as possible, for in the social state the good of the one necessarily constitutes the harm of the other' (E, p. 340n). In such circumstances, the solitary will necessarily be he who comes out best. Rousseau is the forerunner of Joseph Conrad's Axel Heyst: 'I only know that he who forms a tie is lost. The germ of corruption has entered into his soul'.[38]

Again, Rousseau is both with Hobbes and against him. According to *Emile*, above all an educational tract, the ideal education is solitary and asocial. But this means that, given the binding power of social life, paradoxically, what is natural can only be sustained and protected by a form of artifice. Yet in Hobbes, in a sense, artifice is necessary to *overcome* the effects of solitude. Nonetheless, the more one reads Rousseau, the more the praiser *par excellence* of the state of nature seems also a great advocate of human making – above all, when it involves humans making themselves other than they have been and are. Take for example *The Social Contract*. This, if any text of Rousseau's, is ostensibly quite unmisanthropic. Rousseau argues that the social contract is founded on '*the supreme direction of the general will*', which is 'a moral and collective body' (CO, p. 361). What price the collective, one might ask, if true virtue is possible only in the state of nature, and human society odious? But the point is that the civil state constituted by the contract changes mankind, giving their actions 'the morality they had formerly lacked' (CO, p. 364). Alas, however, if the people wills the good of the contract, it often does not see that good itself, as it no longer exists in a state of nature. The people must therefore 'be shown the good road it is searching for' (CS, p. 380). It must be taught to know what it wills. This is the function of 'the Legislator', an extremely rare figure who tends to the maintenance of what is otherwise 'an impractical, speculative chimaera' bearing 'no relation to our nature', and is therefore capable of changing it, of transforming each individual (CO, pp. 381, 392). Through him, the future human – what ought to be – becomes the present one.

Rousseau is scathing about the 'specious maxim' that states that there is no sense in teaching others 'the idea of an imaginary order which is quite contrary to the one they will find and according to which they will have to govern themselves' (E, pp. 457–8). Thus in *The Social Contract* he pursues what he sees as a superior logic, reasoning 'from the existent to the possible' (CO, p. 426). Man is a creature who can infinitely exceed his own boundaries, and no philosopher can say, 'This is the limit of what man can attain and which he cannot surpass' (E, p. 281). Rousseau struggles to think about actual and historical man from the point of view of this infinite excess. Hence what he fears others take to be his 'imaginary and fantastic beings' (E, p. 549) – Emile, the Legislator, the Savoyard Vicar – whom he invents as a challenge to those who dare 'to assign precise limits to Nature and say: here is as far as Man can go, and not beyond it'.[39]

It is *Julie* that provides the great example of this tendency in Rousseau. With their moral elevation, their sensibility ratcheted up to the nth power, their transports that 'elevate' them 'above [them]selves' and 'hearts warmed by a celestial fire', all the main characters qualify as Rousseauian 'beautiful souls' (J, pp. 169, 199, 221). The novel is correspondingly founded on a belief in an exquisite language that exists apart from trivial actuality, risks itself if it manifests itself publicly, and can therefore appear only in private and intimate documents, confessions, diaries and, above all, letters (hence the fact that *Julie* is an epistolary novel). This, the language of the few, the initiates, is the only true language, and the one Rousseau and his characters pit against 'the rest of mankind' (J, p. 316). From the beginning of Part IV, the beautiful souls effectively close ranks, forming an exemplary moral clique, isolating themselves from the world and incessantly congratulating each other on their virtue, delicacy, wisdom, high moral standards and emotional generosity. This is Julie's 'adorable and powerful empire of beneficent beauty' (J, p. 427). But Rousseau has systematically pruned it of all dark undergrowth. No eruption of nastiness, however faint or fleeting – no envy, spite, jealousy, rancour, hostility, scheming, machination, injustice, calumny, self-interest, deceit, covetousness, pettiness or vanity – can trouble the characters' 'felicity', their 'close and sweet benevolence' (J, pp. 423, 541). Above all, there is no manifestation of the furtiveness or indirection that Rousseau so detested. Indeed, if one categorical imperative especially prevails in Julie's Clarens, it is openness, confession. Even at breakfast, writes Saint-Preux, 'We say everything we think, we reveal all our secrets, we constrain none of our sentiments' (J, p. 471).

Julie's Elysium, then, a garden in which those who tend it take 'great care' to 'efface human footprints', would seem not only to be Rousseau's horticultural ideal, but a figure for the novel as a whole (J, p. 461). In the second Preface, 'N', a man of letters, protests that a work of imagination 'must possess traits common to mankind'. But a Julie there has never been. Rousseau's characters 'are people from the other world'. The editor and Rousseau-figure 'R' merely replies, 'Then I am sorry for this one' (J, p. 738). This is scarcely even to reason from the actual to the possible: it is peremptorily to excise the actual. Rousseau is the origin of a modern type of private self-enclosure which encourages the self to nourish its illusions at the expense of the rest of the world. But he also remains the inheritor of Hobbes. What matters in human beings is their capacity to transform themselves or be transformed, a virtual humanity within the real one. Some may feel, as Isaiah Berlin did,[40] that they hear in this a certain moment in the history of an ambivalent form of modern misanthropy that runs from Hobbes to Stalin and Mao Tse-tung, its apogee in art being the epic, dauntless, grandiose figures of socialist realist statuary, in which the new utopian man recreates the human world through force.

Why should Rousseau have felt so intensely that people were just not sufficient as they were? He was torn between two historical cultures, both of which had their attractions but both of which, at the time, were also direly limited. He was born in 1712, in Geneva, a free city, a republic and a member of the Swiss confederacy with a long history of political autonomy.[41] In principle, at least, all its citizens had equal rights. He lived there until he was fifteen, then in neighbouring Savoy until twenty-seven, the period constituting an idyll to which his works repeatedly testify – in *Julie* for example, Claire enthuses over Geneva ('splendid', her *patrie*, a place where 'freedom' has 'taken refuge', J, pp. 644–5) – and from which (according to the *Confessions*) he fell into an increasingly stark and bitter decline. Rousseau himself sufficiently recalled the idyll to keep on inscribing himself as 'citoyen de Genève' on the title pages of his books throughout his life.

It was only in 1742 that he moved to Paris. There were, of course, good reasons for his doing so. To 'a proud Republican', France might seem unconscionably 'servile' (CO, p. 238), but Paris was increasingly the home of enlightened ideas and arts, and especially of the Enlightenment *philosophes*. Geneva was Calvinist, and had been since the sixteenth century, 'a sombre fortress' with an 'austere, repressive ethos'.[42] Its 'enlightened Protestantism' was not incompatible with 'Calvinist misogyny' and a moralism that stifled 'artistic and sensuous delight' (it even suppressed the performing arts).[43] By contrast, Paris was intellectually worldly and broad-minded. Clever, gifted, ambitious, determined, Rousseau was bound to gravitate towards it. But as we saw in Chapter 1, in crucial respects, its culture was considerably more stagnant than Geneva's, as Rousseau was bound to recognize.

Nonetheless, in the 1740s, fashionable society was welcoming the *philosophes* into its bosom, particularly if they turned out to be witty and amusing. Rousseau was not a scintillating conversationalist but, for a while, even he was popular with the salons. They were prepared to overlook his rustic Swiss manners and the freedoms of his behaviour. Yet he felt continually humiliated by patronage. Where he was passionately attached to his ideas, those around him seemed suavely detached from their own. Worst of all, he found in Paris a *beau monde* that, however advanced its ideas were becoming, was still hobbled by manners, courtesies and cultivated formalities, what he called 'precautions and reserves'.[44] These, thought Rousseau, were appallingly destructive of natural sincerity and warmth. But he himself was gauche and untutored, and had none of the relevant social graces. In such a situation, his 'free and republican spirit' could only be a source of torment (CO, p. 294).

If a hankering for Parisian cultivation would not let Rousseau rest easy in Switzerland, then it was the Calvinist element in him that emerged in Paris, its austere sense of principle, its uncompromising seriousness, its refusal to traffic with the world. In 1749, the tensions generated by this inner conflict led to a Damascene moment when, en route to visit Diderot in prison, he had a vision of civilization as a source of corruption, not progress. The rest of his career was the 'inevitable outcome' of that moment.[45] When, not long afterwards, he published his *Letter on French Music* (1753), which claimed that the French were far too sophisticated to be great musicians, *le tout Paris* flew into a huge rage. So, in 1754, Rousseau briefly returned to Geneva, the only city on earth, it seemed, where it was still conceivable that 'justice prevailed and virtue ruled'.[46] Yet there were obvious holes in Geneva's liberal, republican and democratic pretensions. The radical opposition were accusing the governing patriciate of despotism: though the patricians did not exploit the people economically, the latter had no real power. There was no religious toleration, and the dominant morality meant that Rousseau had to pretend that his mistress Thérèse was his nurse. Genevan society was committed to revealed religion, where Rousseau was increasingly turning to a natural one, a religion of the heart.

Rousseau, then, was in large part a Calvinist in Paris and a liberal in Geneva. Neither place was going to work. Later in 1754, he went back to the French capital. He saw that he had to extricate himself from the coteries, and moved to the neighbouring countryside, but this was an awkward compromise. The hermit could not resist staying in touch with the city, and his friends (and enemies) bothered about what he was up to. He steadily fell out, not only with more and more of his old allies, but also with patrons, including those who had provided his cottage. He increasingly suspected the other *philosophes* of treachery, and they in turn increasingly hated him. In 1762, government censorship took on a new lease of vicious life, and singled him out. The *Parlement* in Paris denounced him, and issued a warrant for his arrest.

Rousseau had kept in close touch with developments in Geneva since 1754, and thought of returning. But the Genevans had burnt *Emile* and *The Social Contract*, which seemed inauspicious. He ended up in the nearby principality of Neuchâtel, but there again his domestic arrangements and his views got him into trouble. The locals jeered at him in the street, and pelted his house with stones. He continued to pay attention to what was going on in Geneva, citizenship of which was still 'fundamental to his self-image'.[47] But the authorities upbraided and banned him, and the Swiss Party of Liberty used and betrayed him. In the end, he found the Genevans even more 'disposed to hatred' than the Parisians (CO, p. 588) and came to think of Switzerland as a 'homicidal land' (CO, p. 774). The rejection by Geneva was decisive. From Switzerland he fled to England, in which he had no interest, and where he collapsed into the paranoid delusions – he was constantly spied on; there were plots against him everywhere – that had been imminent for some time. In the words of his long-suffering sponsor David Hume, Rousseau had become a 'real and complete madman'.[48]

Rousseau is obviously a different case to Hobbes and Schopenhauer, but in his case even more than theirs, misanthropy breaks up on the scattered reefs of history. He judged his own thought to be 'too audacious for the century and the country in which I was writing', and he was right (CO, p. 492). The growth of his vast influence, still evident today, began only after his death. Paris and Geneva would be quite different cities after 1789 and the French revolution, not least in becoming cities that idolized Rousseau. In neither city in the 1790s could Rousseau's specific brand of misanthropy have exactly survived. Or, to put matters in a different historical context: one could hardly claim that the Rousseauian values of spontaneity, sincerity and openness are disregarded in our society as they were in Rousseau's Paris. The formality of the social life that Rousseau came to so loathe has largely disappeared from our culture of mates, Twitter, jeans and open-necked shirts, and so equally has the joyless and priggish chilliness of his Geneva. We are in some degree Rousseau's products, and he himself would not have been able to say about us what he says about the world he knew. This does not diminish the power of his philosophy, indeed it testifies to it. But it does raise questions of his misanthropy. It is understandable that Rousseau should have found the two cultures to which he was closest unbearable to live in. But like Hobbes and Schopenhauer, he also converted a historical moment or a social and historical predicament into a generically human one.

4

THE IRISH MISANTHROPIC TRADITION

The first three chapters of this book have not set out to pour scorn on misanthropists. But neither, in the end, have they been able to take the misanthropic insistences we have encountered quite as seriously as misanthropists would presumably like them to be taken. This is because, as we have abundantly seen, the occasions of misanthropy repeatedly turn out to be determined by circumstance. Misanthropy seems unable to persuade us of the full reach of its generalizing claims. The first chapter showed that the great early modern outbreak of European misanthropy occurred in a society whose political features were eminently well suited to encouraging a contempt for human being. The third chapter took this case further, suggesting that the three eminent, misanthropically inclined philosophers it dealt with might have been less gloomy about human proclivities had their own lives taken other courses, or their historical situations been less rebarbative, disquieting or depressing. Given the particularities of their experience, can their larger convictions hold good? In between, Chapter 2 asked whether a truly convinced misanthropist must not ultimately suffer from a condition of organic disgust, a pathological revulsion from human flesh, a paralysis or perversion of the affections, a drastic failure to respond to human beauty and warmth – in other words, a kind of disease. This raises a question more psychological than historical, but which nonetheless hardly shores up the misanthropic vision. It might seem at this point as if the book has already made a sufficient case against misanthropy, and can only repeat its basic argument.

But there are certain points at which the anti-misanthropic case can at least be called in question, and the next three chapters will seek discreetly to do so. This chapter is rooted in one such doubt. Certainly, all grandiose judgements on humanity are finally relative. But are they necessarily vitiated by that? Does the judge have to feel quashed by it? Are all such judgements equally relevant (or irrelevant) to all historical and social worlds? To put matters differently: if we are looking at evidence for and against the general terms of the misanthropic vision, what weight can we give, for example, to Jane Austen's elegant, seductively written romantic comedies of genteel life in Regency England, set alongside, say, Arthur Koestler's clear-eyed, rigorous, infinitely bleak evocation – in *Darkness at Noon* – of the Moscow show trials in 1937–8, of a Russia increasingly caught up in wholesale atrocity? Koestler's is a world gone 'rotten to the marrow',[1] for his Rubashov does not suppose that to admit the monstrosity of Stalin's Russia is also *ipso facto* to hold a brief for the Western way of life. After all, notwithstanding its supposed humanism and liberal democracy, the West has done nothing to aid the miserable victims. Austen shows herself to be at least aware of what is at stake in my question when, in *Northanger Abbey*, Catherine Morland finally dismisses dark and troubling versions of the human world, even if these have come to her from no more profound a source than the Gothic novel:

Charming as were all Mrs Radcliffe's works, and charming even as were the works of all her imitators, it was not in them perhaps that human nature, at least in the midland counties of England, was to be looked for. Of the Alps and Pyrenees, with their pine forests and their vices, they might give a faithful delineation; and Italy, Switzerland, and the South of France, might be as fruitful in horrors as they were there represented. Catherine dared not doubt beyond her own country, and even of that, if hard pressed, would have yielded the northern and western extremities. But in the central part of England there was surely some security for the existence of a wife not beloved, in the laws of the land, and the manners of the age. Murder was not tolerated, servants were not slaves, and neither poison nor sleeping potions to be procured, like rhubarb, from every druggist.[2]

It seems unlikely that Catherine's fragile and limited moral apparatus could withstand any account of 'human nature' more shocking than the one in Gothic novels like Mrs Radcliffe's. She has a hard enough time with that one. Under the delicate irony, however, Austen's point is also that the truth may be altogether too horrible to bear much contemplation anyway, and civilized people are best off ignoring it. If you are fortunate enough to be a member of one of the world's more comfortable parishes, inhabit it as contentedly as you can. To think further is to risk destabilization and even derangement, to no good end.

For Walter Benjamin, by contrast, it was axiomatic that the condition of truth is wholesale destitution. The historical victors, those assured of their place in the sun, will always tell the human story in their own interest or to their own advantage, not least by brightening it up. But its value on their lips is nil. This is equally the case when, seized by conscience or shame, they reverse perspectives and try to tell the tale of the other side. Indeed, anyone who can seek to tell that tale at all already belongs among the victors. The wretched of the earth, the victims of history, the terminally defeated, those that history has left utterly bereft of status or power, even the power to tell their story, have priority in matters of truth, the truth at stake being that of definitive misery and loss. All else is mere glozing. Varlam Shalamov and Aleksandr Solzhenitsyn compile their great encyclopaedias of depravity by heeding the millions of spectres that haunted the Soviet Gulag, watching them, listening to their narratives. They are scathing about the overlords, for whose 'scientific' truths and historical narratives they have vast contempt.

It would seem, then, as though, from a Benjaminian point of view, there might be a certain case to be made for misanthropy, after all, the case of the historical loser, who begins in truth. If so, one fertile source of inspiration is colonial misanthropy. Take for instance the country with the longest colonial history of all, Ireland, not least because it can also lay claim to a rich and diverse tradition of misanthropic writing (though no doubt others can, too; the Irish is the one I know best). The trouble with the passage from *Northanger Abbey* is not so much its lightness of tone as that, burlesque as its intentions are, it ignores reasons for consternation that were closer to home than Italy, Switzerland or the south of France (though, interestingly, it does faintly concede that they may be present in the 'western extremities' of the British Isles). Austen was writing *Northanger Abbey* in 1798. In Ireland, this was also the year of the rebellion of the United Irishmen, which the British army was busily putting down, massacring defenceless prisoners, burning its victims alive and generally convicting itself of the most extraordinary ferocity. If Wicklow farmer Joseph Holt is to be believed, when they found young Irishwomen 'wearing green stuff petticoats', some English militiamen would cut off their haunches and thighs.[3]

From the eighteenth century to Irish independence in 1922, the colonial British regime carried out various forms of experiment in Ireland unthinkable in Britain itself. They also tried out new inventions there. In 1798, they introduced new forms of torture: for example, pitchcapping. Pitchcapping involved pouring boiling tar into a conical cap, which was then placed on the captured rebel's shaved head. His brains seethed. When the cap was torn off, so was his scalp. Half-hanging, too: half-hanging meant exactly that. In an early version of waterboarding, the victim was repeatedly half-hung, each time believing he was going to die. Catherine Moreland on the one hand, pitchcapping and half-hanging on the other: Regency England was by no means the only society to want to draw a veil over the consequences of its political, military and economic dirty work elsewhere. Governments ceaselessly operate on the principle that 'Catherine Morland must not know'. Solzhenitsyn is at pains to stress that the Gulag Archipelago was a vast, shadowy world within a world that knew little or nothing about it. So, too, Ireland was England's squalid backyard, its hidden abattoir. The misanthropist might seem to have at least some reason to suppose that this kind of concealment – and the wilful ignorance that often accompanies it – is typical, and that the underside, the Benjaminian truth, is likely to be bleak indeed.

*

The Ireland of 1798, in fact, was 'fruitful in horrors' to an extent quite beyond Mrs Radcliffe's compass. But then, it had been so for many centuries. The English, or rather Cambro-Normans, Welsh Normans, first invaded in 1169, at the request of a beleaguered Irish king. They were in fact of maverick baronial stock: their predecessors had hurtled down to Wales as quickly as they could, partly to get as far away as possible from the jurisdiction of William the Conqueror. Henry II, however, was not about to let erstwhile vassals establish themselves as a rival power on a neighbouring island, and himself made the trip in 1171 (with fleet and army). Having asserted his authority, he left. (English monarchs never stayed long in Ireland). The Norman barons were free to go hunting for territory, which they promptly did, though the territory in question was duly incorporated into the royal Lordship under Henry's sway.

The Normans were a Viking people, and not noted for their kindly treatment of those they invaded. Yet, strangely, their occupation of Ireland lost momentum, then weakened and came to a halt. The Lordship shrank to the coastal area between Dublin and Dundalk, known as the Pale. Perhaps because of what had been their own rootless tradition, the Normans turned out to be surprisingly open to assimilation. They became 'Hibernicized'. Norman robber barons settled down alongside autonomous Irish princes, fought with but also built alliances with them. They intermarried with the Irish, adopted their language, customs and mode of dress. They wore their hair long, like the Irish. In the well-known phrase, they became more Irish than the Irish. This was so far the case that, in 1366, the English introduced the Statutes of Kilkenny, thirty-five acts that sought to counter what they took to be a process of degeneration. Since, however, the English monarchy had no resources for carrying out any practical programme, the Statutes changed little.

In effect, no stable English kingdom existed in Ireland at this time. The settlers proved increasingly troublesome to the English government, and the Papacy wielded more power than the crown. By the early fifteenth century, it even seemed as though the Gaelic princes had drawn the sting of their Norman neighbours and would overwhelm them. A 'Gaelic resurgence' was taking place, which spelt 'the progressive decline of the English colony', and the actual destruction of some of the centres of Englishness in Ireland. On the eve of the Tudor period, 'the English community in Ireland was in danger of total extinction', and 'the Great Earl', Gerald, Earl of Kildare, was *de facto* virtually master of Ireland.[4]

The man who put a stop to this, and ushered in the truly devastating period of colonial violence, was Henry VIII. Henry thought Ireland was getting more and more disorderly, and the dynasties in Ireland increasingly precarious. When Kildare power collapsed, in 1534–5, the king sent in his troops, aiming to establish central control, direct rule from London and a garrison (permanent army of occupation) to enforce it. From 1546 to 1566, military campaigns took place on a more or less yearly basis. Between 1534 and 1691, Ireland changed from a land of two related nations, the 'Irishry' and the 'Englishry', to a subject kingdom of the British monarchy. By 1691, newcomers – the 'planters' or 'New English' – owned four-fifths of a land that had previously been in Irish hands. They were Protestant colonizers, freshly arrived from the homeland, far more brutal and rapacious than their Cambro-Norman predecessors (and better organized). Theirs was a radical colonial project that involved full-scale, bloody conquest. They strategically uprooted local elites, forcing landowners and their tenants and peasants off their land. From Henry onwards, the English objective was dramatically to reshape Irish culture in government, language and culture, transforming it into a replica of England ('Anglicization'). The English justified this by a gospel of ethnic superiority, according to which the Irish were backward, savage, quarrelsome, tribal, drunken, licentious, unreliable, dishonest, idle and hopelessly second-rate. Many of these stereotypes would subsequently persist for centuries.

As a magisterial James Joyce was later to put matters, 'A conqueror cannot be amateurish'.[5] The English were certainly not. The years from Henry VIII to Oliver Cromwell's departure in 1650 saw the repeated practice of State terror. The Tudors knew they could get away with counter-insurgency measures in Ireland that the English would not stomach at home: torture, massacres, head-hunting, pre-emptive strikes, mass slaughter of unarmed civilians, summary execution, not least of migrants and vagrants, frequent mutilation and dismemberment. The colonizers favoured a scorched earth policy in which lands and crops were put to the torch, leading to widespread famine. Some particularly targeted women and children (to dissuade families from harbouring 'rebels', an interesting word, in this context). 'We killed man, woman, child, horse, beast, and whatever we found', boasted one of Lord Charles Blount Mountjoy's captains. (Mountjoy was Lord-Lieutenant in Ireland in 1603–4).[6] Meanwhile, rogue planters accepted financial inducements to murder, or pursued their own greedy little entrepreneurial wars of annexation.[7] Much of the country was destroyed, left waste. Certainly, there was 'a poisonous dynamic of escalation':[8] the Irish struck back, under provocation but sometimes no less outrageously, notably, perhaps, in the case of the massacre of Ulster Protestant settlers, those who had stolen their land, in 1641. But they were fighting to keep hold of their territory and defend their families, not brutally threatening the livelihood of another people and the world that they had built for themselves.

The invaders used the same methods during the Confederate Wars from 1641, which again pitted the by now better established English and Scots Protestant colonists and their military commanders – General George Monck (English), James Butler, Duke of Ormond (Old English, i.e. originally Cambro-Norman, Protestant), Sir Charles Coote of black legend (New English settler, land-grabber and indiscriminate killer, much extolled in the London press) – against the Catholic Irish. Sometimes the commanders ordered the atrocities. Sometimes soldiers just went berserk.[9] The Cromwellian campaign began in 1649, and included the massacres of Drogheda and Wexford. Cromwell sent the survivors of the first off to indentured servitude in Barbados (they were bartered for sugar and tobacco). He left again, by which time there were hardly more than half a million Irish remaining. The Jacobite War of 1689–91 between William of Orange, the English, settlers and Protestants on the one hand, and James II, the Catholics and Irish on the other, was less remarkable for hellish conduct, perhaps because of the number of nationalities that fought on both sides – the Jacobite war was a European war, not another instance of the more usual local bullying – though the rapparees, irregular Irish pike-bearers, were 'hunted down like wild animals'.[10] At all events, the defeat of the Catholic cause brought peace.

For Irish misanthropists, the consequences of the triumph of the cause of the Anglo-Irish or the Protestant Ascendancy, as it now became known, were bitterly instructive. Founded on horror, the Ascendancy speedily erased the memory of it. As though it felt an urgent need to disprove its own barbarous origins, it devoted itself to culture, excelling in philosophy (Berkeley), literature (Swift), political theory (Molyneux) and science (Boyle). It founded the Dublin Society and the Royal Irish Academy. Trinity College had first admitted students in 1593. Now it came into its own, growing richer, rapidly expanding, putting together a vast estate and developing a formidable reputation it was never to lose (though its orientation long remained colonial, doctrinal and sectarian, sometimes dismayingly so). Dublin also became increasingly well known for its medical tradition (all the doctors being Protestants). Responsible as he had been for some of the most alarming excesses of the soldiery during the Confederate Wars, Ormond was also responsible for initiating a redesign of Dublin which, as far as architecture and city planning were concerned, was to turn it into one of the most interesting and stylish eighteenth-century European cities. The same period saw the emergence of the great Irish country houses. The Ascendancy were not only elegant improvers; they were also shrewd ones, creating an educational meritocracy (if strictly for their own, plus converts) that was important to the success of their culture.

This privileged colonial elite wanted absolute political monopoly, lest the 'rebels', who were unfortunately seditious, bloody, cruel, thievish and predisposed to 'inveterate hatred',[11] should rise up again. So they established a set of barriers between themselves and the lesser race. The Irish were a savage, recidivist people, and it was best to treat them roughly: 'They are like their Boggs', wrote one pamphleteer, 'never to be trusted to by going gently over'.[12] It was clear that what Ireland needed was discriminatory legislation. This duly took shape as the Penal Laws. These were partly military: they disarmed the Irish, with the intention of keeping them that way. But they were economic, too, administering the *coup de grâce* to the Catholic landowning class, which soon owned only five per cent of Ireland. They outlawed all manner of Catholic institutions and practices.

They were also deeply racist, though, in most of Ireland if not Ulster, religious difference served (as so often) as a convenient pretext. Edmund Burke famously described the Penal Laws as 'a machine of wise and elaborate contrivance as well fitted for the oppression, impoverishment, and degradation of a people as ever proceeded from the ingenuity of man'.[13] Yet that machine was designed precisely to safeguard what its beneficiaries took to be a civilization from the mire from which it had supposedly been raised, according to what the Ascendancy called the 'right of conquest'. As the eighteenth century wore on, the ethics of the Ascendancy seemed increasingly to be one of enlightenment and moderation. Yet this coexisted with a 'brutish and indefensible' treatment of its own historical victims.[14] Such conduct went far beyond the Penal Laws, as the practices of many landlords (racking rents, levying outrageous tithes, threatening the always insecure tenure of the peasantry) amply bore witness.

At this point, we are almost back at 1798. We could also go beyond it. Long into the nineteenth century, for the majority of the Irish, life spelt dire abjection. Joyce writes for example of 'the terror of soul of an Irish village in which the curfew was still a nightly fear'.[15] Curfews were associated with Coercion Acts, of which the British government introduced 101 between 1800 and 1921.[16] It would be naive to doubt the excesses they made possible. But worse than coercion was famine: one of the major historical occurrences powering Irish misanthropic writing during the nineteenth century was the Great Famine of 1845–52, which wiped out four million, half the population of Ireland. Here the issue was not so much the degree of responsibility the British bore for the catastrophe, much debated by historians and moralists, but rather the very limited degree of responsibility they took for it. In 1801 the British Parliament had passed an Act of Union making a single kingdom of Britain and Ireland. How was it then that, when Ireland suffered unconscionable disaster, England kept treating it as a separate province? What could Union on such terms mean?

But here we might pause. The Irish had good reason to look upon the English with 'a colder eye', to adopt a term of Hugh Kenner's,[17] and, indeed, for a long while, many of them unflaggingly did. They also had good reason to be at the very least sceptical about the British colonial project in Ireland. The invading power had often behaved cynically if not monstrously. Furthermore, it had proved expert in doublethink and doubletalk. First, treachery: from the Tudor campaigns onwards, the Irish thought of the English as perfidious. Perfidy became a word they particularly connected with Albion, and remained so long after the Tudors. The Tudor forces in Ireland repeatedly promised mercy or clemency and then reneged on their promise. This became traditional: Monck and his soldiers offered 'quarter' (mercy) to the women at the Castle of Blackwood, Co. Kildare – and then, with one of the most chilling puns in history, duly chopped them into quarters.[18] Secondly, the English kept on coming up with specious justifications for shabby doings: God, providence, racial supremacy, all were used to bear out the case. Most ironically of all, the Tudors repeatedly invoked the value of 'civility'. But 'from the Irish perspective savagery and monstrosity were located squarely in the supposed instrument of English civility' itself.[19] The discourse of 'civility' was merely spin, at which the English were always skilled. For centuries, the Irish were to remain distinctly unimpressed by the claim implicit in the concept of the 'Anglo-Saxon civilization'.[20]

Thirdly, the English had one set of standards for Ireland and another for England. Cromwell, for instance, perpetrated no atrocities in England during the Civil War, but Ireland was a different matter. Indeed, the monsters of Ireland repeatedly became and remained English eminences, luminaries and heroes, key figures in the national mythology: Henry VIII, the scorched earth king; Elizabeth I, supporter of ethnic cleansing in Laois and Offaly; Walter Raleigh, involved in the torture and slaughter of several hundred unarmed, defenceless prisoners at Smerwick in 1580, including the hanging of women and children; Edmund Spenser, great, canonical English poet, proselytiser equally for 'civility' and dispossession, transportation, the elimination of the Gaelic elites and the use 'of famine as a military tactic'.[21] The tradition of racist national heroes continued later with the popular British military hero the Duke of Wellington, English-identified Anglo-Irishman who supported the movement for Catholic Emancipation in Ireland, but whose attitudes to the Catholic Irish are captured in his reaction to being described as Irish: being born in a stable did not make one a horse; Palmerston, much lauded in England as the people's minister, who, during the Famine, shipped off two thousand impoverished tenants from his Irish estates – and briskly improved his lands; and, perhaps most unpleasantly of all, the dirtiest name in the Famine, Sir William Gregory. Gregory came up with an amendment to the Poor Law Extension Act (1847) that (as the landlords wanted) facilitated mass evictions from their estates, greatly increasing the sum of Irish misery. He was duly knighted in England.[22] Fourthly, still, the English got away with it. The larger world – or at least, the larger non-colonial world – respected the 'Anglo-Saxon civilization', even when it hated and feared it. But that meant the Irish reputation only suffered further as a consequence. The Irish fiercely opposed a civilization: they must evidently all be wild animals, brutes, hoodlums, gunmen, dynamitards and rebels. By the late nineteenth and early twentieth century, some Irish nationalists were determined strategically to resist what they had come to see as a 'campaign of calumny'.[23]

But resentment, political anger and chronic political scepticism do not amount to misanthropy. Anti-colonial rage does not have the same structure as colonial misanthropy. Indeed, the reverse is likely to be the case: it tends to breed righteousness, like that of John Mitchel in his *Jail Journal* (1854), for example – though he can sound misanthropic – a conviction of the good (one's own). This can be unappetizing, or is easily made to sound so: hence Joyce's refusal to share it. 'I find it a bit naïve', he writes, 'to heap insults on the Englishman for his misdeeds in Ireland ... for so many centuries the Englishman has done in Ireland only what the Belgian is doing today in the Congo Free State, and what the Nipponese dwarf will do tomorrow in other lands' (anticipating Japanese conduct in China thirty years later).[24] This, however chilling, is meant to sound like gritty political realism, a hard, modern resignation to incontrovertible historical and political fact. It emphatically repudiates the tradition of impotent fury and the refuge in pious self-satisfaction.

But Joyce was certainly no misanthropist, and the passage I have just quoted also repudiates the Irish misanthropic tradition, as Joyce was concerned to do throughout his career. This, however, has the useful effect of allowing us to see the tradition more clearly for what it is. One can date the beginnings of the Irish misanthropic tradition approximately to the battle of Kinsale in 1601. This is because Kinsale saw the comprehensive defeat of the forces of the Gaelic Irish, and marked the ultimate stage in the subjugation of the old Gaelic order in Ireland. As we have seen, Gaelic Ireland had successfully maintained its identity after the initial invasion. It had done so, not least, by assimilating the invader. In the late sixteenth century, however, it had been progressively threatened by the Tudor strategy of plantation. Kinsale marked the decisive success of Tudor policy; henceforth the Irish were open to disinheritance and dispossession on a massive scale.

This dealt a death blow to what had previously been a sophisticated, if deeply fissured, constantly warring culture centred on the Irish clans. The clans were structured according to a hierarchical order with a dominant aristocratic caste which had, for example, its own complex and subtle legal system. Above all, this was a culture that profoundly valued poetry, music, literature, storytelling, including the narration of history, and art. Here the key figures were the bards, imposing presences in medieval Irish culture. Poets and scholars were effectively minor nobility patronized by the clan chieftains and aristocracy. They were chroniclers, moral advisers to the chieftains, promulgators of knowledge, responsible for the preservation and cultivation of traditional learning. Though their social role might certainly be conducive to satire – satire was one of the principal concerns of the bards – it was unlikely to breed misanthropy, not least, given the privileges the bards enjoyed. With the collapse of the Gaelic order, however, the bards lost the elevated social position they had enjoyed for centuries, a loss cemented in place as Anglicization made progressively deeper inroads into traditional Gaelic culture. Whether or not, as some historians have suggested,[25] the concept of the annihilation of the Gaelic order should be opened up to question, the bards after Kinsale certainly experienced the destruction of their world. One is left with a choice: on the one hand, a (possibly in some degree) mythological evocation of a historical experience which for the bards was not a myth, but a disaster inflicted on the communal psyche, or what Joyce would later call a 'vastation of soul';[26] on the other, the technical, delicate, sometimes rather soulless discriminations of the pragmatic, moderate, modern historian. Poetry and literature should orient us from the start, here, since they speak hauntingly of psychic disaster, do so again and again.

*

The psychic disaster of the end of the Gaelic order has a number of consequences. With the famous exile of the Irish aristocracy in 1607, the so-called Flight of the Earls, the bards were deprived of their wealthy, noble patrons. They were therefore more inclined to turn to ordinary Irish people both as their audience and for their subject matter. At the same time, while maintaining their learned traditions, they were now deprived of their own privileges and comforts. 'The high poets are gone', Dáibhí Ó Bruadair lamented, 'and I mourn for the world's waning'.[27] The bards frequently became itinerant, impoverished, chronically at risk from the invader. They died in despair and abjection. Bards were publicly hanged, as in the case of Piaras Feiritéar in Killarney in 1653, or murdered, as in the case of the hapless, nameless figure whom an English soldier threw over a cliff.[28] According to the seventeenth-century *Cambrensis Eversus* (by John Lynch), in the invaders' war of destruction of everything Irish, the famous bardic instrument, the harp, 'was broken by soldiers wherever it could be found'.[29] The predicament of the seventeenth-century bards gives rise to a tradition of writing from a position of learned destitution, exquisite and coarse together, that endured well into the last century.

In post-Kinsale Ireland, the tradition of bardic satire now took on misanthropic dimensions, if irregularly, here and there; in other words, a misanthropic discourse now formed part of it. Aogán Ó Rathaille's 'The Merchant's Son', for example, speaks of an Ireland where one can expect 'no welcome, no regard or love'.[30] In Art MacCumhaigh's 'Fair Churchyard of Cregan', a female figure tells the poet:

> You have none left alive,
> No family nor friends,
> Not a jot or a jive
> Do you own.

He should flee a world become a desert for a life with her among the 'fairy race'.[31] Bardic misanthropy, however, is specific in kind. Its specificity is determined by what I shall call an incomplete, failed or blocked identification. The bard knows what he values, but can no longer discover any feature of the human world around him that corresponds to it. If he has any repository of value, it is a historical past which has categorically and abruptly disappeared, flown with the Flight of the Earls, a past which is ghostly, spectral, vanished, at best a murmur of disembodied voices. Physically, materially, in every sense, he is left belonging nowhere.

On the one hand, then, logically enough, the bards excoriate what Ó Rathaille calls 'the alien hordes in land and townland' and the Annals of Connacht the 'evil, false band':[32] the invader, his violence, vengefulness, greed and perfidy, his destruction of their schools of learning, their way of life, their vocation itself, since they can no longer be the poets they were. In this aspect of their art, they reflect what, by the 1640s, had unsurprisingly become 'a general revulsion against all things English',[33] lamenting the catastrophe that has engulfed them and their culture, their departed leaders, the desolation of their territory. In 'No Help I'll Call', Ó Rathaille cries out:

Our land, our shelter, our woods and our level ways
Are pawned for a penny by a crew from the land of Dover.[34]

In his account of an Ireland beset by slaughter, famine, deportation, bribery, false testimony, press-ganging and the desecration of monasteries and churches, Éamann an Duna slides from Gaelic to English in order to convey his impression of the invaders in their words, or rather, words of theirs that are seared into his mind:

Transport, transplant, no mheabhair ar Bhéarla,
Shoot him, kill him, strip him, tear him,
A tory, hack him, hang him, rebel,
A rogue, a thief, a priest, a papist.[35]

But this again does not itself amount to misanthropy. By contrast, when Eoghan Rua Ó Súilleabháin mourns the plight of Ireland 'among blackguards', it is no longer clear which side he means.[36] Here the failure of identification is inseparable from a multiply directed strain in post-Kinsale poetry which qualifies it as properly misanthropic. For if the bards excoriate the English, they also repeatedly and indeed more frequently turn on their own. When the bards curse, and they do, they are as likely to curse the Irish as the English. In Brian Ó Cuív's phrase, they repeatedly express 'shame and contempt for the Irish chiefs who had abandoned their heritage and submitted'.[37] Thus Séathrún Céitinn's 'News from Ireland' accuses the nobles of failure and neglect of their duties, and An Bard Ruadh launches a barrage of 'extraordinarily vituperative' attacks on the most important Irish families.[38] But they equally revile the uncouth and uncultivated classes who now increasingly hold sway, attacking them, above all, for their abject surrender. According to Dáibhí Ó Bruadair, they are wearing English clothes, aping English ways, speaking an upstart version of broken English, and no longer respecting either learning or poetry. Ó Bruadair says as much in 'The Poet Laments His Learning':

O it's best to be a total boor
(though it's bad to be a boor at all)
If I'm to go out and about
Among these stupid people.[39]

Out of this kind of grasp of the historical situation comes the 'Páirlement Chloinne Tomáis', a Swiftianly savage prose satire on the rise of the new uncultured classes who have come to prominence with the disappearance and death of the old aristocracy. These pretentious figures are tamely servile to their English overlords and pathetically mimic them. They are 'off to the fair, any hour of the day', cutting a dash in their beavers, 'tan riding boots and thin polished spurs', while the poet now works in the fields or does odd labouring jobs.[40] Alan Harrison asserts that the comic satire of the 'Páirlement Chloinne Tomáis' leaves its mark on Irish writing to this day.[41] It does so partly as a misanthropic colouring. The poet now sets his teeth against 'the great world', as Tadhg Rua Ó Conchúir calls it, which sees the truth and justice that he urges upon it as mere 'idiot noise'.[42] This is increasingly what Ó Rathaille calls the bards' 'bitter vision'.[43] If on the one hand, as various bardic epigrams suggest, it would be hard for Christ to show 'a snug Saxon that didn't mangle [His] law', on the other, 'the men of Ireland have swelled of late with ostentatious pride', and 'loss of learning' has 'brought darkness, weakness and woe … amid these unrighteous hordes'.[44] The vision is one that easily takes on a religious dimension. Thus in the 'Summary of the Purgatory of the Men of Ireland', Ó Bruadair can detail the monstrosity of dispossessions, transplantations, confiscations and transportations of Irish to the West Indies as slaves, yet insist that Ireland has been damned by the sins of its 'churls' or 'rabble'.[45] Not surprisingly, the bards were more and more inclined to prophesy impending doom. At least one author took the onset of plague in 1649 as a divine punishment of the Irish. At the extreme end of this, Feircheirtne File predicted not only the further evils to befall Ireland, but also the birth of the Antichrist and the end of the world.

Cecile O'Rahilly informs us that bardic poetry repeatedly, specifically blamed the 'disunity and treason' of the Irish for their misfortunes'.[46] But this is also the theme of the massive, three-volume, anonymous history of the Confederate Wars of the 1640s, the *Aphorismical Discovery of Treasonable Faction*, even more than bardic poetry. On the one hand, within a few pages, the *Aphorismical Discovery* can call up a world of English atrocities: pillage and destruction, massacres, including those of women and children, wanton plunder, casual arson, casual executions, English faithlessness and breach of promise and an extraordinary hatred, as in the case of Coote. It records Irish men and women being hunted, 'like deeres, and other savage beastes'.[47] But it reserves its most poisonous venom for the Irish parliament, the Irish Supreme Council, Irish commissioners, chief clerks, judges and attorneys – 'the greatest knaves and chettingest rogues' – and, above all, Irish factionists and traitors and their 'plusquam diabolicall proceedings':

> O enemies of God, King and kingdome, of truth, justice and loyaltie and friends to all treacherie, misbelife, periurie, disloyaltie … O poore nation, O more weake than goshlings that forbears such an inevitable fate, that to the present acte is annexed, but nothinge will be done – och, och.[48]

Certainly, there are heroes here and there, and men of integrity. But they are doomed figures in a gathering darkness who hardly counterbalance what the writer otherwise describes as the 'refuse of human nature'.[49] Again and again, the *Aphorismical Discovery* tells the story of what it takes to be the systematic betrayal of the best, broadening the vision out at moments to include other histories of national failure and devastation, from Greece and Rome to Burgundy and Switzerland.

If, then, the chronicler of the *Aphorismical Discovery* more or less takes it for granted that the English are appalling beyond measure, it is in fact his own side that attracts his most virulent disgust, and by far the larger proportion of it. True, it is the Old English that he most anathematizes – the assimilated English who had already been in Ireland for centuries but who, in his view, are now betraying the Gaelic Irish. But beyond this there is rage and despair at the lack of any 'coniunction and union of the nation' that would save the Irish from 'their everlasting destruction'.[50] In the *Aphorismical Discovery*, as in other contemporary histories and as in the bards, one sees the original colonial trauma already involving the failure of all identification and thus unfolding as self-rending, self-castigation, divisions beyond repair, and therefore as misanthropy.

As Harrison suggests, the poetry that emerged out of the decline of the Gaelic order was subsequently hugely influential in Ireland for at least two centuries,[51] and indeed more. It was so, not least, in the case of this misanthropic strain. The dream of redemption from abroad that was initially focused on the earls who disappeared in 1607 shifted to the Stuart royal family and the Stuart king over the water. From this emerges the late seventeenth- and eighteenth-century *aisling* (dream-poem). The bards had sometimes declared that their only hope now lay in love: only the woman could matter, could save the poet from dereliction and despair, wholesale loathing of the world. They also repeatedly thought of Ireland as a violated woman, 'our mild, bright, delicate, loving, fresh-lipped girl', as Aogán Ó Rathaille put matters, now in the hands of 'that black, horned, foreign, hate-crested crew'.[52] The *aisling* formalized the theme: the poet has a dream-vision of a beautiful woman who represents Ireland, tells him of her plight as a deserted spouse and yearns for her rightful husband, one of the Stuart pretenders. After the collapse of Stuart hopes in 1745, the misanthropic strain in the *aisling* grew still bleaker. As Murray Pittock points out, in later *aislings*, even the dream woman of the vision becomes a rotten, corrupted harlot.[53]

In the nineteenth century, the Irish misanthropic tradition finds various points of transmission: Thomas Furlong, for example, in both his translations of the bards and his own poetry. His first poem was precisely entitled 'The Misanthrope'. It is Furlong, too, who allows us to see again how clearly the bardic theme of the lovers' flight from the world was misanthropic, on the one hand, and related to conquest, on the other. In one poem, the speaker declares that he wishes that 'my love and I/From life's crowded thoughts could fly', like the misanthropes of the French tradition under the Ancien Régime. But here the retreat is supposed to be a place 'where no stranger should intrude/On our hallowed solitude',[54] 'the stranger' being an Irish term for an English colonist. More obviously, there is James Clarence Mangan, for whom, Joyce wrote, life was surely 'a heavy penance', because 'he reads so truly the lines of brutality and weakness in the faces of men that are thrust in upon his path'.[55]

What is remarkable, however, is not the fitful persistence of the tradition in the century of Daniel O'Connell, Catholic Emancipation, Parnell and the Home Rule movement – after all, the Famine seemed to some not only to rewrite the tradition of misanthropy all over again, but to do so in the same reversible terms, contempt both for the enemy and, given the nightmarishly extreme forms of conduct to which starvation drove people, for one's own – but its persistence after 1922 and Irish independence. And yet it is arguably after 1922 that the Catholic Irish tradition produces what are perhaps its finest specimens of misanthropic art, notably in Flann O'Brien and Patrick Kavanagh. O'Brien co-founded the magazine *Blather*, which aimed to achieve 'entirely new levels in everything that is contemptible, despicable and unspeakable in contemporary journalism' in a manner commensurate with everything contemptible, despicable and unspeakable in contemporary Irish life, to wit, 'graft and corruption ... cant and hypocrisy ... humbug and hysteria'. 'In regard to politics', the editorial continued, 'all our rat-like cunning will be directed towards making Ireland fit for the depraved readers of *Blather* to live in', adding with a flourish, 'a plague on all your parties, legal and illegal'.[56] Once again, we return to the absence or impossibility of identification, as is confirmed by setting O'Brien's *The Third Policeman* and *The Poor Mouth* alongside each other. On the one hand, *The Third Policeman* is a vision of unending hell, in which the protagonist is condemned to perform the same loop, caught up in a lunatic logic – that O'Brien treats the lunacy hyperbolically and indeed surrealistically does not change the point; it rather enhances it – determined by the power of State and Church presented as (it would seem) beyond appeal. On the other hand, *The Poor Mouth*, with what Anthony Cronin calls its 'unrelentingly bleak view of human existence',[57] describes an Irish peasantry not without humour but categorically unavailable to redemption or progress. So too O'Brien's contemporary and friend Kavanagh hated the early twentieth-century Anglo-Irish-dominated Literary Revival as 'a thoroughgoing English-bred lie' but, in stripping away the fancy romantic costumes in which the Revivalists dressed up the Irish peasantry, could not but suggest that what he then revealed was deeply depressing: 'Rapscallions of hell', as the priest calls the peasants in *Tarry Flynn*, 'curmudgeons of the devil that are less civilized than the natives of the Congo. Like a lot of pigs'.[58] Kavanagh's mindset changed late in life.[59] But like O'Brien – fascinatingly, both of them tended to cast themselves in the old role of the bard – the younger Kavanagh is left revolving in an empty space that inclines him to pronounce a plague on all houses and produce a generalized excoriation.[60] To some, at least, this position actually takes O'Brien as far as Manichaeanism. Cronin for example suggests that, for O'Brien, 'this world was perhaps Hell, or part of its Empire'.[61] O'Brien himself referred to the possibility that 'the awesome encounter between God and the rebel Lucifer' had, despite all we have been told, in fact 'gone the other way'.[62]

Thus the history was not readily to be thought away. Colonial misanthropy is born of a complex defeat, and, in Ireland, persisted well after independence. Indeed, it is only with the 'Celtic Tiger' and the Good Friday agreement that Ireland might have seemed properly free of it (though many Irish faces would by now grin sardonically at that idea, too). Certainly, the defeat is military, and the character of the military defeats, the frank terror that the English and Scots visited on Catholic Ireland, is hardly likely to improve one's view of humanity, even at this historical distance. Nor is English and Scots treatment of the Irish after the defeats, or their subsequent indifference to their historical responsibility (still very much today as it was then, for all the occasional formal apologies). But this is reason for rage, not misanthropy. The defeat of the Irish was not simply a question of conquest and dispossession. It was defeat for an identity. The Tudors avowedly wanted to extirpate Irish culture, which had thitherto been strong enough to assimilate the English, rather than being assimilated by them. The possibility of assimilation ends with Kinsale. There is thus a Kinsale of the battlefield, but also a Kinsale of the spirit. From now on Irish identity itself is split, fissured, set at odds with itself. The bards and the historians are not to be reconciled with the invader or inclined to yield to the cultural transformation he is proposing. But henceforth the sense of identity which fuels the will to resistance is founded on a void. Nothing will underwrite it, which leaves it turning indefinitely in a circle from which there is apparently no release. It is worth recalling, here, that O'Brien considered an alternative title for *The Third Policeman*: *Hell Goes Round and Round*.

*

However, I have so far only discussed a tradition that is first Gaelic and later Catholic and nationalist Irish. Quite clearly that was not the only tradition. The most famous Irish misanthropist of them all, Swift, was not of Gaelic Irish stock. He was Anglo-Irish and Dean of St Patrick's, the Protestant cathedral. There was an Anglo-Irish or Protestant Irish tradition of misanthropy, too, or, perhaps better, an Anglo-Irish variant of the tradition. This variant picked up the by now traditional structure of Irish misanthropy, the broken, absent or failed identification, but also slanted or skewed it. Why should one assume, however, that the older tradition in some way conditions the later one? Because, from the seventeenth century onwards, Anglo-Irish writers and scholars took a great deal of interest in the very culture that their people had overridden, derogated, humiliated or destroyed. Swift for example was aware of the bardic tradition, and translated Tadhg Gaelach Ó Súilleabháin and Hugh MacGuaran's robustly misanthropic 'The Feast of O'Rourke', among others. Oliver Goldsmith was clearly aware of the bardic tradition, too. But it is worth turning to Richard McCabe's great book *Spenser's Monstrous Regiment*. Spenser was violently hostile to Gaelic Ireland, and famously wrote a *View of the Present State of Ireland*, which argued that Gaelic culture must be rooted out and exterminated. What MacCabe shows, however, is that, while Spenser knew no Gaelic, by a kind of process of osmosis, the bards and their traditions enter into *The Faerie Queene* and their marks on it are repeatedly perceptible. Again and again, Anglo-Irish culture turns out to be more intimate with Gaelic Irish literature and culture than it acknowledges, and there are repeated transfusions of the second into the first.

This is precisely the case with the double-directedness and the failure of identification in the misanthropic tradition. But in the Anglo-

Irish they operate in the reverse direction. Anglo-Irish intellectuals cannot conceivably properly identify with Gaelic Irish culture; in so many respects, it is not theirs. Yet at the same time they find themselves repeatedly alienated from things English, from English culture. This may go as far as a pronounced discomfort with the Englishness in themselves, to which they at times add a strain of covert sympathy with the Gaelic Irish in their sufferings. This makes for special forms of satire, special modes of irony and a strange condition of suspension. Swiftian misanthropy and irony, for example, assume a new dimension once seen in this context. On the one hand, Part IV of *Gulliver's Travels* famously allegorizes the gulf between Anglo-Ireland and Gaelic Ireland; that is, in the difference between the coolly rational, civilized horses, the Houyhnhnms, and the loathsome, filthy, disgusting humans, the Yahoos. (Declan Kiberd points out to me that the Anglo-Irish are associated with horses, not just because they rode them for pleasure and hunted with them, as the Gaelic Irish did not, but because the Irish thought the new invaders' accent was so odd that they heard them as making a neighing sound). Though he was capable of producing a work like *A Modest Proposal*, Swift also shared the later Protestant Irish poet Samuel Ferguson's 'inherited fear' and 'loathing' of the Irish helotry.[63] But what complicates the picture is that Gulliver repeatedly tells us that the English are no better than Yahoos, that their culture is Yahoo-like in its barbarity. Furthermore, there can be no identification with the Houyhnhnms, not just because they are horses, but because it is clear that, under the civilized surface, they operate an economy founded on slavery and because Gulliver, a man, becomes simply ludicrous when he tries to imitate them.

Seen in this light, Swiftian misanthropy thrives on the hole in the middle between England, Anglo-Ireland and Gaelic Ireland. It means he can ultimately declare no allegiance to any of them. The elevated position of the colonist as opposed to the colonized writer is in some sense an empty one, as the bards' sense of prestige is for them after Kinsale, the emptiness being doubled by the fact that they (the colonists) are not compelled to occupy it. The Anglo-Irish misanthropist can have no truck with civilization, because it reveals its underside as barbarism. But he can also have no proper truck with what he takes to be the barbarism of the other, because it is apparently irredeemable. The brutality of England and Anglo-Ireland makes any identification with them impossible. But equally identification with the defeated is impossible, precisely because of the effects of defeat on them.

The same kind of multiple displacement, of an Irish problematics of identification, is evident in Goldsmith. Primrose, Goldsmith's Vicar of Wakefield, is a displaced version of an Irish *ingénu*, at sea in an English world of hard-nosed mercantilism and ruthless economic pragmatism. That is the gist, for example, of his fleecing over the sale of his horses. Primrose is certainly – it is a critical cliché – a benevolist and sentimentalist. But not only is there persistent irony at his expense; the series of disasters to which he is exposed towards the close of the novel more or less confirm the misanthropic perspective against which he has intently defended himself, and which is the obverse of his own. That perspective is articulated in a character, Burchell, who keeps on trying to tell Primrose the truth that he must learn, to the point at which Primrose must admit that 'every day [Burchell] seemed to become more amiable, his wit to improve, and his simplicity to assume the superior airs of wisdom'.[64] Goldsmith is displacing an Irish and colonial problematic and projecting it as a dispute of the English with themselves.

In Goldsmith's earlier work, *The Citizen of the World*, the displacement is still more concrete and glaring. *The Citizen of the World* is composed of colonial letters – not, however, Irish ones, but letters from a Chinese philosopher visiting England, to quote the subtitle, 'to his friends in the east'.[65] What the Chinese philosopher encounters, like Primrose, is an English misanthropist, the egregious Man in Black. The Man in Black particularly accompanies him round Westminster Abbey, where the philosopher learns that, in the Man in Black's phrase, you get an honoured place by 'gaining battles, or by taking towns'.[66] The one tomb in the Abbey over which the Man in Black explicitly pauses, as embodying his case, is that of Monck. As we have seen, Monck was notorious for his exceeding ruthlessness in Ireland. So, too, later in the book, Goldsmith launches a savage attack on the system of Penal Laws: 'When once the work of injustice is begun', says the philosopher, 'it is impossible to tell how far it will proceed. It is said of the hyena, that, naturally, it is in no way ravenous, but when once it has tasted human flesh, it becomes the most voracious animal of the forest, and continues to persecute mankind ever after'.[67] The one system of Penal Laws of which Goldsmith's readers could conceivably have been markedly aware was the Irish system. But, in Goldsmith's text, what we have is a

Chinese talking about Japan. The displacement is self-evident. Or take our philosopher on the Daures, a subject people of China. On the one hand, we are told, 'the barbarous ceremonies of this infatuated people' make them intractable: 'Are these men rational, or are not the apes of Borneo more wise?' Yet at the same time the philosopher deplores the fact that they are subject to abuses of authority, 'unlicensed stretches of power', and incapable of demanding restitution: 'These provinces are too distant for complaint, and too insignificant to expect redress'.[68] It is this kind of knowledge that draws the philosopher close to the Man in Black. Goldsmith was nearer Swift than is sometimes supposed, not least in his more or less unconscious sense of the impossibility of identification.

Here we might turn to a very late example of the Anglo-Irish tradition, if it is any longer describable as that, the tradition at its last gasp, Samuel Beckett. That misanthropic sentiment is a feature of Beckett's work is hardly disputable. One might begin with Hamm (in *Endgame*), afraid that humanity might start up all over again from a flea, and proceed to collect a long list of instances. It is not difficult to find evidence of a Beckettian double-directedness in voices that call down a plague on all houses and are capable of sounding ironical if not scathing equally about power and powerlessness. We might also cite Beckett's recurrent concern with the figure of the tramp, the outcast, the abject victim, a figure brought low, with distinctly superior-sounding, vestigial memories of an abandoned learning. This might make Beckett's Molloy or Malone seem remote from the abject Irish victim. But it also makes them seem close to the bards after Kinsale, who fitfully continued with the bits and scraps of a now futile erudition, the remnants of a world that was still in some sense theirs, the afterlife of an eminent but shattered tradition.

But I want instead to end with Beckett's *How It Is*, a difficult and seemingly abstract work, one still cryptic to us and remarkably if obscurely full of a sense of the cruelty and misery of things. Here the double-directedness and the incomplete identification of the Irish misanthropic tradition are pervasively in evidence. One problem with understanding *How It Is* is that it is not obviously best read in linear fashion, like a novel. It is composed of three parts; that we should initially approach them in orderly sequence is understandable. But we should also read it from the second part, 'with Pim', outwards, because the second part is quite distinct from the first and third. This world is perhaps Hell, or part of its Empire: that is a claim one might exactly make of the world of the second part of *How It Is*. That is what it says about 'how it is'. At the centre of Part 2 is an image of horror: the apparently unending torture of one man, apparently named Pim, by another, seemingly called Bom. That this image has at least some of its roots in the colonial Irish relation, particularly that of the seventeenth century, is likely. Take for example the significance of the mud in which the figures flounder. When the Tudor and Cromwellian planters dispossessed the inhabitants, forced them off their land, they often did so quite literally and pitilessly, in acts of what Bom calls 'sadism pure and simple'.[69] The Irish were driven out into rain-swept landscapes to fend for themselves as best they could. Mud had diverse associations for Beckett, not least the trenches of the First World War. When he owned a small house near the Marne, he described himself as 'struggling' with work in progress in his 'hole in the Marne mud', or 'crawling up' on it from 'a ditch somewhere near the last stretch'.[70] It is nonetheless hard if not impossible to imagine that he was unaware that the image of one man on top of another, hammering him into the mud, was a resonant one in Irish history. Swift was certainly conscious of it, referring to the Yahoos as having a custom 'of wallowing and sleeping' in the mud.[71] Often enough, the dispossessed Irish had been hunted down into the mud. Mud became their element. Writing in 1847, Alexander Somerville remarked on the so-called Irish 'troglodytes' who lived in mud holes in the bleak wet desert of the Bog of Allen, and whom he described as 'living where the worms live, in holes of the earth; crawling as the worms crawl'.[72] They had been there for at least two centuries.

Pim, we are told, is Bom's 'unbutcherable brother' (HII, p. 82). In one of their aspects, the two are variants on the Biblical pairs of Cain and Abel and, more distantly, Jacob and Esau, in both of which the Irish found figures for the colonial relation. Bom thinks Pim may be speaking a foreign tongue, indeed, is 'perhaps a foreigner' (HII, p. 62), 'a thing you don't know' (HII, p. 80). At one point, he notes that he has had 'hardly a word out of [Pim] not a mum this past year'. 'Mumming' meant acting, as in the open-air seasonal folk-plays of the medieval mummers. But it had also come to mean aping the colonist, his language and ways, possibly with all the more reason because 'mumming' itself had not been indigenous to Ireland, but an Anglo-Norman introduction. Bom is the 'bad master' (HII, p. 79). Beckett makes ironical reference to his noble name and possibly noble lineage. Bom's tones on occasions are those of the boisterous, self-assertive colonist, particularly when he speaks of his pride in his ancestry: 'The Boms sir you can shit on a Bom sir you can't humiliate him a Bom sir the Boms sir' (HII, p. 67). So, too, the barbarism latent in the civilizing project is flagrantly at stake: 'From left to right and top to bottom as in our civilization I carve my Roman capitals', says Bom, of his work on Pim's body (HII, p. 77). For Irish nationalists, Imperial Rome was long a trope for Imperial Britain. But the passage that seems most peculiarly evocative in this context comes when Bom reflects on Pim's as

> that life then said to have been his invented remembered a little of each no knowing that thing above he gave it to me I made it mine what I fancied skies especially and the paths he crept along how they changed with the sky and where you were going on the Atlantic in the evening. (HII, p. 80)

From historical erasure and oblivion ('that life ... invented remembered a little of each') to colonial appropriation ('he gave it to me I made it mine what I fancied') to the figure 'creeping along' paths by the Western seaboard, the fate of so many of the dispossessed Irish who had been chased there, to mass emigration ('where you were going on the Atlantic in the evening'), the words summon up residues of a historical scenario that the Bom-Pim relation represents and replicates. So, too, that grimly, violently capitalized sentence in the book – DO YOU LOVE ME CUNT (HII, p. 99) – expresses the final, exquisitely perverse, obscenely wrong colonial demand.

So Part 2 of *How It Is* appears to offer a rather stark identification of the colonial disaster and Beckett's position relative to it, as contrasted with the obfuscation or allegorization of the colonial situation more common within the Anglo-Irish tradition, as in Swift and Goldsmith. But it is not possible to sustain the point. The materials I have picked out from Part 2 are mixed with others that adulterate them, thin them out, leave them only as a set of sometimes faint and ambivalent traces. This in itself represents a new late turn within the Protestant Irish tradition, in that Beckett puts, not so much the identification itself as the question of identification or, more precisely, of the incompleteness, impossibility or failure of identification, right at the centre of *How It Is*. Identification with the colonized is at stake, but also more largely, identification in the sense in which we associated it with the bards: where if anywhere can I conceivably imagine myself belonging (any more), as taking my stand? In other words, at the heart of *How It Is* there is a fleeting identification from which Part 2 intermittently retreats, and about which Parts 1 and 3 are, in complex and differing ways, reticent and evasive. Perhaps Bom's most revealing moment comes when he declares, 'How I can efface myself behind my creature' (HII, p. 58). With an irony characteristic of Beckett, *How It Is* declares its meaning through what is in large measure a process of such self-effacement, as is clear if we now turn to Parts 1 and 3.

Part 1, 'before Pim', is dominated by a set of procedures by which Bom both approaches or sidles up to Pim, edges towards an identification of colonial atrocity, and backs away from it. Beckett manages the relations between these procedures with consummate subtlety. There are at least four discourses at stake in Part 1, two pointing in one direction, two in another. On the one hand, there is a Bom already anticipating a confrontation with the atrocious particularity of Part 2 and thinking forward to 'the words of Pim his extorted voice' (HII, p. 23), to the work of extortion itself. This tips over into a classic misanthropic discourse, as when Bom refers to those who have 'sought refuge in a desert place to be alone at last and vent their sorrows unheard' (HII, p. 14). But there are also two other Boms. One thinks of himself as not a 'monster of the solitudes' at all, but as belonging 'above in the light' (HII, pp. 8, 14). He projects, fantasizes or appears to recall a life lived there. This Bom is still endowed with learned references – Malebranche, Heraclitus, Milton, Dante, Haeckel, Klopstock; he will not appear again, after Part 1 – though their very slightness indicates the tenuousness of his purchase on them. He can exclaim, sardonically, 'The humanities I had my God' (HII, p. 33). Alongside him, however, there is a Bom inclined to subsume his predicament under a pompously generalized rubric, or what he calls the 'great categories of being' (HII, p. 15). This Bom thinks in terms of 'vast tracts of time' or 'the joys and … sorrows of Empires' (HII, pp. 7, 13), 'abject abject ages each heroic'.[73] He thinks of the mud as 'primeval' (HII, p. 12). He seems remote from the horror in which he will participate in Part 2, though, in a way, he is clearly already disposed to find alibis for or extenuations of it.

Part 3, 'after Pim', returns to the four discourses in Part 1, if in rather different versions. First, there are gruesome flashbacks to Part 2.

Secondly, there are bleak abstractions from the vision of Part 2 into a generalized misanthropy, a world given over to darkness and death, to the 'great shears of the black old hag older than the world born of night' (HII, p. 114). Thirdly, there is Bom's refuge in a (now extremely meagre) version of his 'humanities' and a pathetic, fleeting, clearly hopeless resort to 'the humming bird known as the passing moment' (HII, p. 111). Fourthly, the 'categories of being' reappear. But to the retreat into the generality of the categories, Bom adds two further strategies, which dominate the last part. The first is that he generalizes the tormentor-victim relation. All are tormentors, all victims. But Beckett knows very well that this notion is a fantasy and a subterfuge. Part 2 is altogether fixated on a one-way relation, Bom as tormentor, Pim as victim, which has at least some of its roots in the colonial relation, and from which the tormentor–victim system can only seem like a specious, self-protective extrapolation.

The second 'additional strategy' involves mathematical descriptions of suffering, including the 'tormentor–victim system'. But this strategy is no more convincing than the first. It is demented, and meant to sound demented, demented in the manner of Swift's projectors in *Gulliver's Travels* and 'A Modest Proposal'. It is the voice of Ascendancy science, of the airiness of Ascendancy reason, the chatter of a voice with no purchase on the incalculable seriousness of the historical world in which it is lodged, but nonetheless concerned both to place and supersede it. We hear the same chatter gushing from the English entrepreneurial adventurers sizing up commercial opportunities in the West of Ireland in the 1850s, when the Famine had cleared the land. We hear it in different, more august and milder forms in the Victorian commentators, from Mill to Carlyle to Thackeray, who sought to bring (a self-appointed) reason to a scene that no English reason could possibly reduce to terms, since it was unable adequately to acknowledge a founding unreason or incur the intellectual debt that unreason imposed. This is the voice of rationalization where the idiom of rationalization is grotesquely, shockingly inappropriate.

How It Is is very much about misanthropic vision and incomplete identification, in that, in Part 2, Bom effectively declares himself, but in Parts 1 and 3 also withdraws from, re-translates or disguises his own self-identification. He can neither admit the truth, that he is an instrument of a fundamental, ineradicable injustice, nor entirely efface his existence as such from the parts of the book that seek to advertise it. *How It Is* is a deeply disturbing work, in that, most of the time, it is about non-confrontations with the most disquieting levels of historical experience it articulates. This, however, does not make of it a book that alleviates or dilutes Irish misanthropic tradition. Rather, the reverse: the conclusion at which it urges us to arrive is that it is in the very negligence with which we dismiss the misanthropic vision that we may most bear it out. Beckett achieved this with a singular and perhaps inimitable black brilliance. If, to come up with two final quotations, 'the ancient without end … buries mankind to the last cunt', and one might as well give up on 'the old business of grace in this sewer' (HII, p. 68), on the evidence of *How It Is*, that is because 'mankind' will not confront either the sewer as its own element or its own responsibility for it, its own complicity in producing it – as was supremely evident, perhaps, in the colonizing race and the colonial classes in Ireland.

One objection at least will remain in many minds: with obvious exceptions, like Swift, the Irish tradition is not essentially misanthropic, because its scope is confined. But this in turn invites a Benjaminian riposte, that certain local and particular histories may be all we need to know, that the truth-value of other perspectives born of power, privilege, wealth, comfort, ease is effectively zero. With the Irish tradition, we recognize that misanthropic discourse need not of itself make universalizing claims. Misanthropy can be local if the local constitutes its only horizon. If a villager who knows of nothing beyond the horizons of his or her village loathes fellow villagers without exception, he or she is in effect misanthropic. Misanthropy turns out to be a local concern presumed to be universal. The argument that the local and particular, whatever our definition of it, is all that can be available to us is not uncommon at the present time. But what if the local and particular indefinitely points a tale of horror? Can we dismiss the victim who insists that such a tale is the only one that finally needs to be told, not least because the victims are always there, they do not go away? On what grounds, exactly? The happiness of the greatest number? Progress?

5
WOMEN, MODERNITY AND MISANTHROPY

It is difficult to see, then, how the case for misanthropy on the basis of the experience of those who have suffered extreme historical damage should make absolutely no appeal to us. How exactly would one dismiss an Irishman or woman who asserted in 1900 that the Irish people had for many centuries suffered gross historical injustice and maltreatment at the hands of a nation that took itself and was taken by others to be one of the world's great civilized powers, had neither been able to save themselves nor been rescued by anyone else, and therefore had good reason not to think highly of humanity? But I want to pause for a moment and underline the fact that, in the work of O'Brien, Kavanagh and other modern Irish writers, Irish misanthropy persists *after* liberation from British rule. In O'Brien and Kavanagh, the misanthropy that springs from a history of victimization resists the narrative of ready emancipation from it, refuses to grant it any weight for thought. There is a misanthropy that carries on through the modern drive to emancipation, lingers within, survives, may even be born of and nourished by it. This chapter is about such a misanthropy, and my examples will be modern women.

Any woman reader of this book may well have been bubbling with increasing irritation at its masculine focus. The texts I have been quoting stubbornly keep on equating humanity at large with man. My book has seemed from time to time to mimic them in this. But it has also repeatedly asked questions about the defensibility of the misanthropic attitude, in effect sounding sceptical about what has been, historically, a predominantly masculine orientation. Surely, then, misanthropy was in fact a function of backwardness. If, as must self-evidently be the case, until the modern age, more or less all the misanthropists, or those we know about, were men, didn't women just know better (and wouldn't they have said so, given half a chance)? The rise of the modern feminisms calls time on misanthropy, or so the argument might seem to go; misanthropy swiftly becomes irrelevant, obsolete. With the integration of women into the modern, democratic constituencies, humankind redefines itself, and for the better. But has the continuing emancipation of women remade the world effectively enough to keep the misanthropists at bay? Suffragette Emmeline Pankhurst proclaimed that 'men were responsible for the present [dire] state of affairs', but that women would successfully 'undo' their 'terrible mistakes'.[1] Have her hopes been borne out? Not all our contemporaries have confidently thought so. This chapter, however, is about some great modern women who never shared her optimism in the first place.

The women's movement, or what is sometimes known as 'first wave' feminism, particularly in Britain and the United States, began in the 1860s and 1870s. In Britain, the National Society for Women's Suffrage was founded in 1872. But the constitutionalist suffragists that emerged from this made comparatively little headway until, with the emergence of the suffragette movement – Emmeline Pankhurst founded the Women's Social and Political Union in 1903 – the militants arrived on the scene. They and the constitutionalists worked together until 1912. This produced a mood of moral buoyancy and uplift, a distinctively modern mood of 'revolutionary' elation if not exhilaration. In countries, too, that, as far as enfranchisement was concerned, were rather in advance of England and America – New Zealand, most of the Scandinavian nations – at the beginning of the twentieth century, a new and widespread modern confidence was emerging, reflected in the foundation, in 1904, of the International Woman Suffrage Alliance. History everywhere was apparently on women's side.

The new optimism in early twentieth-century feminism cannot be separated from its humanism, progressivism and reformism. Sandra Stanley Holton has shown in detail how far the dominant strain in modern English feminism descended from Enlightenment political philosophy and nineteenth-century liberalism, notably through Mary Wollstonecraft and John Stuart Mill.[2] In its inception, it was humanistic: women deserved equal rights with men because they shared common human attributes. As Mrs Hugo Reid put the point, 'The ground on which equality is claimed for all men is of equal force for all women. ... It is the possession of the noble faculties of reason and conscience'.[3] For all her radicalism, Emmeline Pankhurst was still restating the same theme as late as 1914: 'Human values must be restored' via the suffragette movement; respect for 'the value of human rights' must be established through its work. After all, 'the moving spirit of [feminist] militancy' was 'its deep and abiding reverence for human life'.[4]

The suffragists, and particularly the suffragettes, did not just want the vote. They also had a raft of other demands, which pointed them beyond equal franchise (in Britain, granted partially in 1918, fully in 1928). In general, they looked forward to 'better laws' and 'happier lives' for women.[5] There is no necessary reason why subscribing to a significant political or moral sequence with a particular and important goal, as suffragism undoubtedly was, should require that one espouse any larger theory or narrative of progress. But, like most twentieth- and indeed twenty-first-century liberals and radicals, the early twentieth-century feminists did. Pankhurst, for example, anticipated 'the times to come, in all constitutional countries of the world', when the emancipation of women would have had pervasive and far-reaching effects encompassing 'the welfare of humanity'.[6] This progressive mindset is equally evident in the work of the suffragist novelists: May Sinclair, Gertrude Colmore, Elizabeth Robins, Evelyn Sharpe. No self-respecting heroine in a suffragist novel can fail to make some kind of advance. Robins's *The Convert* (1907), Colmore's *Suffragette Sally* (1911) and Constance Maud's *No Surrender* (1911), for example, all emphasize resolution, struggle, work and personal development, overcoming oneself and circumstances. The form of the personal is a microcosm for the political story. The characters change precisely in the interest of furthering the cause, the great movement forward, 'the march towards the vote and political awareness' (the onward march is a recurrent image).[7] Indeed, for some of them, and for some sympathetic men, the women's cause was representative. On the issue of the enfranchisement of women, wrote Brougham Villiers, 'the character of the whole progressive movement in England depends'.[8] If, then, for suffragists and suffragettes, getting the vote was crucial, it was also merely a stepping stone, the struggle for women's rights a link in an emancipatory 'continuum'.[9]

But plenty of intelligent and articulate women were in some degree anti-suffragist, and often anti-progressive: Marie Corelli, Mary (Mrs

Humphry) Ward, Charlotte Yonge, Florence Bell, Beatrice Webb. This is hardly a gallery of dimwits. As Julia Bush remarks, 'The anti-suffrage cause was extremely fortunate in its women writers'.[10] For the anti-suffragists, women's reality, while by no means inferior to men's, remained separate and distinct from it. In the world of women, the priorities were family affairs, the domestic sphere, 'gendered duties and responsibilities', emotional life.[11] If these writers have dated, it is because they too often sounded tamely conventional: their preoccupations were frequently religious, moralistic and commonplace. But beneath such emphases, on occasions, lay a profounder and more trenchant misgiving. Mark Winnington gives voice to it, in Mrs Humphry Ward's *Delia Blanchflower*: 'The vote? What is it actually going to mean, in the struggle for life and happiness that lies before every modern Community?' One can only be 'oppressed with its impotence for the betterment of life'.[12]

The larger emancipatory drive may finally turn out to be powerless, whether or not any project for the liberation of a partial interest succeeds in its aims. The modern problem is somewhere else, somewhere apart from the political project as conventionally established in liberal minds however well meaning, and categorically inaccessible to the meliorists. (According to the OED, the word enters the language during this period). Emancipation has an intractable remainder which threatens to turn the taste of liberty to ashes in the mouth. Rebecca West (in *The Judge*) and Virginia Woolf (in *Night and Day*) dwelt on exactly this issue. On occasions, such scepticism can sound quite close to classical misanthropy: extreme suffragettes like Christabel Pankhurst and Cicely Hamilton even began to doubt whether relations with men could ever be other than destructive for women.[13] *Vir feminae lupus*? But there were also good reasons for reservations about the suffragists and suffragettes: they 'laid claim to the mantle of empire',[14] avidly supported the war effort between 1914 and 1918, frequently became bustling feminist entrepreneurs and often had little interest in women beyond the white middle classes.

Certainly, by the 1920s and 1930s, as Holton puts matters, there had been 'a considerable moderation of the high optimism of the suffrage movement'.[15] The 'New Feminists' of the times were altogether more pragmatic and down to earth. But there were also other, different and more powerful manifestations in women's writing of the collapse of pre-war buoyancy. If anti-suffragism was often anti-progressive, it was not misanthropic. None of the writers just discussed seems likely to tip over into misanthropy (though Christabel and Cicely's forebodings seem unencouraging for the future of sexual relations). It is in the twenties and thirties that the strain of scepticism within feminism itself grows darker. The period witnesses the emergence of the great misanthropically focused novel as written by modern women. This misanthropic female tradition then re-emerges elsewhere, above all in France, at another moment of historic moral uplift, the Liberation in 1944. There are later manifestations of it in Britain and America. By the late sixties, however, so-called 'second wave' feminism spreads so widely and proves so successful that the misanthropic tradition in women's writing fades into obscurity, and it would be hard to find significant examples of it today.

I shall turn to five women writers whose work seems strikingly indifferent to the modern progressivisms and meliorisms (without being at all indifferent to women's sufferings and sexual wrongdoing). Modern female misanthropy is bred less of disenfranchisement than of emancipation itself, not least because of the radical opening and extension of horizons it brings with it. That does not make it reactionary. Indeed, even when unmixed, modern female misanthropy may well point in the opposite direction. If the line of misanthropic descent had been overweeningly patriarchal, certain modern women writers took hold of it as such and, with extraordinary vitality and ingenuity, recast it, thought it afresh, made it their own without abandoning its fundamental premise, that the good of and in the human thing is neither self-evident nor assured. I shall look at five principal strains in modern misanthropic female writing. I shall call them the shocked appropriation of the world at large; the private world as theatre of war; wastelands of new solitudes; the malignancy of tropisms; and 'dying like a woman'. Together, they constitute a major new reinvention of misanthropy.

*

Edith Sitwell, Ivy Compton-Burnett and Jean Rhys all show scant awareness of even belonging to the same world as contemporary suffragists, suffragettes and feminists, and seem possessed of an immunity to the progressivist mindset almost as complete as their ability to make great writing out of savage, destructive, vengeful, malevolent, forlorn and melancholic emotion. Compton-Burnett's middle-class background and university education (Royal Holloway College,

London, women-only at the time) might have led a young woman to suffragism. But Hilary Spurling's massive, vastly assiduous biography of her contains no reference either to suffragism or to feminism.[16] It is as though, for Compton-Burnett, an extraordinarily brilliant and tough-minded woman, they scarcely existed. Edith Sitwell was perhaps a bit too upper-crust for suffragism. But it would have fitted in with her politics in the twenties and thirties, which were leftist, pacifist and anti-imperial.[17] She had very good reason for abhorring patriarchy: aided and abetted by a manufacturer (male) and a surgeon (male), her father attempted to cure a curvature of her youthful spine by encasing her in a painful orthopaedic brace, a cage that ran from her armpits to her hips, with steel boots (and steel leggings and locks at night). For a period, she also had to wear a steel nose-truss (family friends came and gawped).[18] Yet, though she later vilified her three benefactors, she seems to have taken no interest in the women's cause *per se*. Jean Rhys was Dominican Creole. She came to England from the Caribbean in 1907. But she went to a school where she had to read Charlotte Yonge aloud each night after supper as part of an anti-suffragist education, which, given her temperament and disposition, might swiftly have bred an inward resistance.[19] As her biographer Lilian Pizzichini shows, she may very easily have been subsequently exposed to suffragist ideas.[20] But there is no indication that they were ever important to her, and her turn to the theatrical world brought her into contact less with advanced ideas than with a sexual culture quite beyond the experience of most of the suffragists.

Sitwell provides my example of 'a shocked appropriation of the world at large'. It would be absurd to suggest that, before the 1920s, women writers did not think beyond provincial horizons. George Eliot, for example, decisively broke with any such assumption, most strikingly in *Daniel Deronda* (1876), which ranges through Europe, exposes its readers to foreign worlds and opens them up to new intellectual vistas (Zionist and Kabbalistic ideas, modern European philosophy and music). But Sitwell in effect asserts that women are as capable of extreme thought as men, that they can stare without flinching at what another woman writer with occasionally misanthropic tendencies, Stevie Smith, called 'the general view'.[21] Women's writings, too, can be vehicles of a grand, prophetic, modern indictment of the whole show, as say, some of Conrad's, T. S. Eliot's and Waugh's were. This conviction underlies Sitwell's novel *I Live Under a Black Sun*, and *Heart of Darkness*, 'The Waste Land' and *A Handful of Dust* loom alongside it like sombre monoliths.

Sitwell's spinal problem led her to identify with the great Augustan poet Alexander Pope, who suffered from an acute curvature of the spine, and, through him, with the darker aspect of the Augustan vision, notably in no less a figure than Swift. The central character in *I Live Under a Black Sun* is a modern version of Swift called Jonathan Hare, and it quotes Swift liberally. Its vision, like Swift's, is without sweeteners. The 'general view' is the novel's baseline and its insistent groundswell. It takes its larger sense of things from the urban context. Sitwell's city is the *città infernale*, and the city is where one confronts essential truth; nature, by contrast, is incidental, exists as nooks and byways. In the urban 'circles of hell', Sitwell writes, all the forms of misery congregate together.[22] Here one learns all one needs about the 'old tyrannies and cruelties', 'the rankness of all human nature', 'this muddle and waste that we have made of the world' (BS, pp. 19, 38, 175). Cities are places where 'men have created and known fear' as a consequence of 'the man-made chasms' between them (BS, p. 19). This is notably the case with the 'two nations' that 'alone inhabit the earth, the rich and the poor', walking 'in opposed hordes' in 'their endless pursuit of nothingness' to their death (BS, pp. 29, 105). This, says Sitwell, stonily, is all we have been capable of creating out of 'the oceans of blood that have been spilt for us, from all the worlds that have been laid down for us' (BS, p, 137) – so much for a world that has supposedly been 'made safe by [the First World] war' (BS, p. 104). But in any case, it is not war-free; memories of 1914–18 bulk large in it. One might better imagine the whole panorama as 'laid waste by the Plague', thick with 'infections from the world's fever', haunted by shapes from prehistoric life, 'worm's spawn beginning in the worm's shape, ending with the worm' and thriving in the 'morbid pomp' of the sun (BS, pp. 38, 110, 138, 140). All of this Jonathan Hare apparently grasps with an unfathomable intensity, 'a black unknowable power' (BS, p. 13).

One crucial moment in the novel comes more or less at its midpoint, when Jonathan shrugs at one of his two women, Anna:

'Little tendernesses!' he said to her. 'Small marks of consideration! They are for small men, Anna. But that is what women want; that is all they care for. They know nothing of the vastness of life, and they care nothing; they are incapable of a great conception'. (BS, p. 120)

I Live Under a Black Sun itself emphatically repudiates this condescending assumption of small-mindedness (not least in the figure of its author). At this point the novel turns increasingly against Hare. Darkness overtakes his women, first Anna, then Essy, then Anna again, more profoundly, and it is Hare, we increasingly see, who is responsible for smashing them up. He battens on, consumes, destroys them. In his most precious relations with women, he is himself the very instance of the fatal human virus he excoriates. Sitwell has long foretold that the 'black unknowable power' might 'at any moment' rise 'to such vast and uncontrollable strength that it would turn on him who had been its master and destroy him' (BS, p. 13). Like Swift, Hare goes mad, but in Sitwell's narrative this final disintegration seems the direct result of his treatment of women. The havoc Hare has everywhere so lucidly perceived has finally become one both with the havoc he has caused and the psychic havoc in which he ends.

Sitwell had a very profound understanding of Swift's irony. She saw that it fuelled and confirmed his misanthropy in that he was able to turn the huge, despairing rage he felt towards humankind equally on himself, since he knew that the malignity and destructiveness he saw everywhere were also his own, and recognized his own 'craze for power' as, like humankind's, a lunacy (BS, p. 17). Hare's irony has the same double edge. But Sitwell supplements it with her own, which is as baroque as Swift's, but in a different manner. She reproduces Hare's black panorama, understands it both from within and without, but also draws a limit to its purchase insofar as women are its needless sacrificial victims; and yet again, she also extends and deepens it in a final, Sitwellian version of it. For she brings us back from the 'polar silence' of Hare's madness to a realm of psychic paroxysm which becomes indistinguishable from the pandemonium into which the world is plunging, turning us back to the apocalyptic vision that dominated the first half of the novel (BS, p. 244). Not surprisingly, the novel ends extremely starkly:

Let them fight. Let them destroy each other.
Then will come Darkness,
Darkness.

(BS, p. 254)

The point is not that there is no serious gender politics to Sitwell's novel, but rather that it is held and integrated within a great catastrophic vision – precisely, a shocked appropriation of the world at large – not urged upon on us as a liberal moralism.

*

If Ivy Compton-Burnett had little or nothing explicit to say about suffragism, here and there, the novels make some of her views quite clear. She would surely have agreed with Miss Basden in *Pastors and Masters* 'that women often equal and surpass men in literary achievements'.[23] She wrote the novel only a few years after women won the vote, and obviously approves of a society increasingly 'equalizing the position of women' (PM, p. 86). But she would also have taken any notion of 'equalization' as meaning that the world was getting better to be frivolous, and she would quite possibly have despised any special pleading as basically feeble. She had quickly moved well beyond the feminisms contemporary with her. In what is perhaps the most granite-hard of all her novels, *A Family and its Fortune*, she says of the ferocious Matty that 'she had never met a man whom she saw as her equal'.[24] Quite a few of Compton-Burnett's female characters share Matty's attitude. Like many women of Compton-Burnett's generation, they radiate sheer force of character and an acute intelligence in a language so gripping and distinctive as to be almost foreign to us today. But it is no exaggeration to say that they can also kill. Indeed, from time to time, they do.

Self-evidently, for Compton-Burnett, patriarchy was a violent and ludicrous contraption. Her contempt for its worst representatives – the monstrous Duncan Edgeworth in *A House and its Head*, Andrew Stace in *Brothers and Sisters* – is patent, however loudly they sometimes make us laugh. In *Pastors and Masters*, Mr Bentley's terrifyingly frigid view of himself and his sons – 'I have never met a man so unfortunate in his children' – to which one of the 'unmitigated nincompoops' responds by gallantly summoning up an occasional pathetic little caper, sends a cold shiver down the spine (PM, pp. 66–7). Brothers can be as bad as fathers. Take the opening lines of A Heritage and Its History:

> 'It is a pity you have not my charm, Simon,' said Walter Challoner [to his brother]. '… Can it be that you have death in your heart? What a different thing from charm! To think of the gulf between us!'[25]

Much of the detail of Simon and Walter's relationship in the novel will seem to run counter to the narcissism and offhand, devastating cruelty of this; and yet we cannot be sure that, heavily disguised, it does not underlie the relationship throughout. The jocular tone only makes the intensity of the masculine standoff all the more chilling.

This, however, is only to push gently at a door that yields a bestiary. Compton-Burnett turns in exactly the opposite direction to Sitwell, contemplating the nucleus, not the vista: hence her fiction is my example of 'the private world as theatre of war'. She focuses on small worlds, chiefly the family, sometimes in combination with a genteel or (upper-)middle-class community. In twenty superficially similar novels, she has one interest above all: to conduct a sustained, intense, microscopic, almost clinical scrutiny of the workings of the human monster in a domestic context. In the period of 'first wave' feminism, home and the family were very much political themes. Suffragists were calling the domestication of women radically into question. For their part, anti-suffragists were insisting that women belonged in the home and at the hearth, which was where true value lay. Josephine Butler wrote, for example, of the political need for 'free opening out and giving forth of the influences of homes, as reservoirs of blessings for the common good'.[26] Compton-Burnett clearly had no particular interest in the suffragist politics of liberation from the home. With rare exceptions, almost all her characters are confined to it, equally – women and men. But she was also certainly no defender of woman's domestic role, and the effect of her novels on the idea of the 'reservoirs of blessings' is approximately that of a nuclear bomb.

Thirty years before Compton-Burnett published her first major novel, Henry James wrote: 'I have the imagination of disaster, and see life as indeed ferocious and sinister'.[27] Ruthless, predatory beasts prowl through the Jamesian jungle, intent on their own purposes, however obscurely so. They are the more likely to seize their prey in that the jungle does not look like one. It sets a premium on the civilities. But the beasts can flourish there the more successfully in that they have no need to show themselves for what they are, can go about their business by indirection. Yet James was not a misanthropist. As he himself said, his whole interest was in rescuing a presumption of innocence or virtue and its redemptive power from the wilderness. It took modern women writers to strip away the Jamesian consolation, and to imagine the disaster proper. In Compton-Burnett's novels, as Joseph Baines has noted, 'Justice is neither done nor contemplated', not least, justice to innocence and virtue.[28] Compton-Burnett repeatedly denied James's influence, but this is not surprising. She must have thought that he had chickened out.

In *Elders and Betters*, Anna disobeys her Aunt Sukey's instructions and burns her will in favour of her sister Jessica and her family, preserving the one that leaves everything to Anna herself. Sukey then dies, and Anna inherits, much to the surprise of the other characters. She brazens her way through some difficult exchanges, with everyone trying 'to get in some little poisoned shaft',[29] and then confronts her Aunt Jessica. Jessica, perhaps the only remotely decent and sympathetic character in the book, if a weak one, actually wants to find out more about her sister's state of mind in the closing stages of her life. Anna, however, thinks she is challenging her over the will, even, perhaps, that she is provoking her to admit the truth. She therefore sets out briskly to destroy Jessica both emotionally and psychologically, by showing her, not only that she chronically failed Sukey, but that she has chronically failed her own family, too. Not long afterwards, Jessica commits suicide.

Similar sequences recur in other novels: in *Men and Wives*, for example, Matthew directs such extraordinary aggression at his mother Harriet that she subsequently threatens to 'smash up our affection and our daily life',[30] then suffers a mental breakdown and spends months in a home. When she returns – or so it appears – Matthew discreetly feeds her a tablet that kills her, in order to secure his relationship with Camilla, which he fears his mother will break up. In both novels, readers are left incredulous, rubbing their eyes at what they have witnessed. In *Elders and Betters*, Anna's case against Jessica is plausible, coherent, lucid, psychologically penetrating, strenuously made, even civilized, apparently energized by real conviction; and yet it is impossible not to suspect that she goes on the offensive for defensive reasons, that the zeal with which she takes Jessica apart is a reflection of her own fierce need to cover her tracks, not least because she has set her cap at Jessica's idle if articulate son Terence, who is unlikely to agree to marry her without money, since he does not intend to earn any.

Compton-Burnett repeatedly makes us do such double takes. These are conversation novels consisting of people 'bandying words' (MW, p. 108), with little or no intervention from the narrator, which means that no voice will even pretend to vouchsafe any truth of things to the reader beyond what the characters say in their articulate, educated and sometimes awesomely clever manner. But conversation in Compton-Burnett is almost unfailingly a means of avoiding contact with others, of not admitting what is likely to be at stake in relationships. The family is the crucible of this stark vision. Behind the cut and thrust of family exchange, there are often hints of an extreme callousness towards others' feelings that is the predictable corollary of the unrelenting self-intentness the characters generally share. Alternatively, emotional lives seem insignificant to the point of nullity. Thus, at the end of *A Family and its Fortune*, the hapless Dudley, one of Compton-Burnett's most egregious victim-figures, finally recognizes this of his brother Edgar: '"You had nothing to give. You have nothing. There is nothing in your nature. You did not care for Blanche [Edgar's wife]. You do not care for your children. You have not cared for me"' (FF, p. 236). Compare, in *Elders and Betters*, Benjamin's 'incredulous gratification' at the seeming fact that at least one of his children 'did not desire his death' (EB, p. 124).

But we should press the point further than this. Compton-Burnett comprehensively ruins the ordinary human persuasion that there is at least one sane, healthy normality that we can take for granted. The family and home are in fact scarily *unheimlich*, unhomely or uncanny. The general idea is familiar from Freud, but Compton-Burnett pursues the Freudian understanding of the family deep down and all the way down. Can the sophisticated voices we hear really be connected with the misdemeanours and horrors we fear we may have glimpsed? With financial skulduggery, certainly, this is England, but drastic cruelty? Psychological torture? Incest? Murder? The point is, not that the answer to such questions must be a resounding yes, but that Compton-Burnett leaves her readers exactly balanced on the point of the question. This is the uncanny in action.

As such, we might hope to keep it in a certain proportion. But if the smooth, formulaic to and fro of language leaves us wondering if the characters ever mean anything they say, sooner or later, abruptly, violently and often for no apparent reason, someone does, and then the results are shocking if not cataclysmic. Compton-Burnett had an expert ear for the savage and peremptory fashion in which, merely through an elegant choice of phrase, the English middle classes can skewer their weaker and more vulnerable members. Matty's brusque demolition of her impoverished companion Miss Griffin is an obvious example. As with Jessica or Harriet, the point with Miss Griffin is that anyone who does not quite share the social idiom, or get it, or cannot sustain it, does not know how to keep the ball in play, or makes a mess of doing so and, as a consequence, lives too much in honest feeling, is likely to be crushed out of hand.

But this in turn illuminates the nature of the idiom. The triumphs of wit or exquisiteness to which others' sensitivities are casually sacrificed may be very entertaining. Compton-Burnett knows that, and knows her readers know it, too. But conversation in her novels is also interminably fractious. Everybody takes issue with others, however lightly and amusingly. Everyone wants to steal a conversational march on everyone else, to top the last remark. We might fleetingly call Schopenhauer back to mind: in Compton-Burnett, conversation becomes a succession of minuscule surges of will, a constant skirmish for power, an endless stream of petty self-assertion, a series of tiny territorial gains which yield a small and transitory but psychologically necessary gratification. The doomed are those who miss this, who do not understand the art of the riposte, who fail to recognize that the other is always tinder for one's flint and steel.

Once again we ask ourselves, can people really behave like this to each other, even when they hardly seem to be doing so, or are apparently so unaware of it? But our incredulity is the author's point. There is a second kind of uncanniness in Compton-Burnett's novels, the uncanniness of people's refusal directly to confront or to express the meaning of what they nonetheless see and obscurely grasp. Because hers is a social world in which adherence to certain norms of civility or urbanity is *de rigueur*, the characters can get away with being implacably furtive, oblique or discreet, and therefore contrive to keep the unmentionable unmentioned. The idea that Matthew has quietly murdered his mother cannot be borne in a world which, after all, began with Sir Godfrey loudly proclaiming 'the great, unbreakable bond of family love and fellowship' (MW, p. 5). The official bombast will no longer exactly prevail at the end; what rather ensues is a complex and subtle cover-up which admits of doubts and hesitations, but nonetheless sustains appearances. It does so, however, not just because the family needs to pass muster socially, but because no one in the novel wishes to conceive of himself or herself as living in a world to which Matthew's deed or the emotions that drove him must be recognized as integral. So, too, Compton-Burnett surrounds Anna with an array of characters none of whom quite want to broach the thorny question of her conduct, of what may be staring them in the face. They all have their own interests to consult, their own comforts to attend to, their personal horizons beyond which it is easier not to look, and these take precedence. So what they know is also what they prefer not to know, the degree of individual evasion and disingenuousness being the sole variant factor; and here, the characters become their readers' surrogates or mirror images.

One of the most artful features in Compton-Burnett's novels is the regularity with which the characters come out with misanthropic judgements – on the irreducibility of egoism, human nature red in tooth and claw, the general prevalence of malignity, self-regard and complicity – that the novels constantly suggest but refuse to quite confirm. 'We all prey on each other', says Emma in *Mother and Son*. 'The jungle is never dead'.[31] Such cynical aphorisms accumulate, gaining ground ominously as the novels draw towards their conclusions, with many if not most of the characters contributing to their continuing plausibility. Yet Compton-Burnett's people never quite see their misanthropy through to the bitter end. Terence declares that 'there is horror in every heart, and a resolve never to be honest with anyone else' (EB, p. 223), and this would seem to be a conclusion to which *Elders and Betters* inexorably points us – except that, in the very diligence with which it sticks to the surface, it shields us, too, as perhaps we too wish to be shielded.

Compton-Burnett, then, is a superb manipulator of a kind of incipient misanthropy. She encourages the imagination of disaster but also refuses to fix it in place, understanding that both her characters and readers will be tempted by it and nurse misgivings about indulging it. The degree to which those misgivings might be just is never quite ascertainable; the mode of the conversation novel ensures that. Nonetheless, one might think of Compton-Burnett as issuing a wry rejoinder to an imperial and masculine tradition in the novel, running from Conrad and Kipling to Greene, Waugh and Golding, that took male protagonists halfway round the world to encounter its heart of darkness in exotic locales. For hearts of darkness, she seems to say, seek no further than the next room. Elizabeth Bowen grasped the point very acutely when she wrote that, during the war, 'to read ... a page of Compton-Burnett dialogue [was] to think of the sound of glass being swept up, one of these London mornings after a blitz'.[32] But it is poor Dudley who might seem to point us to the necessary conclusion: '"It is a pity we have to be human. ... Human failings, human vanity, human weakness! We don't hear the word applied to anything good. Even human nature seems a derogatory term. It is simply an excuse for everything"' (FF, p. 30).

*

'Good morning midnight', runs the epigraph to Jean Rhys's novel of that title, 'I'm coming home'.[33] For Rhys, 'coming home' involves a special abnegation, an acceptance of an absolute and inescapable solitude which also involves giving up on or growing away from others. The other person is not there, will never be there, to *combler la béance*, to fill the void. Above all, there is no completion or fulfilment in love, and indeed we could have no idea what that might mean. It is hardly new to suggest that solitude is a major theme of modern literature. But from Byron to Baudelaire to Conrad to Camus the crucial figure in this tradition is man, spiritual hero, intellectual pioneer and metaphysical adventurer. With the major emergence of modern women writers, however, it becomes possible to invent new wastelands of solitude, to think solitude in new ways. In particular, Rhys's characters become the focus for understanding a drift so far to the margins of the world that, in effect, it and its denizens cease to exist. In Rhys's case, according to Pizzichini, 1913 was the significant year. By the end of it, she had reached a state that, in some degree, always remained with her, 'of dawning unconsciousness, of not having to try any more, to comprehend, react, parry words, enter the incomprehensible world of other people'.[34] Rhys herself puts the point more figuratively: 'Everywhere there are placards printed in red letters: This Way to the

Exhibition, This Way to the Exhibition. But I don't want the way to the exhibition – I want the way out' (GMM, p. 12). From the point of that recognition onwards, solitude empties the world as effectively as a pandemic, leaving no survivors.

Rhys lived under the shadow of her mother's grim admonition: 'Nothing is fair'.[35] As in Compton-Burnett, there is no justice here. Rhys took this truth to heart; she conceived of herself as living in a world absolutely deprived of justice, yet was also quite unable to hold the soothing unction of good works or political commitment to her soul. Since she was burdened with a preternatural sensitivity to injustice, this left her with 'a bitter mistrust of the world'.[36] Other people often intimidated, brutalized, victimized and humiliated her. Yet she also repeatedly won a certain kind of attention and personal respect, and this was not just a matter of sexual interest, though she had enough of that, nor even the beauty of her writing, but rather of others' more or less embarrassed sense that she was willing to take certain questions a lot further and more seriously than they were. We can grasp the connection between Rhys's moral *jusqu'au-boutisme* and literature in the fact that, for her school friend Myrtle Newton, she was one of those rare creatures who could read aloud from a Shakespeare play as though she felt extremely intimate with and intensely alive to its meaning, as though she lived in it more than she did in the world.[37] There was, in the end, a radical idealism to all this, and naturally its consequence could only be suffering from beginning to end.

Rhys was a courageous woman who was not afraid of herself or even, possibly, of what she finally wanted. She derives an exceptional power from defeat, utter depletion, terrible helplessness, the decisive 'j'en ai assez' (GMM, p. 112), the ineradicable conviction that she is not 'of the fold'.[38] But its corollary has to be terminal disconnection. There was an immensely dreary side to this: the later obscure life in Beckenham, Cornwall and Devon, the domestic rows, court cases, endless fights with neighbours and indeed neighbourhoods, most of them alcohol-fuelled. But it was also what drove her to write and kept her writing. The world was monstrous beyond belief, and writing alone could bring it to terms. Naturally, it almost goes without saying, men are 'swine, deary, swine' (Q, p. 14). But 'You want to know what I'm afraid of?' says Sophia:

All right, I'll tell you. ... I'm afraid of men. And I'm even more afraid of women. And I'm very much afraid of the whole bloody human race. (GMM, p. 144)

What initially underlies Rhys's misanthropy is her acute eye for 'human misery' (GMM, p. 155). She was unremittingly conscious of it, hunted it down everywhere, not in the places most ostentatiously deserving of charity, but in obscure holes and corners that the good prefer not to notice, like the prison in which Stefan is incarcerated in *Quartet*. 'When you come out', he begins, then adds, 'but you don't come out. Nobody ever comes out' (Q, p. 106). Rhys fastens melancholically on the myriad zones of blight, because they are infinitely more significant and expressive than those of light, the parties, fairs and carnivals, the public rejoicings and official celebrations, the respectable and comfortable world of solid citizenship, prosperous circumstances, responsible toil and satisfied conscience, good lives well led.

For the trouble with the zones of light is that they dazzle one so much that they make what lies beyond them invisible. The law of the world at large, the 'malignant world', is in the first instance cruelty (Q, p. 28). As Rhys's Sophia murmurs (again): 'Homo homini lupus' (GMM, p. 21). Hence Rhys's own special version of 'a room of one's own': 'A room', as Sophia says, 'is a place where you hide from the wolves outside and that's all any room is' (GMM, p. 33). All of Rhys's heroines know how crucial it is to be able to flee to one's room. But the room of one's own is not only a bolthole from cruelty. Nor is it just a refuge from the inexorable rule of an injustice which determines that cruelty shall not matter. It is a haven from those who shrug indifferently, the 'inscrutable people, invulnerable people' (Q, p. 79). For 'they are without mercy' (GMM, p. 146). Where exactly does one otherwise go, in a world which can observe dispassionately that a princess was once left screaming for ten days while rats ate her? 'The mean things they got away with – sailed away with – smirking', thinks Marya, in *Quartet*. 'Nobody caring a bit' (Q, p. 29). The roots of Rhys's misanthropy partly lie in her belief that she inhabits a world of radical untruth.

What most terrifies Sophia about people, however, is not their cruelty, though she knows that they are 'horribly cruel', but the fact that it is 'rosy, wooden, innocent cruelty' (GMM, p. 81). The image is of a painted doll or effigy: see below. But Sophia's point, here, is not rank cruelty or rampant self-interest but rather what she otherwise exclaims against as naivety. The naivety of people as manifested in their clichés and above all their belief in their clichés is peculiarly disturbing. For clichés, received ideas both disguise ignorance and make it serviceable. Furthermore, they work. Best therefore to learn to 'gabble without thinking as the others did', as schoolgirl Antoinette ruefully muses in *Wide Sargasso Sea*.[39] Marya's 'vague and shadowy fear' in *Quartet* is of something cruel but also '*stupid*' in people 'that had caught her and would never let her go' (Q, p. 28, my italics).

People, in fact, are idiots, and the world is idiotic. (Idiocy is an insistent refrain in *After Leaving Mr Mackenzie*). As philosopher Clément Rosset emphasizes, the Greek root of the word idiot, ἴδιος means private, one's own, particular. Only subsequently does it come to mean deprived of intelligence or reason. That which is idiotic is singular unto itself. It has a blank or expressionless surface; it cannot communicate or register a fellow communicator. It is incapable 'of appearing as its double in the mirror'.[40] The great sources of Rhys's imagination lay in Dominica and, more loosely, the Caribbean. She spent her whole life working towards a full recognition of that inspiration. *Wide Sargasso Sea*, her great Caribbean work of fiction, was published some thirty years after its predecessor, but many of its imaginative features were already present in the earlier writing. For Rhys, the Caribbean is the site of extreme beauty. But its beauty is that of an evil flower. There is the original, historical evil: 'French and English like cat and dog in these islands for long time. Shoot, kill, everything' (WSS, p. 80). There is the evil done in return. 'The people here hate us', says Mason (WSS, p. 27). The blacks shun Antoinette and her Creole family as 'white cockroaches' (WSS, p. 20). This is a deeply poisonous world (though *Wide Sargasso Sea* destroys any presumption of a superior, anthropological understanding of the nature of the poison).

'The devil prince of this world', says Godfrey (WSS, p. 16). Rhys's Caribbean swarms with monster crabs, cockroaches, giant ants and snakes. But it is also a world of zombies, voodoo, effigies, *obeah*, curses and spells and blood-sucking vengeance. According to Pizzichini, 'Jean spent much of her childhood screaming, crying or collapsing in terror'.[41] She did this less in her later years in Europe, but the same sensibility is never far away. In Rhys's fiction, vision is inextricable from hallucination; it is hard to know which is which. Demonic forces are always close at hand, if seldom palpable. Compare Sophia on the struggle for life:

> I'm not talking about the struggle when you are strong and a good swimmer, and there are willing and eager friends on the bank waiting to pull you out at the first sign of distress. I mean the real thing. You jump in with no willing and eager friends around, and when you sink you sink to the accompaniment of loud laughter. (GMM, p. 10)

But who is laughing? The lost or fair-weather friends? Bystanders? Or demons (who may have taken their forms)? Rhys's marvellous, eerily subtle talent is to deliver a world in which human beings discreetly mutate and appear as the alien spirits they really always were. People are ghosts, shadows, obscure presences, djinns. Above all, they wear masks. Indeed, there are moments 'when all the faces are masks and only the trees are alive and you can almost see the strings that are pulling the puppets' (GMM, p. 75). The mask is even the truth of the face, inexpressive, uncommunicative, definitively indifferent, singular unto itself. Sometimes people's eyes seem to turn to stone. 'How terrifying human beings were, Marya thought' (GMM, p. 76). This is 'hell', the hell of the human thing possessed, where the incubus is more real than the shell it has taken over, and the only salvation from it is 'the heaven of indifference' (Q, p. 57). But in what indifference of their own can Rhys and her characters themselves trust, given that the rest of the world is indifferent already? Rhys, it seems, found little salvation. But she left behind her an astonishing secularization of voodoo vision, the black arts as a misanthropic mode of imagining the human world.

*

Like Rhys's, the world of Nathalie Sarraute's fiction offers us a world of creepy-crawly people, but creepy-crawly in a different way. Sarraute has no interest in the satisfactions traditionally provided by the novel: plot, character, psychology, development. The novelist, she says, must rather deprive the reader 'of all indications of which ... he takes hold in order to fabricate [such] illusions'.[42] Her concern was rather with what she called tropisms. Tropisms are 'inner "movements" ... hidden under the commonplace, harmless appearances of every instant of our lives'.[43]

We are 'hardly cognizant' of them. They 'slip through us on the frontiers of consciousness in the form of undefinable, extremely rapid sensations. They hide behind our gestures, beneath the words we speak and the feelings we manifest, all of which we are aware of experiencing and are able to define' (PR, p. 8). They are more basic than 'our conversations, the personality we seem to have, the person we seem to be in one another's eyes, the stereotyped things we believe we feel, as also those we discover in others' (PR, p. 9). They seemed to Sarraute to 'constitute the secret source of our existence, in what might be called its nascent state' (PR, p. 8). They are not individual, however, and do not individualize. They are like tremors in 'a substance as anonymous as blood, a magma without name or contours' which courses through all of us and is present 'in all men and in all societies' (ES, p. 1586, 1593). This substance is 'an indefinable, anonymous matter of which all humanity' is 'composed' (TAS, p. 1588). So Sarraute's, again, is a 'general view', and she obscures clear distinctions between her people precisely in order to make it appear so.

The formless and often nameless figures who clutch tentatively at others in Sarraute start out from lack. Their founding condition is 'nothingness … an interior void'.[44] Since, whatever the notions of character, personality and changeless traits that they and others may invent, they are as amorphous as a flow of lava, they suffer from a deep-rooted insecurity, a fear that they have no being. No one escapes this condition. Those who seem solid and substantial, whose identity appears to be anchored in some special way – 'compact and hard … as immobile as one could wish'[45] – invariably disappoint: the novel *Martereau* hinges on the breakdown of such an illusion (about Martereau himself). However, the subject is also driven by an imperious 'instinct for self-preservation', and this makes the Sarrautean predicament seem unbearable (M, p. 50). The only possible way of dealing with it is by appropriating the outside world to fill the subjective hole. Thus Sarraute's people are always groping towards others, as plants grope towards the light: Sarraute actually tells us that the tropisms in her novels 'resemble the movements made by certain living organisms under the influence of outside stimuli' (PR, p. 9). The work of appropriation, however, is bound to fail, because others invariably suffer from the same condition and are themselves tropistically feeling their own way outwards.

This makes Sarraute's world and her people horrible. First, her people are mean. The issues at the centre of the novels are almost always bourgeois and petty, though the responses to them are *hypersensible* (hypersensitive, a favourite word of Sarraute's). The father in *Portrait d'un homme inconnu* broods profoundly on what he believes to be his daughter's theft of a slice from his soap bar. When Tante Berthe in *Le Planétarium* discovers that workmen have fitted an 'appalling nickel handle' to her front door, the 'soft, warm world in which she had been so snug' flies to bits, 'and on the smoking ruins, crushing them beneath their feet, the conquerors advanced. ... They installed a new order, a new civilization, whilst she wandered miserably amidst the ruins' (LP, pp. 2, 14–15). This is the kind of collapse into grand panic that takes place when the subject's effort to plug the inner gap by taking hold of the world has failed.

Secondly, since tropisms 'hide behind our gestures', the really important processes in Sarraute's world tend to take place surreptitiously, beneath the surface, which makes her people chronically furtive and secretive. Furthermore, the aspects of themselves that they strive to conceal are usually displeasing if not repellent. This is not surprising, since Sarraute's characters are concerned with the outside world only insofar as they imagine it may supplement their own lack of being. Sarraute found the same preoccupation with concealment in her favourite novelists. In Kafka, she writes, '"others" are half-human beings with identical faces, whose infantile, incomprehensible gestures ... conceal a malign cleverness that is at once wily and obtuse' (ES, p. 1574). According to Sarraute, Ivy Compton-Burnett (no less) tells us of 'a savage game' in which 'there is concealed danger in these sweet-sounding sentences, murderous impulses worming their way into affectionate concern, an expression of tenderness abruptly distils a subtle venom' (ES, p. 1606). In Sarraute, the concealed impulses may be violent: Alain in *Le Planétarium*, for instance, imagines using his fists on 'the enormous, immobile mass' that is his aunt (LP, p. 187). But they are more likely to be resentful, grudging, nosy, intrusive, self-insinuating, self-regarding, deceitful, obsessive, coldly destructive, brusquely crushing, disproportionately intense, deeply paranoid yet pathetically shamefaced and diffident – or just plain weird. It is hard, if not impossible, to find a single honourable, serious emotion in Sarraute's novels. Her subterranean creatures never rise that far. After all, for Sarraute, human behaviour 'has more in common with that of ants and plants than with free moral agents'.[46]

But what is most loathsome in Sarraute's world is its texture. The metaphors she finds for tropisms repeatedly make them seem repulsive. Tropisms lurk and crouch, like hyaenas or spiders.[47] They uncurl themselves like snakes (see PHI, p. 36). They seethe, swarm, squirm and wriggle, like dung-beetles or cockroaches in their lairs, 'repugnant creatures crawling in humid darkness amongst foul odours' (PHI, p. 48, M, p. 132). They resemble 'leeches' and 'slugs'. They slime things 'with their ignoble understanding'.[48] The novels pullulate with images of snails, lampreys, toads and frogs, caterpillars, carnivorous plants, larvae, 'spectres and ghouls', vampires and 'hungry, pitiless parasites' (PHI, pp. 52, 64, 71, 114, 128, T, p. 17). It is equally a world of the fluid and the viscous, oozing, seeping and trickling things – 'sticky slaver' (T, p. 5), 'gluey coatings' (PHI, p. 111), vitriols and poisonous or acid secretions – as it is of dire infections, ugly contagions, sickening smells, morbid excrescences, 'miasmas, fatal emanations' (M, p. 290). Sarraute, however, has a special fondness for images of underwater creatures, particularly polyps and invertebrates, those with 'soft little suckers' that cling and palpate (M, p. 169), 'tiny tentacles that at every instant stretch out towards the nearby partner' (ES, p. 1575). They suit her because they seem appropriate to the groping movements of tropisms. Since Sarraute's creatures are much inclined to observe other people's 'means of defence' (PHI, p. 112), with their hard shells and their tendency to stay under cover, crustaceans figure a great deal, too.

'Why am I a misanthropist? Why that?' asks one of Sarraute's speakers in Tropismes (T, p. 7). The answer is not far to seek: Sarraute's creatures feel abandoned 'in a hostile universe' (T, p. 8), and are rebuffed by others, whom they are therefore bound to hate. The hatred and distrust will necessarily be reciprocal. In Sarraute, both social life and the psyche sometimes seem altogether given over to sado-masochistic drives, if usually of a rather surreptitious kind: hence her frequent resort to images of teased and tormented animals. The point is not that the subject cannot recognize the other person's tropisms. Rather, he or she needs to see the other as an alien (and cruel) fixity with a 'fearful, implacable' will to destruction, whereas the other takes itself to be 'the

frightened little animal that hides as best it can at the bottom of its hole'
(M, pp. 23, 33). At all events, contentment in relationships is mere self-
persuasion, self-preservation, a repression of the tropisms. Our natural
state is mutual wounding, not least through language.

*

Neither Sarraute nor her characters take their chronic misgivings about
other people as far as a desire for death. But the interest in killing oneself,
or imagining one's own death, 'dying like a woman', is repeatedly present
in the work of various modern women misanthropists. Indeed, the other
themes we have identified with these writers often seem to point in
that direction. Dying like a woman is not like 'dying like a man'. The
second of course is a familiar concept, often with heroic implications,
whether the heroism in question be military, athletic, intellectual, artistic
or bohemian. Dying like a woman does not share in this ethos. It is
not first and foremost a promotion of the woman's supposed courage,
strength, adventurousness, awesome intellectual extremism or genius.
It is rather a testimony to the failure of the human world *tout court*.

Dying like a woman has two principal features: first, absolute and
uncompromising sensibility. From 1935, Virginia Woolf was increasingly
a hostage to this.[49] There had always been strains of misanthropy in her
work. In the context of the novel in which it appears, for example, *Jacob's
Room*, Rose Shaw's judgement – 'life is damnable, life is wicked'[50] –
carries a great deal of conviction the novel finds it hard to resist. Woolf's
fiction in general repeatedly balances delicately between a cynic,
pessimist, melancholic or misanthropist (Helen Ambrose, Katherine
Hilbery, Septimus Smith, Rhoda), and a character or characters who
might seem close to sharing his or her premises but who refuse to take
the same path. That structure seems to reflect a hard-won equilibrium
in Woolf's mind. If so, however, in 1935, it began to fail. Her husband
Leonard would later write of both of them as suffering 'the erosion of
life by death' in the 1930s, 'a process which gathered momentum as
we went downhill to war'.[51] With Hitler's invasion of the Rhineland in
1936, theirs was becoming a 'world of horror'.[52] Not for the first time,
the guns were getting near to Woolf's private life. She had even grown
to hate her beloved London ('crowded, arid, sordid, unhuman').[53] When
war broke out it was, she said, 'the worst of all my life's experiences'.[54]
While she remained obstinately unpatriotic and a pacifist, many of her

erstwhile friends and allies now backed the military effort. Meanwhile, she was reading Freud for the first time, and finding in him confirmation that 'we ourselves are like primeval man, a gang of murderers'.[55] 'World aggression', she now believed, had 'psychological, deeply buried, inherited human sources'.[56] In the end, only one response to it seemed possible. As Julia Briggs puts the point, 'driven by mass murder, hatred and cruelty' towards 'those darker aspects of our inner life that we normally resist or dismiss',[57] on Friday, 28 March 1941, Woolf walked out of the house and died like a woman.

Virginia Woolf tended a tiny little utopian flame of her own in the teeth of the radical insufficiency of the world around her. When that flame was finally, brutally snuffed out, the misanthropic nightmare became total and the pain was unbearable. There is however a second mode of dying like a woman that is different from Woolf's. This involves a kind of staging or performance. Here, dying like a woman becomes a masquerade, or better, a counter-masquerade, since, if as Joan Riviere and later Lacan suggested, femininity itself is a masquerade that defines the identity of a woman, even her womanhood as such,[58] then the masquerade of dying like a woman passes judgement on the masquerade of living a woman's life.

Even as the women's movement was taking its first faltering steps in America, a great American woman poet was turning away from the human race. From the 1860s onwards, Emily Dickinson decides to speak to her visitors only from behind a door. She refuses to have direct contact with human beings any longer. There is certainly a strain of misanthropic sensibility in Dickinson:

> One anguish – in a Crowd –
> A minor thing – it sounds –
> And yet, unto the single Doe
> Attempted – of the Hounds
>
> 'Tis terror as consummate
> As Legions of Alarm.[59]

Hence the importance in her poems of entirely solitary places, settings and situations. 'I took', she writes, 'my Power in my hand –/And went against the World' (EDP, Poem 660, 2.643). For her principal concern is with her own spiritual life. The masquerade of dying is thus a function of the struggle towards the 'lonelier thing' that finally escapes 'the mind of man' (EDP, Poem 570, 2.567, Poem 1343, 3.1162).

But the enterprise is clearly laden with risk. 'Much madness' may conceivably be 'divinest sense', but it is a sense to which the world is not only obtuse but fiercely hostile:

> Assent – and you are sane –
> Demur – you're straightway dangerous –
> And handled with a chain –
>
> (EDP, Poem 620, 2.613)

This inclines Dickinson, as it were, to conjure with death. 'Dying like a woman', performing one's death, has a logic, and that logic is misanthropic. Dickinson tells us: 'Living hurts', but 'Dying – is a different way –/A kind behind the Door –' (EDP, Poem 528, 2.536). The poems experiment with that logic in a manner that life itself does not permit. The famous 'Because I could not stop for Death –' (EDP, Poem 479, 1.492-93), for example, enacts death as a stately progress beyond all things human in which mortality is paradoxically welcomed as a release from one's surrounds. In more senses than one, it is about 'fail[ing] from Man' (EDP, Poem 568, 2.565).

But the woman writer who looms largest in this context and most completely thinks of 'dying like a woman' as both a performance and the logical consequence of sensibility is surely Sylvia Plath:

> Dying
> Is an art, like everything else.
> I do it exceptionally well.
>
> I do it so it feels like hell.
> I do it so it feels real.
> I guess you could say I've a call.
>
> ('Lady Lazarus')[60]

Again and again, Plath's poems rehearse and play out death and the reasons for choosing it. These are various. Her experience had turned her, she said, into 'a misanthrope … a nasty, catty and malicious misanthrope'.[61] But misanthropic knowledge and the will to die have 'no *singular* origin'. Jacqueline Rose suggests that the 'component of psychic negativity' in Plath is irreducible to a sole explanation, both inwardly and outwardly determined.[62] Intimate relations are fraught with horror ('Father, this thick air is murderous', PCP, p. 93). Love offers only a 'golden hell' (PCP, p. 310). But the vital principle itself is not to be trusted, as mushrooms indicate:

> Nudgers and shovers
> In spite of ourselves.
> Our kind multiplies.
>
> We shall by morning
> Inherit the earth.
> Our foot's in the door.
>
> ('Mushrooms', PCP, p. 139–40)

In a historical period far more anxious about the future overpopulation of the planet than the present one (not necessarily wrongly), this disquieting version of the life-force self-evidently takes on an extra dimension.

Plath's Lady Lazarus chooses her art of dying partly because she needs 'to annihilate' the 'trash' of 'each decade' of her life (CP, p. 245). But right from the start, as her juvenilia demonstrate, the poet also dreamt of a more general annihilation:

> Then hurl the bare world like a bluegreen ball
> back into the holocaust
> to burn away the humbug rust
> and again together begin it all.
>
> ('Song For a Revolutionary Love', PCP, p. 323)

'Holocaust' no doubt has more than one meaning here, but the allusion is clearly partly to the camps. In Plath's later work, the Holocaust of 1939–45 becomes, not an exceptional historical 'trauma', but the very core of human history, a historical essence that we cannot circumvent, the 'gorgon-grimace/Of human agony', which is the very meaning of history (PCP, p. 83). The 'thin people' are 'always with us', she tells us. 'We own no [misanthropic] wildernesses deep and rich enough/ For stronghold against their stiff/Battalions' (PCP, pp. 64–5). Plath was gripped by a compulsion to 'know the *worst*', immediately. It was the only way one could be adequate to history and its numberless lost souls.[63] But the compulsion was always likely to end in misanthropy, and because, for Plath, the historical essence is inseparable and inextricable from private worlds, because, as Rose says, subjectivity, history and politics are fatefully intertwined, this misanthropy shuttles indifferently between the public and private domains. Thus mother, grandmother and great-grandmother 'reach hag hands' to 'haul' her down with them (PCP, p. 70), and father and husband come to embody the Nazi spirit. Plath cannot free her imagination from the fear of authoritarian violence in her personal life any more than in the public world:

> I made a model of you
> A man in black with a Meinkampf look
>
> And a love of the rack and the screw.
> And I said, I do, I do.
>
> ('Daddy', PCP, p. 224)

In the personal as in the public world, 'havoc' threatens the 'bankrupt estate', and the poet is left groping for a 'ceremony of words' that might patch it (PCP, p. 21). That is the logic that produces 'Lady Lazarus' in particular, and Plath's performances of 'dying like a woman', in general. But such equilibrium as Plath established for herself was at best precarious. On 11 February 1963, she chose to die like a woman for real, placing her head in the oven, with the gas turned on.

Why should one be inclined to take the misanthropy of the woman writers especially seriously? The answer is at its clearest in the case of Sarraute. Sarraute nursed her misanthropy at the very heart of emancipation. Indeed, emancipation enables it. She published her most significant fiction between 1948 and 1963. This is precisely the period, not only of the liberation of France (from the Germans), but also of the emancipation of Frenchwomen, at least insofar as, on 21 April 1944, Charles de Gaulle's Provisional Government of the French Republic belatedly granted them the vote. Before the war, Sarraute had worked for the feminist cause, and she was pleased by its success. Yet her work has little or no connection with women's issues, and she was fiercely hostile to women who wanted to separate off women's writing from men's and treat it as a particular case.[64] Literature was about the 'general view', or it was nothing.

For in between her feminist activities and April 1944 loomed the war. Sarraute witnessed the speedy military defeat of France, the German occupation of the north, the presence of the Gestapo, the proto-fascist Vichy regime, its collaborations, betrayals and denunciations, its persecution of 'aliens' and its deportations of Jews (Jewish herself, Sarraute was sacked from her job and went into hiding), its surreptitious outbreaks of civil strife, its inanely vicious propaganda; then the vast confusion of the liberation by the allies; and finally the anarchic, uncontrolled, sometimes random, chronically unjust and even murderous violence of the Purge (of alleged collaborators), bizarrely punctuated by the pompous triumphalism of the new ruling elite. Given this, it is hardly surprising if her imagination, like those of quite a few of her French contemporaries, turned away from the emancipatory hope, which must have seemed singularly forlorn at the time, and towards a misanthropic vision that would supply its own logic of the human catastrophe.

Sarraute no doubt wished the continuing emancipation of women well. But by 1944 her mind was elsewhere, still deeply buried in recent history and its aftermath. Marx's peculiar, even quaint, nineteenth-century optimism led him to assert that revolution, Communism and the proletariat would supply human beings with the opportunity to escape what he called their prehistory. By contrast, by 1934, Walter Benjamin is commending Kafka precisely for his evocation of a prehistorical world from which there is apparently no escape. Sarraute reads Kafka in this way too, as describing a world 'without exit, enlarged to the dimensions of an endless nightmare' (ES, pp. 1573–4). Her own world, too, is prehistorical, in Marx's and Benjamin's sense. With her 'deep incursions into forbidden, dangerous zones', she became extremely aware of 'the often monstrous, hardly believable iniquities' of which human history is largely made up (ES, pp. 1562, 1591). She lived in an age of suspicion, she felt – not surprisingly, in Vichy and Gaullist France – and there is no one in her fiction who is not open to suspicion. Indeed, for Sarraute, suspicion of the other person would seem to be not only fundamental to us all, but at all points logical and necessary.

If Compton-Burnett, Rhys, Sitwell and Plath still have a serious reputation and the ideologues whom I cited at the beginning of this chapter, both suffragist and anti-suffragist, do not, this is not because they cede any ground on women's equality with men, any more than Sarraute did. The point is axiomatic for them. None of them assume, however, that its political, legal and cultural embodiment actually has anything to do with progress. (In 1944, Sarraute must have seen this all too starkly). What is so arresting about the women's misanthropy is that it has nothing of defensive conservatism about it. It both resists the very enlightenment the writers value and in which they would want to believe and, at the same time, is paradoxically integrated within it. They are prepared to think the unthinkable: that feminism can be right, and yet its triumphs make no difference, at least, beyond a disturbingly unimaginative and restrictive historical and political conception of the world, one deaf to the sheer magnitude of suffering beyond the finite scope of a specific political trajectory. They recognize – there is no other way of understanding them – a profoundly retrograde element at work in human life that is grimly refractory to any significant progress, any decisive resolution of human predicaments. From this retrograde element we have never had any conception of how to emancipate ourselves. We need not give up on the emancipatory projects for that reason, but it does have implications for their tone. The next chapter will make it very clear what I mean.

6

MISANTHROPY AND THE NEW WORLD

But Sarraute seems obviously to be another case of a misanthropy produced by particular historical circumstances, a misanthropy that can presumably therefore also be eclipsed by changes in them. This hardly seems an adequate basis for exempting the misanthropy of modern women from the historicist stricture. There is at least one recurrent problem, however, with granting historicism any absolute or final purchase, in that it tends to give too much credence to what Georg Jellinek called 'the normative power of the factual'. By this he meant, not the power of fact as opposed to fiction, but the human drive 'to assign normative authority to existing states of affairs', states of affairs that are immediately present and to hand.[1] People respond to the vagaries and vicissitudes of history by confining their imaginative orientation to the latest historical set-up, to which they grant a superior reality because it is the latest and their own. Historicists might seem not to do this. But there is actually a more or less conscious drive within historicism – certainly within contemporary historicism, perhaps above all in its language and style – to withdraw imaginative weight from what for the past were its essential truths, in assuming the privilege of a present whose concrete fullness, better wisdom, greater meaningfulness and more conspicuous virtue the historicist does not appear to doubt. It is only very rarely that historicism is doubtful or humble about the perspective its own historical position supplies. It rarely seems aware that its own historical authority is possibly negligible. Michel Foucault was an exceptional example to the contrary.

Art and philosophy, however, constantly raise doubts about 'the normative power of the factual' in both its present and, by implication, its future forms. The Greek Cynics, again, are an excellent example, particularly in Foucault's description of them (in *Le Courage de la verité*).[2] Foucault describes the Cynics as putting contemporary schools of thought into radical question. For the schools turned out to be incapable of structuring the life around them according to principles or moral precepts that might raise it to the level of the philosophical life. Though the Cynic has no answers to the questions at stake, he refuses to detach his thought from philosophical or properly moral principles, however scandalous and abrasive a figure it may make him. This functions in effect as a powerful Cynic (and misanthropic) riposte to the historicists. In historical terms, it means seeking to avoid engaging with history through a contemporary filter. The misanthropist finally poses his or her question of 'the factual' in all its forms. The modern women writers decline to award automatic prestige to *any* present that has no obvious intellectual and moral right to claim it, that cannot plausibly counter their negativity. Why not misanthropy, in effect, the misanthropist might ask, if the best conceptions of the good proposed to us have only the interests of a given present at their root (and not, we might add, the perhaps compelling interests of the future, or indeed the past)? Thus certain kinds of misanthropy actually start to whittle away at the historicist challenge. They share the historicist's sceptical attitude to the grip of past truths, but don't allow us to suppose that the truths of any present should automatically seem more persuasive.

If the strain of misanthropy in Sarraute, Sitwell, Compton-Burnett, Rhys and Plath seems close to Benjamin and Kafka's insistence that we are not yet out of prehistory, it is in acting as a radical brake on historical buoyancy or self-congratulation. In fact, modern misanthropy has long been serving as a corrective to the facile modern optimisms that begin with Leibniz (and his conception of ours as 'the best of all possible worlds'), Hutcheson, Shaftesbury and eighteenth-century Pelagianism.[3] As we have seen, it often accompanies emancipation, emerges out of a profound alienation, not from the concept of emancipation itself, but from the readiness with which, in declaring new freedoms as promptly as it does, emancipation also repeatedly betrays itself, as though a particular instance of emancipation were anything like a sufficient gain. Here misanthropy becomes cautionary, chronically disbelieving, both a curb, and a gauntlet thrown down.

Just a month before Samuel Beckett's death, the Berlin Wall was finally dismantled. By then, Beckett was an inmate of Le Tiers Temps, an old people's home in Paris. Rather than identifying with the celebrants in their cork-popping moment, he appeared to be disturbed. Having watched some television footage from Berlin in his room, 'he emerged very agitated' and exclaimed to the *directrice*, Isabelle Jernand, '*Ça va trop vite*'.[4] Beckett had seen the effects of other grand liberations before, in Ireland in 1922, and then, like Sarraute, in France in 1944. He knew what they amounted to, knew that, as usual, the latest one, too, would be followed by a hubbub of voices announcing the advent of a new world order. He had lived through the inception of several old new world orders before, and understood that new worlds were not immediately there for the taking. The rich and various strains of misanthropy in his work serve precisely to combat such delusions. So, too, the stark closure of the women writers' worlds asserts that any truly significant transformation will not appear as another step forward down the same road, an advance on what is already there. If anything, it will rather puncture or cut dramatically across Plath's 'bankrupt estate', a world hermetically sealed and, more or less unbeknownst to itself, surrendered to death.

There is thus a third category of misanthropy that might give us pause for thought: the misanthropy that grows in the shadow of boosterism. Most nations, societies and cultures are perhaps boosterist, certainly the ones that, in Pascal's terms, have found their place in the sun. They do not just flaunt the tokens and spoils of their historical success. They talk themselves up, keep on telling themselves and others how good and indeed pre-eminent they are. They do this routinely, unthinkingly. They boast their own virtue, their *modus vivendi*, the superiority of their systems of knowledge and value and their own unique means of arriving at happiness and truth. The most vigorous boosterism naturally tends to emanate from power and wealth, for it is only to be expected that the wealthy and powerful should be boosterist about a world that has done handsomely by them, and to which all their immediate interests commit them. But the tone can also emerge in other domains, the academy, for example, and may be, and often is, deeply populist. One obvious contemporary example of it, part of the 'normative power' of our particular 'factuality', would be the language of advertising, a language usually inflated, that habitually banishes litotes, talking itself up as and through the seemingly infinite cornucopia it dangles before our eyes.

The misanthropy in this chapter radically disputes such a mindset. It might seem easily confused with the misanthropy in Chapter 4, and indeed the misanthropists here, too, may well partly identify with the interests of the historically defeated and disempowered. But they do not belong with them, and their principal concern is not historical injustice, nor are they always reacting against a progressivism. They call in question a culture of which they are a part, but that they present as in thrall to boosterism, which means opening up differences with a semiotics, a rhetoric, a language that tints Hobbes's *inanis gloria* in the garish colours of an *inanis euphoria* and involves a failure of mind, seriousness (though also humour) and aesthetic taste. Here intellectual and moral persuasions become inseparable from one another, and from questions of style. To the misanthropists, in their fervent attachment to their goods, intellectually, morally and aesthetically, boosters have no conception of what might be for the best, and no interest in exploring it, which means that boosterism spells mediocrity. My examples of such misanthropy will come from one of the very greatest and most insidiously absorbing of all misanthropic traditions, the American one.

Boosterism is an American word. In the nineteenth century, it denoted a specific historical and material phenomenon: new American small townships started making inordinate claims about themselves and their future, thus 'boosting' their own prospects. They aimed to attract new residents to their areas, keep up the spirits of communities and raise the value of real estate. Boosterism subsequently came to mean self-promotion, whether of a town, city, business, company or American society and culture in general, the promotion in question going well beyond mere truth-claims. The most notorious American enemy of boosterism, the one who gave the term significant currency, was Sinclair Lewis.

In *Babbitt* (1922) – the eponymous hero of which is a realtor – Lewis portrayed a world in which everyone is a booster, whether of himself, his business or company, his church or other institution or his wife, family, friends and associates, or just 'Uncle Samuel, U.S.A.'[5] The booster's world is one given over to the 'religion of business' (B, p. 10) with only a single register, promotion, for human living and being, and which is philistine, barbarous, vulgar, emotionally and aesthetically dead.

Furthermore, boosterism is a way of turning away from and failing to acknowledge profoundly unpalatable truths. The 'vision' of boosterism beautifies and thereby justifies all trashiness, not least in the case of morality, or what Lewis's boosters prefer to call 'ethics'. Not only is it the case that, as Paul Riesling says, 'this sweet, clean, respectable moral life isn't all it's cracked up to be' (B, p. 48); it isn't sweet, clean or respectable either. As businessmen, Babbitt and his cronies repeatedly if discreetly engage in one form of moral shabbiness or another, in corruption, unscrupulous or sharp practice, 'dirty little lickspittle deals' (B, p. 183). The flip side of the booster's zip, zoom, zing, zeal, zest and zowie is the fact that 'all we do is cut each others' throats and make the public pay for it' (B, p. 48).

For its Babbitts, the city of Zenith is precisely that, a zenith, a peak of civilization, a consummation of progress, a representative city in what Lewis knows is fast becoming the richest and most powerful nation on earth, its boosterism 'the spiritual and mental side of American supremacy' (B, p. 65). Here positivity becomes a nightmare, a trap into which all must fall, an arrant delusion to which everyone must nonetheless pay tribute, since the system determines all the forms of individuality on offer. Boosterism is self-evidently disastrous for the obvious social sufferers, the poor, the destitute, those who have not made it, because it writes them off as of no account (or, worse, as having deserved it, as in American 'prosperity theology').[6] But for Lewis it is also a disaster for the boosters themselves. What keeps boosterism upright is 'oratory', 'whooping it up', the booster's narcissistic pleasure in 'the sound of his own vocabulary' (B, p. 56). But the prop is flimsy, so the booster is always in danger of seeing that he has merely been the addict of a 'poisonous energy' and abruptly confronting the gap between rhetoric and the world, a cleft which then suddenly appears as reality itself (B, p. 115). Hence Babbitt comes to recognize not only that he is not 'the ideal type to which the entire world must tend' (B, p. 139), but that, deep down, the people of Zenith actually 'hate the whole peppy, boosting, go-ahead game, and they're bored by their wives and think their families are fools' (B, pp. 48, 50). In short, the booster system is a fraud, as, under their posturing, the boosters know: secretly, they loathe business, and eat, drink and smoke far too much, commit suicide or go to war as an escape. This is the ultimate meaning of the 'new type of civilization' (B, p. 141), its unprecedented grandeur and vast inanity together. But nowhere else is any better: Lewis's presentation of the Englishman Sir Gerald Doak summarily kills off any notion of the superiority of European cultivation, suggesting, in good misanthropic fashion, that he thought that fraudulent systems were equally the norm beyond America.

*

American boosterism, however, is not just a comparatively recent phenomenon. In some ways, America had 'whooped itself up' from the start, because it seemed to promise a new liberty unprecedented in history that arthritic old Europe could not, because its founding discourses were of particular religious kinds, and because the New World was itself so very extraordinary, and seemed to plead for a language commensurate with its magnificence. The concept of America as the new Eden, a garden of unexampled plenitude where, because America had been 'freed from the cynicism of the Old World',[7] innocence became possible again, went back as far as the early English explorers and had (still has) wide currency. So, too, the idea that America was the new Jerusalem prophesied by Ezekiel and described in the *Book of Revelation* stemmed from the Puritan fathers of the seventeenth century, who took themselves to be building it. 'We shall be as a citty upon a hill', declared John Winthrop, governor of the Massachusetts Bay Colony, in 1630. 'The eies of all people are upon us'.[8]

The conviction shared by many that America was altogether special, that Americans could think of themselves as exempted from the common humanity with which other peoples were burdened, must have always seemed distinctly ironic to some, since the country was founded on fierce and often scandalized resistance precisely to class societies that, in Europe, had allowed privilege to lift itself above the common herd. The belief was nonetheless extremely powerful, and assumed various historical forms: 'Manifest Destiny', for example. This was the nineteenth-century belief, from Andrew Jackson (President of the United States, 1829–37) onwards, that, because of the patent spiritual and moral distinction of its people and its institutions, America's destiny was to spread itself and its power throughout the American continent as a whole. Theology even appeared to underwrite this imperative, certainly, if one understood that the American task was to build the New Jerusalem – a 'Land without Evil'[9] – on a corrupt old earth. Manifest

Destiny was integral to God's purposes. Thomas Jefferson believed in it. Even Abraham Lincoln partly subscribed to it. It became a principal justification for American expansion (initially, westwards).

In time, this led to the doctrine of 'American exceptionalism'. The exceptionalist case again was that America was not a nation like others but was the first new nation on earth, the first truly to come out of a revolution, to establish itself on the founding principles of liberty and equality, and therefore lifted free of the messy historical impediments that held back others. In the twentieth century, exceptionalism became inseparable from the idea of the American Dream[10] – the term first appeared in 1931 – with the belief it sustained in limitless possibility, the right of every individual American citizen to fulfil his or her potential. Everyone could arrive at their own Jerusalem. After all, in the words of a present-day American cultural historian who actually still seems to believe it, 'We are a chosen people assigned a unique and special purpose'.[11] Indeed, according to some, far from finally choking itself back, the American Dream has by now gone global.

Of course, notions of the unique distinction of the American way by no means remained uncontested inside America, let alone outside it. There were compelling reasons for this. From the start, the New Eden was both harrowed and harrowing.[12] The early settlers invaded the hunting grounds of the indigenous peoples. They treated the country as theirs. Before long, they were driving the Indians from their ancestral lands, infecting them with the viruses they brought with them from Europe, destroying their villages and crops and killing and mutilating captives. After the American Revolution, Washington and Jefferson planned to 'civilize' and thus assimilate the Indians. But the Indians were wedded to their own traditions and culture, and there was less dialogue between them and the new 'civilization' than mutual incomprehension. In 1830, Jackson signed the Indian Removal Act, which licensed ethnic cleansing, the forced relocation of the Indian nations to the west of America: hence the infamous 'Trail of Tears', along which so many Indians failed, sickened, starved and died.

Within a few years, the belief in Manifest Destiny was justifying wholesale colonial expansion westwards, and even leading to calls for extermination. Indians were herded like cattle, quarantined like beasts and massacred. Meanwhile, the whites assumed their world, often initially through treaties that merely defrauded the natives, with 174 million acres of Indian land passing into white hands between 1853 and 1856 alone. There were subsequently plenty of high-minded philanthropic efforts to 'improve' the Indians' lot. Nonetheless, to recall the Joycean adage, conquerors cannot be amateurish. America and the American Dream were founded on atrocity. Slavery with all its attendant monstrosities increasingly flourished in colonial America, and the Constitution of the new Republic protected it. According to the census of 1860, just five years before it was outlawed, there were four million slaves in the New Eden. The gulf between modern American boosterism and the historical realities was vast. To say, however, that the first existed to conceal the second would be too simple. In a sense, boosterism became as extravagantly hyperbolic as it did precisely because the history was so extreme. If the American project were to continue – or so the logic of the political unconscious ran – it required a rhetorical juggernaut to defend itself from itself, a Cadillac among rhetorics, a rhetoric worthy of NASA. That rhetoric was boosterist.

A very different tradition altogether, however, a much darker one, was originally dominant in America and loomed sombrely within American life and culture, the Puritan tradition, which stemmed from the theology and mœurs of the first settlers in New England, and became 'one of the continuous factors in American life and thought'.[13] The Puritan settlers derived much of their orientation from the Calvin who inherited from St. Augustine: they believed in the doctrines of original sin and total depravity. Humanity was intrinsically rotten. According to Samuel Willard, 'the unhappy Fall hath Robbed man of ... perfection, and filled his heart with perverse and rebellious principles, tending to the Subversion of all Order and the reducing of the World to a *Chaos*'.[14] So parlous was man's state that, for Thomas Hooker, it was a wonder that the 'great and Terrible God' did not 'pash such a poor insolent worm [as man] into pouder' and send him 'packing to the pitt'.[15]

Men were enslaved to their degenerate condition, and incapable of saving themselves from it simply by referring to 'right reason', which meant that 'only the grace of God' could redeem them.[16] However, God vouchsafed his grace to few (they were few even within the Puritan communities).[17] According to the doctrine of election, these few were the chosen ones, the elect, those whom, in his sovereign pleasure, God had singled out to be worthy of him. God not only chose the elect, but predestined them to their election. The Puritan theorists of New

England helpfully supplemented orthodox doctrine with a Covenant Theology explaining how and why some people were saved,[18] but even the elect had to qualify for eternal bliss, to confirm that they deserved their hallowed status.

It was by no means self-evident to the Puritans that they would indeed qualify. They feared lest the canker of depravity, what John Cotton called 'man's perverse subtilty in inventing ways of backsliding',[19] be eating away within their own communities. Willard warned that even the elect in the New World were not behaving like an elect at all.[20] Cotton suggested that the top guns themselves, the 'Magistrates and Officers in Church and Common-wealth', should be aware that there is 'a straine in a man's heart, that will sometime or other runne out to excesse', and to which they might abruptly find themselves in thrall.[21] No one could trust to their own virtue, and true Puritans had therefore to submit their consciences to the most minute and searching analysis, to interrogate their innermost being without stint or mercy, not in order to ensure that they were inherently virtuous, since they most certainly were not, but the better to perceive the 'loathsome abominations' that lay 'in [their] bosom', the 'very nest' where the lusts were 'hatched and bred', the winding snares of Satan within.[22] Hooker thought that the 'lusts' sent up 'dunghill steams which distemper the mind', making it wander, encouraging the vanities.[23] Only constant vigilance could sufficiently protect one from oneself.

Such thinking was bound to lead to a misanthropic political theory. The Puritans' America was not a land of the free. They greatly distrusted freedom. Winthrop, for example, opined that 'liberty makes men grow more evil, and in time to be worse than brute beasts'.[24] The Puritans were convinced that, at its deep dark core, the world was immutable, and immutably bad, which meant that, without the law and its agents, there could only be infinite criminality, which in turn meant that men and women had to be controlled, harshly if necessary. True, the Puritans' conception of criminality had greater scope than ours: Increase Mather wrote approvingly of the execution of the man in Scripture who was sentenced to death for 'gathering a few sticks upon the Sabbath day', and thought that sleeping during (his?) sermons was sign enough '*that the nature of man is wofully corrupted and depraved*'.[25] Nonetheless, it was clear that, whatever the 'crime' in question, unregenerate humanity required the severest authority and discipline, in effect, dictatorship. In the New England communities, this meant the dictatorship of the few, the holy and regenerate.

*

In American literature, boosterism repeatedly breaks up against the Puritan inheritance, the Puritan temperament and imagination, the most obvious example being Nathaniel Hawthorne. Hawthorne's major fiction is a dark critique of both the boosterism contemporary with him – (Manifest Destiny thinking) – and the whole tradition of American boosterism. Thus *The Scarlet Letter* provides an austere critique of the dream of the New Jerusalem, and *The Blithedale Romance* writes off the dreams of modern American utopians. The hope of Blithedale – that it will be 'the one green spot in the moral sand-waste of the world'[26] – is brusquely and cruelly dashed.

Hawthorne's principal focus was the Puritan past. He turned the bleak austerity of the Puritan vision on itself, amply suggesting that, as the Puritans themselves feared, they harboured proclivities that were as unpleasant as those they saw in the mass of humanity. Hawthorne's Puritans are not only bowed down by guilt, joyless, bigoted, obsessed by dogma, sexually extremely repressed, hostile to the faintest liberalism and authoritarian, but are actually impious, unholy. This is particularly the case with their treatment of those who think otherwise than they do. They whip Quakers and Anabaptists, cut off the ears of blasphemers, exile Antinomians and execute witches, often in the most brutal and peremptory fashion, and flog their sinners and those who dissent from Puritan orthodoxy into line. All of this was historical fact. Hawthorne repeatedly points to a cold, self-righteous, self-gratifying, deeply rebarbative and perverted sadism in the Puritans.

Thus the moral sand-waste devours the supposed oases. The Puritan pessimism that founds Hawthorne's critique of American exceptionalism becomes self-reflexive, and finally expands to include the major foundational ideologies of America *in toto*, and the communities that trusted to them. But Hawthorne has no real belief, either, in the pleasure seekers who run counter to Puritan doctrine or the rebels who defy the communities, in that the first are trivial, and the second must end up sadder and wiser than they started out. Their causes are necessarily doomed. Hawthorne leaves us circling in a void, in that he implies that we can at least hold fast to the value of Puritan seriousness, but not to the system of thought and value that underwrote it.

One can see, then, why Herman Melville took 'the grand truth about Nathaniel Hawthorne' to be that 'he says NO! in thunder'.[27] Hawthorne was resisting what he took to be groundlessly or unwarrantably positive voices, and Melville was conditioned by the same Puritan heritage as Hawthorne, ending up sharing the same principle of radical disbelief. For both of them, America was strictly a 'ruined Eden'.[28] The ruin of Eden is always Melville's concern, whether his subject is directly American or not, and his works all pursue that theme, the serpent in the supposed garden repeatedly turning out to be race. Melville published his first novel, *Typee*, in 1846, just after the first use of the term Manifest Destiny.[29] The narrator Tommo doubly abandons America, firstly by shipping on the whaler *Dolly*, and secondly, since there could hardly be a less Edenic life than the one the 'tyrannical' usage on board the *Dolly* offers,[30] by deserting, ending up among the Polynesian Typees. Tommo is a swingeing critic of an America that prates about democracy but has no sanctions against wantonly autocratic rule on its ships, and the crew of whose men-of-war seem like a summation of 'pent-up wickedness' (T, p. 229; compare the later *Whitejacket*). He is equally scathing about white 'civilization' in general, arguing that it does not subdue 'our wicked propensities', but frees them up and gives them greater power of action, though it also isolates and scapegoats those whom it takes to embody them (T, p. 31). The civilized evils are 'unknown' to other races, but the white race cannot see that the so-called 'barbarous peoples' may possess more virtue than themselves. They rather contaminate, corrupt and 'extirpate' them (T, pp. 145–6).

This clearly begins to point *Typee* towards misanthropic conclusions, but these are offset by the Typees themselves. Tommo stoutly maintains that, if other races seem barbaric, it is because the 'horrible cruelties' of whites have 'exasperated' them into 'savages' (T, p. 41). The Typees, however, have had little or no contact with whites. True, they are cannibals, which is less than heartening. But Tommo knows about the cannibalism and initially has no qualms about it, since he assumes that the tribe only eat the bodies of dead enemies, which is no reason to disqualify them as a prelapsarian people. In Typee valley, it must be, Eden survives. It cannot be true that the Typees prepare live victims for cannibal orgies, this is a derangement, the macabre fantasy of a white mind incapable of trust, always on the lookout for 'inconstancy and treachery', even in primitive innocence (T, p. 93). Tommo decides not, in the end, and flees, at which point the Typees respond in a manner that altogether bears out his misgivings, and leaves him finally 'appalled by their violence' (T, p. 277; cf. p. 279).

Typee is about trying to save a belief in a corner of Eden in the midst of a general moral devastation whose source in the novel, initially at least, is America and American institutions. Tommo seeks to preserve some confidence in humanity through an identification with a different race, but his effort fails. Melville's early pessimism subsequently deepens, as the novels *Omoo* and *Mardi* in their different ways demonstrate, and as any residual faith in non-white peoples steadily erodes. *Redburn* sustains the pessimism but largely drops the race theme. Wellingborough Redburn's progress takes him from innocence to experience, and the bleak convictions to which it leads. The young Redburn is both an American dreamer and an American booster, impatient with 'cheerless' people.[31] On board ship, however, he finds himself 'a sort of Ishmael' – the Ishmael of Genesis 21, outside human society (R, p. 114). He nonetheless persists in believing in 'the triumph of sound policy and humanity', and even continues to trust to a(n American) future 'which shall see the estranged children of Adam restored as to the old hearthstone in Eden' (R, pp. 223, 239). What finally throttles this romanticism is a recognition of the irremediable, forgotten suffering of others, which is 'enough to turn the heart to gall; and make a man-hater out of a Howard' (R, p. 253).[32] Redburn is bound to conclude that Eden is not restorable, but that people doggedly refuse to see and know it: 'We are blind to the real sights of this world; deaf to its voice; and dead to its death' (R, p. 383).

Two years later, in *Moby Dick*, Ishmael is the name of the central character. *Moby Dick* is partly about trying to escape misanthropy. Ishmael takes to the seas when his 'splintered heart and maddened hand' are 'turned against the wolfish world', when his 'hypos' (morbid depressions of spirits) 'get such an upper hand of me that it requires a strong moral principle to prevent me from deliberately stepping into the street, and methodically knocking people's hats off' (MD, pp. 1, 52). Since he ends up on a ship hell-bent on natural destruction, with a monomaniacal captain and a crew unable to restrain or resist his insane singleness of purpose, indeed, who are caught up in it, the project seems destined to go horribly wrong, and indeed it does. Captain Ahab, the crew and the *Pequod* are partly an allegory for an America in principle democratic but profoundly compromised by the exclusion of women, slavery and ethnic cleansing, and in practice all too often at the mercy of immensely powerful, shadowy forces. Significantly, Melville told Hawthorne that a belief in 'unconditional democracy' was not incompatible with 'a dislike to all mankind'.[33] He was also inclined to believe that America was just the latest phase in the history of 'a wicked world, in all meridians' (MD, p. 58). Here 'sin that pays its way can travel freely' (MD, p. 44), there is 'no folly of the beast of the earth which is not infinitely outdone by the madness of men' (MD, p. 394), and 'we are all killers, on land and on sea, Bonapartes and sharks included' (MD, p. 144). The early Puritans would have agreed.

In his late fiction, Melville not only brings these various themes together but also focuses them on a particular aspect of boosterist discourse. As far as race was concerned, by the time he wrote 'Benito Cereno', he had no life-raft left to cling to. Captain Amasa Delano is a liberal American, buoyant and optimistic, 'a person of a singularly undistrustful good nature' who is not liable 'to indulge in personal alarms, any way involving the imputation of malign evil in man'.[34] As a result, Delano gets everything wrong, right up to the point when, in a last act of consuming despair, the misanthropic and apparently half-mad Cereno throws himself off his ship and into Delano's boat. The black slave cargo on Cereno's ship has revolted and taken it over, murdering the passengers and most of the crew and committing various iniquities, then forcing Cereno to lie systematically to his guest. Delano intuits nothing of this, rather scoffing mildly at Cereno's 'insane terrors' as the hallucinations of a sick mind (BC, p. 216). So complacent is Delano's liberal, upbeat benevolism, so inert and closed the language in which he articulates it, that he is comprehensively incapable of perspicacity, sound judgement or moral insight, a study in bland self-deceit. The past 'is passed', says Delano at the end, to Cereno,

'why moralize upon it? Forget it. See, yon bright sun has forgotten it all, and the blue sea, and the blue sky, these have turned over new leaves.'

'Because they have no memory,' [Cereno] dejectedly replied; 'because they are not human.' (BC, p. 246)

It is abundantly clear which character has got things right.

Critics have sometimes deplored what they have taken to be the story's racism. But the later Melville is a misanthropist, not a racist. His rebel slaves are not inferior. Where Delano does not possess 'more than ordinary quickness and accuracy of intellectual perception' (BC, p. 164), the slaves have impressive reserves of cunning, intelligence, subtlety and ruthlessness. Far from elevating himself on to a racist pedestal, Melville slyly puts Delano there, in that Delano's liberalism actually amounts to little more than a genially indulgent view of the blacks that is steeped in sentimental condescension and ultimately dehumanizing. Melville had no faith in any pedestal. In work after work, he flayed what he took to be the ignoble, self-exculpating hypocrisy of modern Western and especially American culture. However, he also gave up on any belief in the intrinsic virtue of the ethnic other and the supposed moral pre-eminence of victimhood. That is a Delano-type idea. When Delano exclaims, 'Ah, this slavery breeds ugly passions in man!' (BC, p. 214), Melville ensures that we hear a quite different meaning to the one his character intends: in the words of W. H. Auden, 'Those to whom evil is done/Do evil in return'.[35]

So, too, 'Bartleby' takes a narrator similar to Delano, temperate, well-meaning, liberal-minded, considerate and kind, but decidedly limited in that he is inveterately attached to a clutch of sanguine beliefs and reflexes, and runs him up against a man, Bartleby, whose relationship to the world is clearly and painfully deprived of all palliatives. Bartleby stubbornly allows the narrator's reassurances no purchase whatever, rather sticking to his own version of the thunderous no, an unalterably melancholic refusal of cooperation in and with humanity: 'I would prefer not to'.[36] In his drastic repudiation of other people, Bartleby is as immovable as the 'dead brick wall' at which for long periods he stares. The 'best affections' which the narrator believes human misery encourages in him crumble, yielding to 'a certain hopelessness of remedying excessive and organic ill' (BA, p. 22), a dreadful intuition of the logic to unbreachable solitude and despair. 'Ah Bartleby! Ah humanity!' (BA, p. 41): finally, it would seem, there is no more to say.

Thus Lawrance Thompson is quite right to suggest that Melville's vision ultimately 'narrows down to the sharp focus of a misanthropic notion that the world was put together wrong'.[37] The process culminated in *The Confidence-Man: His Masquerade*, Melville's great, final demolition of American boosterism. The Confidence-Man boards a Mississippi steamer and systematically fleeces and bilks an array of different American types, speciously winning their trust through plausible talk. He deceives them about himself, but also about themselves. He is the Devil incarnate, and the Devil plays the best game in town, is even gambling with the house's money. For Melville, finally, America gives no reason for any of the nineteenth-century versions of Babbitt's confidence, still less for the empty language in which they were expressed. Having confidence in people is a mistake.

Melville stands as the central figure in what we might call post-Puritan or, broadening it out, East coast misanthropy. From him we might turn to the figure who, though not without competitors, could claim to be the American Diogenes, Melville's contemporary Henry David Thoreau. Thoreau was born and educated at the heart of post-Puritan New England, and clearly belongs to the American Puritan tradition, if rather differently from Hawthorne and Melville. Thoreau loved nature and solitude, altogether preferring them to people. 'To be in company', he asserted, 'even with the best, is soon wearisome and dissipating'.[38] By contrast, he wrote stoutly on behalf of the 'wonderful purity' of the nature invaded and profaned by man.[39] In 1846, he delivered himself of his own great thunderous no, retiring to Walden Pond, where he lived the simple life, in a lonely hut he had built for himself.

'Society is always diseased', wrote Thoreau, 'and the best is the most so'.[40] Like a good Puritan, he was a moral absolutist who supposed that complete sincerity, truth and integrity were vitally important in human dealings, but found all three in scant supply. In reality, his world was that of The Confidence-Man, and he came to expect nothing of others. This encouraged a doughty, Crusoe-like, Protestant independence, a conviction that his salvation was in his hands alone. Giving up on others, however, did not exactly mean ignoring the contemporary American scene, and Thoreau nourished an immense contempt for its shoddiness and was scornful of its pieties. He turned values right around: if he behaved well, he thought, it was because a demon possessed him (see W, p. 10). On that holiday of holidays, 4th July, Independence Day, he bustled about moving his few belongings to the Pond, in effect asserting that he alone knew what independence really meant, setting as little store by the publicly hallowed date as Dickens's great misanthropist, Scrooge, does by Christmas. Nonconformity was his habit and his rule. In his great moment of defiance of the State, in 1846, he refused to pay his poll tax (and was duly arrested).

Thoreau was no democrat, certainly not in the contemporary sense. Majority rule was just a matter of might, not right. There was no reason to credit the views of the mass of men, since they served the State, and 'not as men mainly, but as machines, with their bodies'. There were others who served it with their heads, but they were not capable of making moral distinctions, so were 'as likely to serve the devil'.[41] Class after class of human beings falls before Thoreau's scythe: legislators, office holders, bureaucrats and (notably) politicians – that politics seemed 'all the rage' with 'the Indians now' merely gave him to suppose that 'a row of wigwams, with a dance of powwows, and a prisoner tortured at the stake, would be more respectable than this'.[42] Farmers only bothered about agriculture, not humanity. None of these were 'real men'. They were self-interested ciphers. But above all, there were the merchants. Thoreau loathed what he took to be America's 'exclusive devotion to trade and commerce and manufactures' as being extraordinarily and unnecessarily wasteful and betokening an obsession with luxuries, inessentials, trivia. American commerce, he lamented, 'whitens every sea in quest of nuts and raisins',[43] while the 'factory system' existed chiefly to enrich the corporations (W, p. 26). Nothing, 'not even crime', was 'more opposed to poetry, to philosophy, ay, to life itself, than this incessant business' (LWP, p. 104).

Thoreau shuns humans because they will not live up to 'higher laws', about which he has quite a lot to say (W, pp. 210–22). He thinks far more of men as they might be than of men as they actually are. Nonetheless, for all his recommendations of the 'higher … intellectual flights' (W, p. 107), the most exquisite accounts of higher things in Walden are actually loving descriptions of what are, from an anthropocentric perspective, lower ones, the myriad natural phenomena that he sees around him. Walden resounds with hymns to natural beauty that spring from attentive observation, are rhapsodic and clinical together. Thoreau knows exactly how rapidly blackberries can 'deepen their tints' (W, p. 156); he has watched them do it. He can hear a puff ball burst. He develops an intimate relationship with beans. He thinks of himself as 'partly leaves and vegetable mould' (W, p. 138), and the few people he is at all drawn to similarly gain from being half-human, like the French-Canadian woodchopper who is 'cousin to the pine and the rock' (W, pp. 146–7).

Thoreau was not a loveless man. It was merely human beings that he could not love.

Beneath all this was a serious if not unambiguous Thoreauvian politics, which, once again, as in the case of other American misanthropists, was partly a politics of language. Thoreau was appalled by and persistently condemned slavery and the wars in the west, refusing to pay his poll tax partly because the government was prosecuting an expansionist war with Mexico. The invasion of California and the Gold Rush were 'the greatest disgrace on mankind' and, as the two edges of the world appeared to touch, he asked incredulously whether this was really 'the ground on which Orientals and Occidentals meet' (LWP, pp. 108–9). But no one else seemed to care about America's self-abasement. What Thoreau heard instead was rhetoric, rousing voices, the 'cheap wisdom and eloquence of politicians' (CD, p. 19), the 'din of religion, literature and philosophy' in the 'pulpits, lyceums and parlours' (NHM, p. 194), the speechifying produced in transient and superficial moods of excitement, everywhere, the authentic sound of men imposing on themselves and others for their own advantage. It was all profoundly discouraging. For no discourse could be in the least uplifting if it were not 'steady and cheery', yes, but in the manner of 'the creak of crickets' (ibid.).

*

One could extend an account of East coast misanthropy much further, going back again to Dickinson and Plath, both of them Massachusetts women, or turning to Boston-bred Robert Lowell ('each of us holds a locked razor').[44] But I want rather to mention Dorothy Parker, though she is half-Jewish and in essence a New Yorker, and doesn't really fit into the Puritan tradition. Parker's short stories are full of dull, uncultivated, conventional, superficial people who have 'sedulously effaced all trace of individuality'.[45] They are spiritually and imaginatively dead. They may travel. They may read books, and even write them. None of this saves them. They are pusillanimous, and Parker treats them with chilly detachment. 'What've I got to live for?' moans the woman in 'Dialogue at Three in the Morning' (CS, p. 48). The answer, as is all too clear from the whole drunken, repetitive exchange of which the story is chiefly made up, is nothing; nor could anyone conceivably supply a reason. Parker's focus tends to be on certain American types, particularly

New Yorkers. But she knows her La Rochefoucauld,[46] and her vision frequently broadens and deepens. Mrs Legion in 'A Certain Lady', for example, appears to be the 'Heiress of the Ages' both because she is an exceedingly wealthy New Yorker, and because she is exceedingly vacuous.

Parker's people frequently behave very badly indeed. Mr Durant in 'Mr Durant', for example, contemplates his short-term lover's unexpected pregnancy and subsequent abortion with remarkable complacency, then hypocritically arranges the quick dispatch of the dog his children very much want to keep, because of the 'disgusting' possibility that they may find it reproducing (CS, p. 29). Not only do people behave like this, in Parker's world: they do so lightly, gaily, frivolously. In 'The Wonderful Old Gentleman', for example, Mrs Whittaker cheats her brother and sister out of their inheritance ruthlessly, quite pleasantly, and without turning a hair. Parker's people are at best sublimely indifferent to others, at worst cruel, brutal and exploitative. This rubs up harshly against their pathetically desperate need for relationships. But such relationships are commonly motivated by insecurity, and therefore don't stand a chance of succeeding. 'Why does there have to be so much hell, all the time?' asks Mobie, in 'Dusk Before Fireworks' (CS, p. 152). Hell indeed: Parker's shrill and unnecessary people repeat their patterns, as they do their hypnotic and disastrous litanies, with an almost lunatic regularity, like infernal creatures trapped in their own circles. Parker repeatedly said that the American style of bonhomie had turned its possessor into 'an overzealous salesman' avidly promoting its 'wares of good humour and vivacity' (CS, p. 34). Her reality, by contrast, though it is very largely that of people sufficiently privileged to enjoy the luxury of confirming the American myth, rather sweepingly discredited it.

But rich New Yorkers were hardly the most significant example of American realities giving the lie to the American myth. The histories of the Indians and slavery did so with incalculably greater force. Other aspects of American history also had a similar effect. In particular, life in the parts of America where the exceptional character of the new nation was emerging, newly settled lands and the (much romanticized) American frontier, was often direly un-Edenic: lonely, filthy, lawless, violent, rapacious, racist and misogynist, beyond all moral inhibitors. From William Gilmore Simms's *Guy Rivers* (1834) to the anti-Westerns – Peter Fonda's *The Hired Hand* (1971), Robert Altman's *McCabe and Mrs*

Miller (1971), Robert Benton's *Bad Company* (1972), Dick Richards's
The Culpepper Cattle Company (1972), Jim Jarmusch's *Dead Man*
(1995) – American literature and art has darkly borne witness to this.[47]

Frontier misanthropy overlapped with and fed into Southern
misanthropy. Like the East coast version, Southern misanthropy
emerged, on the one hand, out of a chronic gap between ideals and
realities – the wretched failure of the realities of Southern life to live up
to Southern romance or genteel Southern expectations – and, on the
other, the gloomy legacy of puritanical churches, notably, perhaps, the
Southern Baptist. Two writers immediately come to mind, here: Mark
Twain and William Faulkner. Right from the start, the comic surface
of Twain's work keeps cracking open to reveal great gulfs of horror.
This stems from two sources: his experience of the frontier and his
familiarity with Southern (and Western) frontier culture, and his gift
of childlike vision, the imagination with which he adopted the child's
point of view. In *The Prince and the Pauper* (1882), for example, he has
little prince and little pauper exchange places so that they can both
confront the awfulness of each other's lives. The pauper is oppressed
by the world of power and status, and through him Twain lays bare
its underlying reality: false pomp and circumstance and self-inflation, a
paralysing conventionality that forbids all candour and spontaneity, and
a casual indifference to the lives and sufferings of the less fortunate.
For his part, the prince is deeply shocked by his encounter with low
life in Tudor England: violence, brutishness, anarchy, dire deprivation,
crass, random and sadistic injustice ('To think that these should know
the lash! … Not just in Heathenesse, but in Christian England!').[48] Even
in this early novel, it was finally only the children's story format and the
child's tone that saved Twain from the misanthropic plunge.

Life on the Mississippi (1883), Twain's memoir of his experience as
a Mississippi steamboat pilot, is lively, humorous and anecdotal, and
hardly qualifies as a misanthropic text. Yet it contains portents of things
to come. Twain sardonically juxtaposes historian Francis Parkman's
great romance of 'the mystery of [the] vast new world' with a tight-
lipped acknowledgement of Indian dispossession as approved by the
king and 'piously consecrated' by the priest.[49] He is withering about an
authentically Southern boosterism, the grandiose hyperbole, appallingly
bad taste and absurd pretentiousness to which he thought Southern
romance led, particularly the sentimental Southern devotion to Sir

Walter Scott, which he demolishes partly by means of a vast footnote stuffed with unsentimental Southern facts: feuds, vendettas, gunfights, public killings, often publicly approved (LM, pp. 236–8).

The Adventures of Huckleberry Finn (1884) grew out of *The Prince and the Pauper* and *Life on the Mississippi* together. Its greatness lies in its obstinate and rigorous exclusion of all grandiosity, but the sheer clarity and resolute unpretentiousness of Huck's demotic idiom also turns the novel into an incipiently misanthropic book that can only rescue itself through child's play. Huck and the runaway slave Jim escape the unflagging violence of Huck's father and Miss Watson's unappealing blend of Christianity, respectability and racism, and embark on their journey downriver. Like Redburn's, however, the journey downstream is less into the untrammelled freedom of the wilds than into sick knowledge. 'Sick' is a word to which Huck returns. There is a lot in his world to make him sick. The banks of the river are populated by 'quarrelsome people and all kinds of mean folks'.[50] Huck watches on helplessly, for example, as, with striking equanimity, two long-feuding aristocratic families wallow in yet another bloodbath, which for them is quite reconcilable with their puritanical Christianity and a belief in 'brotherly love' (HF, pp. 293, 297). He sees the novel's *eminence grise*, Sherburn, coldly gun down the reckless but harmless old Boggs. With a touch of misanthropic genius, Twain both grants Sherburn an eloquent indictment of the average human being – critics have repeatedly taken it to be Twain's own – and leaves Huck so nauseated by Sherburn that he has to sneak off to the circus to recover.

This is a world that will accept the trade in others (blacks) with, at best, two-faced furtiveness, at worst, unscrupulous zeal, but in either case without compunction. Its people speedily resort to enthusiastic lynching, yet are 'greenhorns' and 'flatheads' who easily fall victim to arrant con men (HF, p. 329). Here the worst can fleece the best, and one must flatter 'low-down humbugs and frauds' in order to survive (HF, pp. 305–6). Twain tries finally to lighten the gathering murk by bringing Tom Sawyer into the novel and having him draw Huck into an elaborate, Scott-influenced rigmarole whereby they 'free' Jim from slavery when he has in fact already been freed. But Tom is just playing games: this is Twain the novelist's equivalent of Huck and the circus. It is a charming but patently inadequate response to the issues that his novel has broached. For the Huck who has started to feel 'ashamed of the human race', the necessary conclusion must be different: 'I guess I got to light out for the Territory *ahead of the rest*' (HF, pp. 338, 447, my italics). He ends by articulating the classic misanthropic dream of desert solitude, its bleakness mitigated only by its being cast in the captivating (and revocable) terms of a child.

As Twain grew older, his misanthropy threatened to become all-embracing. He founded the Damned Human Race Club. In 'The Man Who Corrupted Hadleyburg' (1899), he let loose a vindictive character with a grudge upon a supposedly incorruptible American township that has long boasted of its honesty and integrity, and gleefully watched it go rotten in his character's hands. 'Why, you simple creatures', gloats the nemesis of Hadleyburg, 'the weakest of all weak things is a virtue which has not been tested in the fire' (pp. 46–7).[51] Hadleyburg is, in a sense, unworldly, but chiefly about itself, with disastrous consequences. Significantly, the final humiliation of the town takes place in front of a crowd including reporters, who will expose the unreality of Hadleyburg's boosterism and its language to the American public at large.

In 'The Mysterious Stranger' (1916), like Melville, Twain finally turned to the Devil incarnate, surrendering the world to a beautiful if rather idiosyncratic Satan who runs the show with total indifference, recognizing that humans are altogether dispensable and replaceable, their sufferings both necessary and arbitrary, inconsequential. Satan never has 'a kind word' for the 'paltry race', and bridles at any attempt to confuse it with animals.[52] Animals do not pretend to virtues they do not possess. This is 'the monopoly of those [creatures] with the Moral Sense' (MS, p. 78). The Moral Sense flatters human beings with a belief in their own superiority, because it allows them to choose, but in fact they almost always choose wrong: think for example of the average businessman or factory-owner, says Satan, who knows very well he should not exploit others, yet persists in doing so. Thus where animals sin innocently, man continually turns out badly, the failure of the Moral Sense degrading him 'to the bottom layer of animated beings' (ibid.). Satan bears this out by showing the narrator a pageant of human history from Cain and Abel through numberless wars, murders and massacres to an endless future steadily making progress in 'the deadly effectiveness of ... weapons of slaughter' (MS, p. 106). No interruption of this history is possible, because the race is 'made up of sheep ... and follows the handful that makes the most noise' (MS, p. 110). None of these truths will it face, because it dupes itself 'from cradle to grave with shams and delusions' (MS, p. 116).

But the work that is surely key to understanding Twain's misanthropy and his later development is the earlier *A Connecticut Yankee at King Arthur's Court* (1889). The younger Twain had sometimes waxed enthusiastic over American ideas of advancement, and this had helped keep his misanthropic inclinations in check. His Connecticut Yankee, Hank Morgan, is a Northern progressive and a booster, a republican committed to democratic process, a capitalist, entrepreneur, meritocrat, believer in industrialism, consumerism, free trade, a free press, freedom of religious worship and the self-made man. All of this he readily talks up. By contrast, Arthur's kingdom is clearly a composite of Twain's favourite targets, a romantic but morally and materially backward South, a benighted old Europe, and a modern Europe still bedevilled by class distinctions, restrictive codes and obscurantism. It is a world of cruelty, gross inequality, slavery and superstition. When Hank finds himself in Camelot, he decides to give it a good, 'uplifting' blast of American modernity.[53] Since he is shrewd, practical and scientifically and technologically adept, though he encounters resistance, he also makes headway.

However, at a crucial turning point, in order to 'scour the country and familiarise [themselves] with the humbler life of the people', he and Arthur disguise themselves as freemen (CY, p. 241). Alas, the experience of common humanity threatens to turn into one of universal braggadocio and pretension. The people keep on taking the wrong side, and can quickly turn into a vengeful mob. Worse still, in spite of all Hank's efforts, 'the magic of fol-de-rol', superstition and mediocre forms of belief survive in them (CY, p. 363). Hank eventually arrives at a point at which he not only can declare a republic in Camelot but also backs the republic up with Gatling guns, mines and electrocution. Increasingly, the tables turn: he puts his own nobles in elite positions and consolidates his system through violence, even having his knights 'remove' (i.e. kill) those who won't buy his products (CY, p. 365). He is not above suppressing the very freedom of speech he formerly claimed to value. Beneath Hank's boosterism, a bit of him has always feared that 'human muck' is not transformable at all, and been half-inclined 'to hang the whole human race and finish the farce' (CY, p. 283). When the flower of Arthur's knighthood rebels – supported, significantly, by the people – he and his henchmen massacre them. Ultimately, however, the victors also destroy themselves. Hank dies.

By this point, boosterism, humanity and the American way have fallen through a hole in the middle of the novel. The prison-house of the past yields to a progressive historical logic, but that logic turns out to be implicitly catastrophic, in a manner quite beyond the understanding or control of the most dynamic historical agents. In this respect, it is hard not to think of *A Connecticut Yankee* as an extraordinary product of a gift too little appreciated at the current time, prophetic intuition. Once again, boosterism does not survive the test. 'He is useless on top of the ground', writes the whimsical eponymous hero of another of Twain's late, dark novels, *Pudd'nhead Wilson* (1894), of man, 'he ought to be under it, inspiring the cabbages'.[54] The cynicism is rooted in revulsion from boosterism. Hence another of Wilson's maxims parodically and pointedly declares that while 'it was wonderful to discover America … it would have been more wonderful to miss it' (PW, p. 147). Native Americans would doubtless have agreed with him.

Faulkner saw himself as writing in Twain's wake: Twain was 'the father of American literature'.[55] Faulkner himself is often celebrated as in the first instance a modernist genius. In fact, he is a great dark saga-maker, a historian-poet of the deep South, chiefly the Mississippi he knew so intimately, above all, in its post-bellum decline. The South after the Civil War was a defeated, shell-shocked and profoundly demoralized culture. The war had been fought almost entirely on Southern soil; the fatality rate among Southern soldiers had been extremely high. The North had smashed the Southern economy – then the Northern project of 'reconstruction' failed. In any case, Southerners harboured a deep resentment of Northern intruders like the carpetbaggers intent, at least officially, on importing Northern ideas of modernity and progress. As for the freed slaves, the Black Codes, Jim Crow laws, segregation, continuing disenfranchisement and 'white terror' came close to making a mockery of the very ends for which the war had ostensibly been fought. The issue of race did not for a moment disappear. The South became a benighted, poverty-stricken backwater.

Faulkner's world is haunted by a conviction that his South labours under a 'fatality and curse'.[56] It is chiefly composed of a degenerate elite that frequently pretends to an 'odorous and omnipotent sanctity',[57] but is actually growing steadily weaker, more brittle and febrile with succeeding generations, and even, like the Compson family in *The Sound and the Fury*, more abandoned and insane; recidivist, often whisky-sodden and casually violent white sharecroppers; and ignorant small townspeople infected with a peculiarly virulent, hypocritical and brutal strain of the puritan virus, given to 'meddling' (a favourite Faulknerian word) and, as their preposterous certainty of their own civic virtue boils over, banding together and taking the law into their own hands, as in *Light in August*. There are plenty of blacks in Faulkner's fiction, too, but they seldom occupy the foreground, this mirroring the founding evil of the South, which, politically and culturally, reduced them to spectral presences in a cruelly damaged land.

Given such a configuration, that critics have repeatedly accused Faulkner of 'misanthropy and despair'[58] seems understandable enough. One of his most searing insights into social evil is the element of complicity it involves. Social evil drags everyone in; no one remains immune, not even those who would protest. 'Dammit, say what you want to', as Horace Benbow declares, not without self-awareness, in *Sanctuary*, 'but there's a corruption about even looking on evil, even by accident; you cannot haggle, traffic, with putrefaction' (S, p. 103). This means that the holdout positions are always already emptied from within, that the good people clutch only empty husks. As Benbow himself recognizes when Lee Goodwin, the man he defends from a charge of murder, is not only unjustly found guilty but also subsequently lynched, his objection to Goodwin's pessimism – 'You've got the law, justice, civilization' (S, p. 105) – is not worth beans. All one can hope for is a bitter peace: 'Night is hard on old people', [Benbow] said quietly, holding the receiver. 'Summer nights are hard on them. Something should be done about it. A law' (S, p. 239).

Thus boosterist Northern ideals get short shrift at Faulkner's hands. *Absalom, Absalom!*, for instance, is a savage satire on the American Dream, the fantasy of the land of opportunity and the type of the self-made man transplanted to the South. Born into a poor white family in West Virginia, Thomas Sutpen thrusts, hacks and hews his way to affluence, ownership of a plantation and a mansion and the rank of colonel in the Confederate army. In his wake, he leaves a trail of devastation and abuse of anyone who is touched by his demented personal project, notably women and blacks. '*Given the occasion and the need, this man can and will do anything*' (AA, p. 38): the history of the

Sutpen principle is one of 'outrage' (another favourite Faulknerian word). But Faulkner's most astringent critique of the impact of Northern values on the South comes in the Snopes trilogy (*The Hamlet, The Town, The Mansion*). The Snopes family crawls into the light of Yoknapatawpha County as an unprepossessing gang of sharecroppers, barn-burners and casual vandals. The clan grows steadily, revealing itself to be by turns malevolent, predatory, treacherous, intimidatory and lacking in scruple and sensibility. The dogged persistence and low cunning of the Snopeses have made for a 'long tradition of slow and invincible rapacity'.[59] This is above all the case with Flem Snopes, whose implacable rise is at the centre of the trilogy.

The Snopeses are, in a way, beyond good and evil. They spread and multiply like a cancerous growth, behaving 'like colonies of rats and termites', yet also forming a single organism, moving by 'osmosis' (T, pp. 37, 352). They invade Jefferson 'like an influx of snakes or varmints from the woods' (T, p. 440). But if they are a serious menace, it is because the opposition is so largely comprised 'of little weak puny frightened men' (T, p. 407). The South in its decadence can offer no significant weapons with which to resist them. They get what they want because the local people are passive, inert, stupid and manipulable. But they also 'besmirch' and 'contaminate' those with whom they come into contact (T, p. 380), undermining the gratifying certainty of moral superiority that their fellow townspeople might otherwise be inclined to feel. This process culminates in *The Mansion*, when Gavin Stevens, one of the few resisters, finally declares that 'there aren't any morals' (M, p. 1044) and helps thug, murderer and long-term jailbird Mink Snopes to kill Flem.

As Faulkner presents matters, however, the parasitic growth that is Snopesism is inseparable from the slow but relentless incursion of Northern culture. The Snopeses, chiefly Flem, understand the moribundity of rural Southern culture and see that it is all too openly exposed to a bracing injection of Northern economics. They are obsessed with profit and consumption, consumers themselves who encourage the consumerism nascent in others. So contemptuous is Faulkner of this development that the Snopes family takes on a double function. When Faulkner describes the first car in Jefferson, Mr Buffaloe's 'stinking noisy little home-made self-propelled buggy', as being for Jefferson's youth 'an augury, a promise of the destiny that would belong to the United States' (T, p. 354), he is both having a joke at their expense and lampooning the grandiose Northern myths to which they are becoming subservient. The Snopeses are at once a loathsome *nec plus ultra* of Southern decay and a burlesque *reductio ad absurdum* of the Northern mentality. The names of some of the Snopes children – Wallstreet Panic Snopes, Montgomery Ward Snopes, Watkins Products Snopes – tell the tale. So, too, it is the hapless and incoherent I.O. Snopes who most explicitly parrots the boosterist gospel, squawking phrases like 'Competition is the life of trade' (H, p. 64).

In his Nobel Prize acceptance speech, Faulkner presented himself as the champion of the 'inexhaustible voice' of a humanity capable of 'compassion and sacrifice and endurance', of 'courage and honour and hope and pride'.[60] But he was briefly surrendering to a particular form of moral boosterism, posing 'as a humanist' while actually having written 'as a misanthrope'.[61] In Faulkner's imaginative world, the 'inexhaustible' virtues seem very largely the preserve of a vanished antebellum and wartime past but, since he rarely writes about the past in itself, the virtues remain mythical, the stuff of legend, unreal. In any case, if they manifested themselves at all, it was in a generation Faulkner repeatedly refers to as doomed. Those characters in whom a fainter version of them survives are a flawed if well-intentioned few whose struggles to stave off disaster are all too likely to prove vain. As she contemplates Ruby Lamarr's baby in *Sanctuary*, a Schopenhauerian-sounding Miss Reba gets closer to the mark than the Nobel Prize winner: 'It better not been born at all … None of them had' (S, p. 168). There is 'a *sickness somewhere at the prime foundation*' that no intervention can cure (AA, p. 137). The one virtue that Faulkner stressed in his speech that is also conspicuous in his writings is endurance: '*Endure and then endure, without rhyme or reason or hope of reward – and then endure*' (AA, p. 119). He associates it chiefly with women and blacks.

If there is a major contemporary heir to Twain and Faulkner, it is Cormac McCarthy. McCarthy is conceivably a version of 'the true and living prophet of destruction' Sheriff Bell refers to in *No Country For Old Men*.[62] What Faulkner does for Mississippi, McCarthy has long been doing for the borderlands of Texas, Mexico and New Mexico. From *Blood Meridian*, which addresses the Wild West of the 1840s, to the *Border Trilogy*, which is concerned with an increasingly modern and democratic post-war West, to *No Country for Old Men*, which focuses on an almost contemporary West, to *The Road*, a phantasmagoric, post-Apocalyptic revision of *Huckleberry Finn* set in an America of the future, McCarthy mounts a ferocious assault on a range of America's Enlightenment-rooted, positive understandings of itself, from its founding experiences and principles to its progressive modernity to its Manifest Destiny to its boundless future. What he everywhere reveals in doing so is an underside of immense stupidity, barbarity and desolation.

The archaeological work at the site of the first English settlement in America at Jamestown, Virginia, has recently discovered that the earliest settlers in fact resorted to cannibalism. This was no solitary instance. McCarthy's vision has a starkness of this order: the romance of the colonization of the West concealed a strictly unspeakable history. *Blood Meridian* is rawly determined to see things straight (its author did his research). Like almost no other, it is a blood-soaked book. McCarthy is acutely aware of a historical monstrosity so extreme that the human thing itself becomes monstrous in thought. The protracted revulsion the book engenders is a deliberate effect, and is a token of McCarthy's revulsion both from American history and the determined evasion of it: '*The stories get passed on and the truth gets passed over. As the saying goes. Which I reckon some would take as meaning that the truth cant compete*' (NC, p. 285).

Misanthropy is an ungainsayable consequence of McCarthy's mode of historical analysis. Monstrosity is what survives in *Blood Meridian*: the most monstrous of all its figures, Judge Holden, is its last man standing, as an injured Chigurh is still thriving at the end of *No Country for Old Men*, bleeding but not killed, an obstinately durable lump of motiveless malignity. McCarthy's brooding imagination makes both Chigurh and Judge Holden seem larger than themselves, embodiments of some evil beyond the pale that is in fact more profoundly American than what opposes it, but also more than just American, too. The two central figures in *The Border Trilogy*, John Grady Cole and Billy Parham, seek to traverse and even emerge on some other side of the inhumanity of man. But there is no 'other side', only, as Billy learns, 'an enormous emptiness without echo'.[63] Ultimately, there is nowhere to go beyond Judge Holden and Chigurh, or (in *All The Pretty Horses*) Alfonsa's radically un-American historical pessimism:

There is no one to tell us what might have been. We weep over the might have been, but there is no might have been. There never was. It is supposed to be true that those who do not know history are condemned to repeat it. I don't believe knowing can save us. What is constant in history is greed and foolishness and a love of blood.[64]

Thus, convinced as McCarthy is that his band of murderous filibusters in *Blood Meridian* are 'itinerant degenerates bleeding westward like some heliotropic plague', carrying 'war of a madman's making onto a foreign land'[65] – the real madman, in the first instance, was the execrable William Walker – native Americans and Mexicans fare no better at his hands; which brings us back to Auden, and the perpetrators of evil passing it on like a plague to their victims. In McCarthy's terms, colonial depravity is beyond all moralisms, but what equally appals him is the insistent will to draw a veil over it, and the advantage that always grants the monsters, for 'the wicked know that if the ill they do be of sufficient horror men will not speak against it' (TC, p. 604). Even more chillingly, McCarthy appears to fear that human beings 'have made of the world a lie every word'.[66] He has little to offer to allay such fears, save his own intransigent resolve to keep on staring the Gorgon in the face.

McCarthy brings us up as far as the contemporary scene, the subject of my final chapter. There we shall come upon John Gray. Gray argues that America is the last great Enlightenment nation left on earth. If so, McCarthy seeks to engineer its collapse as such: a collapse, that is, into anti-Enlightenment misanthropy. If America has sustained certain Enlightenment faiths, and therefore repeatedly affirmed itself as an outstanding example of the truth of progress, from slavery to Vietnam to G. W. Bush and Donald Trump, the evidence of this has hardly been conclusive, clear or unequivocal. Hence, again and again, boosterism comes into play, because it pastes great swathes of positivity over the insufficiency of the evidence. American misanthropy functions as a rejection of a current but conventional and fraudulent rhetoric whose main purpose is to conceal the traces of a wholesale flight from reality. It appears thus particularly in literature and art.

American misanthropy tends to reverse terms, to insist on a bedrock of negativity beneath positive appearances, implying that the grim truth goes overlooked and unexpressed, chiefly because America has no investment in acknowledging it. 'Ah, happiness courts the light', as a sadder and wiser narrator says at the end of 'Bartleby', 'so we deem the world is gay; but misery hides aloof, so we deem that misery there is none' (BA, p. 40). Two centuries earlier, Hooker had referred his congregation to Ecclesiastes 7.4: 'The heart of the wise is in the house of mourning; but the heart of fools is in the house of mirth'.[67] Redburn takes the case further: we will make no moral progress unless we learn the truth 'that one grief outweighs ten thousand joys' (R, p. 383). Amidst the heedless parade of the world about its pleasures, it is misery alone that counts. The willingness to risk a sobering knowledge of the pervasiveness and profundity of misery and its causes – where those who 'court the light' will always set them at naught and prefer another tale – is integral to the logic of American misanthropy. But we might finally also ponder the split between a line of thought, running from eighteenth-century rationalists to contemporary managerialists, technocrats, cognitivists and social democrats, that tells us that mankind can be clear about itself and even its destiny and control both for the good, and another line that runs from Christ through the great theologians to psychoanalysis, Michel Foucault and Slavov Žižek, that, in Christ's words on Calvary, says of human beings that 'they know not what they do' (Lk. 23.34). The first is presently fashionable, the second inconveniently, repeatedly and disastrously borne out by history. If the implications of climate change are to be believed, the future may also confirm it (and with it the misanthropic case, or so some might think). Contemporary culture has wagered massively on a conviction that ancient conceptions of historical logic, as in Galatians 6.7 – 'Be not deceived; God is not mocked: for whatsoever [a] man soweth, that shall he also reap' – are just fuddy-duddy, old-guy stuff, and clearly past their sell-by date. As we shall see, however, like McCarthy, not all our contemporaries are quite convinced.

CONCLUSION: CONTEMPORARY CULTURE AND THE END(S) OF MISANTHROPY

To recapitulate, by way of summing up: at least three conditions of the misanthropic vision seem crucial: a failure or absence of democracy; hatred of, or at least disaffection from, the body; and a lack of historical consciousness. By this token, contemporary Western culture ought logically to have surmounted misanthropy and made it a thing of the past. First, ours are societies that, broadly speaking, pride themselves on representing a gain for democracy. The evils of the France of the *Ancien Régime*, or so conventional wisdom might have it, are imaginable only on the edges of the West of today, those border zones of Western culture in which democratic values have yet fully to establish themselves. Secondly, in the West, at least, we get the *soma*. We understand and are relaxed about pleasure, about the principle of everyone taking their pleasure and as much pleasure as possible, as never before. This would most obviously be the case with sexual pleasure. Within such a regime, Swiftian physical disgust seems pathological, an extraordinary aberration, if (one hopes) curable. Thirdly, ours is a historically conscious age, increasingly aware of the determining force of historical circumstance. It is no longer nature that we cannot think beyond, as in Hobbes, but historicity, as in Richard Rorty. Nature is precisely what we cannot know and remains beyond our compass. The grandiose generalities of misanthropy are unavailable to anyone thinking properly within the horizons of contemporary intellectual modesty. All in all, misanthropy should surely be defunct.

There is a great deal around us that would seem to testify to the death of misanthropy. One would be hard pressed, to say the least, to find much explicit trace of it in the dominant culture, the boosterist world of political discourse, business and finance, corporate management, advertising companies – though they may all be working from misanthropic premises, like Richelieu – and government service, think tanks, the press, the media, museum and gallery culture, even, increasingly, the academy and contemporary arts. It is not clear, however, that, elsewhere in the culture, misanthropy is dead at all. The opposite appears to be true: at other levels, or in subcultures, like malaria, now threatening a major resurgence, misanthropy is flourishing, diversifying and assuming new forms. Hence, to take just a couple of initial examples almost at random, this time from the Nordic countries, the Schopenhauerian misanthropic tradition persists in the work of Norwegians Hermann Tonnessen and Peter Wessel Zapffe, and continuing interest in it since their deaths, and the films of Lars von Trier preserve the misanthropic tradition in Scandinavian cinema represented by some of Ingmar Bergman's work.

I shall focus principally on three types of contemporary misanthropy, though they are certainly not the only ones (the terms are mine). First, the dark radicalisms: these tend to come out of the tradition of 'radical philosophy', defining themselves against its other contemporary mutations, abstracted and remote from any practical efficacy as they seem (the scattered, twenty-first century, [extremely] late Marxisms, Simon Critchley's rigorous love, or faith of the faithless).[1] Secondly, the post-liberalisms or post-progressivisms: these are academic more often than not, and emerge out of a bleak, melancholic, disbelieving if sporadic implosion of contemporary liberal faiths. The disbelief is understandable from a number of different points of view, but one would be the extent to which, as Howard Hotson has brilliantly shown, progressivism has by now become the official ideology, for example, of vast, impersonal outfits like that 'global consortium of large transnational corporations', the World Economic Forum, with its 'commit[ment] to improving the state of the world'.[2] The third type, popular misanthropies, is by far the most fascinating and significant, and I shall spend the most time on them. Contemporary culture abounds in assertions of indifference to humanity, declarations of humanity's categorical inadequacy and expressions of a desire to see it come to an end or be superseded by other life forms. They may not always quite fit with the standard definition of misanthropy. But if they are not exactly an expression of a rooted hatred of human beings, and are therefore not misanthropies in a classical sense, they also grant little or no value to humanity in either its past or its present forms, and here coincide with misanthropic tradition.

By 'dark radicalisms' I mean what Steve Fuller calls 'dark ecology', which he thinks of as the 'higher misanthropy'. 'Dark ecological' thought abandons 'our need to identify with the human altogether'. It promotes the assumption that 'that there may be something fundamentally unreliable about being human'.[3] Thus, for example, in *The Dark Enlightenment*, philosopher Nick Land argues that the very advances in science, medicine and technology that have so clearly improved people's lives over the past two centuries and more have also led to a heedless and ever more ravenous consumption of the world's resources and, unsurprisingly, to new forms of political conflict and international warfare. According to Land, democracy itself exhibits a 'relentless trend to degeneration', not least in that, 'essentially tragic ... it provides the populace with a weapon to destroy itself, one that is always eagerly seized, and used'. In fact, 'Every major threshold of socio-political "progress" has ratcheted Western civilization towards comprehensive ruin'. Land unnervingly suggests that we should welcome and hasten this process, for it is the moment of utter calamity that will finally allow humanity to get beyond itself, in a self-transcendence by now imperative. In other words (a startling thesis), 'Emancipation requires the programmatic destruction of independence'.[4]

Elsewhere, too, certain strains in contemporary philosophy have pushed it closer to an incipient misanthropy than it has been, perhaps, at any time since Schopenhauer. Fuller particularly remarks on the currency of 'object-oriented philosophy', notably in the work of Graham Harman. Harman calls for an end to modern thought. For even in the case of the so-called 'linguistic turn', it leaves humans 'in absolute command at the centre of philosophy'. We should focus instead on 'inanimate reality', the infinitely diverse and various forms of objects and their transformations.[5] The human subject no longer serves a useful function as a priority for thought, and must be evacuated from it. Compare the other philosophers who, along with Harman, were briefly known as the speculative realists: Quentin Meillassoux, Ray Brassier and Iain Hamilton Grant all urge us to think beyond the human parenthesis. They require that we think a different time, a time beyond both the scope and the historical experience of the human world, a time indifferent to it. This is the time that modern science has increasingly borne in on us, a 'cosmological time' within which 'anthropomorphic time' is 'nested'.[6] Meillassoux calls it 'ancestral time'.[7] It exists beyond the human world as and in objects, not least 'arche-fossils', materials that bear the traces of 'phenomena anterior even to the emergence of life ... such as the starlight whose luminescence provides an index of the age of distant stars'.[8] The timescales and historical transformations involved are beyond 'the phenomenological capacity not only of individuals, but also of any and all species'.[9] Nature does not descend to the systemic level of any one of its products, whether human or other.

Thus humanity does not serve as a limit or defining point for anything in nature. The reverse is rather the case: nature – one fears that this might be self-evident – will extinguish humanity as it has stars, and equally produce wholly new species. Speculative realists insist that the question is what thought, logic can make of our knowledge of nature's 'other temporality', a time anterior and posterior to and outside *the possibility of* [human] *experience*'.[10] Bracketed within the vast expanses of objectively existent, non-human time, the human intellect and its creations are nothing. The philosophers think this soberly and without pathos. Brassier in particular appears not only to write off anthropocentric thought, but to be in effect indifferent even to a degree zero of the human thing. Philosophically, it merits no regard.

*

The 'dark radicals' are patently at odds with contemporary boosters. They have equally no investment in present-day liberal ideas. But postmodern liberals are themselves haunted by their own misgivings. Take queer theory, for example: it might seem by now to have founded a practically exemplary postmodern ethics, one easily reconcilable with law, government and the accepted way of doing things (gay vicars, gay marriages). Yet it has also been exhibiting a strain of misanthropy, notably in the work of Judith Halberstam and above all Lee Edelman. This attitude is born of the conviction that, contrary to many contemporary persuasions, queer desire and experience do not fit into conventional moulds at all, and repeatedly leave gays and lesbians unhappily beleaguered and at odds with a hostile world. In Halberstam's (rather cumbersome) terms, such thinkers continue to assert queerness 'as a mode of critique rather than as a new investment in normativity *or life* or respectability or wholeness or legitimacy' (my italics).[11] This amounts in effect to turning one's back on the community – like a good misanthropist.

Halberstam takes fierce issue with what, in an excellent phrase, she calls the 'toxic positivity of contemporary life' (QA, p. 3), a culture with a tone and indeed a rhetoric audible everywhere around us. Toxic positivity is a 'mass delusion' that lazily colludes with capital and 'normativity' together (QA, pp. 2–3). It imposes emptily selective but overweening 'logics of success' (QA, p. 19). Against them all, like Beckett, a key figure for her, Halberstam values failure and stupidity, losers, oddballs, eccentrics, wayward minds. The structure here is that of classical misanthropy, but with a peculiar, contemporary twist, a kind of exceptionalist thought in the negative. This might not seem to make Halberstam an example of misanthropy, and indeed she does tend to slip into another form of toxic positivity herself, that of 'the subversive intellectual' (QA, p. 19). However, she also dwells on what she readily admits are 'wholly improbable fantasies' of alternatives to where we are now (QA, p. 21). These alternatives inhabit the murky waters of a dark, counter-intuitive realm of 'critique and refusal' (QA, p. 2). They are inseparable from a work of negation. Thus Halberstam ransacks 'the archive of anti-social feminism', and scours 'the bleak and angry territories of the anti-social turn' (QA, p. 110). She writes about gay and lesbian novelists and artists who commit themselves to queer negativity, and feminist subjects who refuse to cohere, speak, even 'quite simply to be', where being has already been defined for them (QA, pp. 126, 140). She sinks into the archive of abjection, 'the brutality and narrow-mindedness of the human', notably in the case of Nazi homosexuality, and art that refuses to forget it. This art finally 'lets no one off the hook' ('The killer in you is the killer in me', QA, pp. 171, 182). One of her select group of *eminences grises* is Renton in Irving Welch's *Trainspotting*: 'Choose life. Well, ah choose not tae choose life. If the cunts cannae handle that, it's thair fuckin problem'.[12]

Edelman is still more extreme. He stakes his claim 'to the very space that "politics" makes unthinkable', right outside what we take to be the human domain, 'the place of the social order's death drive'.[13] Of course, liberals strive to dissociate gays and lesbians from this place. But gays should accept and even embrace it, as a negativity 'opposed to every form of social viability' (NF, p. 9). For the normative order cannot underwrite any good, predetermined as it is against homosexuals from the start. Homosexuality is irreducibly linked to the aberrant or atypical, to the *isolato* who wanders outside the human norm and fails to fit with normative conceptions of human being. In particular, in *No Future*, Edelman argues that we should abandon what he sees as the ubiquitous politics of 'reproductive futurism' as an 'organizing principle of communal relations' (NF, p. 2). Our culture endlessly commits itself to an endlessly future-oriented thought in the figure of human reproduction and above all the child. (Here Edelman sounds just a little like St Augustine). It thinks of the child as the germ of a future and an image of progress that must be nurtured and protected and to which the present must be endlessly sacrificed. Thus the child 'has come to embody for us the *telos* of the social order and come to be seen as the one for whom that order is held in perpetual trust' (NF, p. 11). This, we assume, is human life itself.

But such thinking ensures, seemingly *in perpetuo*, the dominance of heterosexual norms and anthropocentric humanism together. Properly self-identified gays and lesbians alone remain outside this syndrome, but as disquieting representations of an alien irony and negativity, of the death drive, like Shakespeare's great melancholics and misanthropists, haunting the edges of the scene, a question posed to the human project itself. So, too, the queer misanthropist is pro-abortion, not because she or he is pro-choice, but because he or she is genuinely opposed to reproduction, against life. Hence Edelman sides with two great fictional Victorian misanthropists, Dickens's Scrooge (in *A Christmas Carol*) and George Eliot's Silas Marner (in the novel of that name). With his 'stingy, reclusive, anticommunitarian ways' (NF, p. 42), says Edelman, 'disengaged from every form of human fellowship and every act of social intercourse' and well-nigh rebuffing 'the very warm-bloodedness of mammalian vitality' itself, Scrooge is actually a 'futuricide', in that he 'refuses the social imperative to grasp futurity in the form of the Child' (NF, pp. 45–6, 49). Silas Marner, that 'solitary, miserly, misanthropic man' who sets at naught 'the interconnections of which the social fabric is woven', turns his back 'on humankind' (NF, pp. 54–5) and refuses human life. Those homosexuals who have grasped what has set them so singularly beyond the pale will likewise refuse to conspire in humanity's inexorable delusion of its progress.

Queer misanthropy seriously challenges any assumption that contemporary Western culture is going anywhere or is the product of a history that has been doing so. In Edelman above all it reaches a point of extreme scepticism about our present world as a pre-eminent or at least laudable achievement. In one sense, we might say the same about contemporary post-humanists. But the post-humanists also conjure up a historical break with what they take to be the human past, drawing a line under humanity and heralding an era in which it surpasses itself, or fades from the scene. They fall into three main camps: techno-prophets, catastrophists and critical post-humanists.[14] The third group is the least relevant of the three, because it tends to occupy a moderate, rational, cautious middle ground. The other two groups are opposed, but also oddly united.

The techno-prophets include 'transhumanists' like Marvin Minsky, Hans Moravec and Ray Kurzweil, who believe that science and technology, particularly information, cognitive, bio- and nano-technologies, are by now showing that they have the power to transform human beings and make their old, recidivist forms redundant and forgettable.[15] Not surprisingly, perhaps, transhumanists tend to base themselves in California. Note for example the 'extropians', who had their own institute for a while before it wound itself up, distantly recalling Hawthorne's *A Blithedale Romance*. Extropians lay particular emphasis on the human capacity for self-shaping through scientific and technical revolution – 'artificial intelligence, nano-technology, genetic engineering, life extension, mind uploading, idea futures, robotics, space exploration, memetics'[16] – as a grand reversal of the corrosive work of entropy, that key concept of recent but bleaker and more unstable years; hence their name. They even celebrate the possibility (as they take it to be) of human beings achieving immortality. Humanity can proceed to ever greater things, but only by leaving itself behind (though to judge by extropian writings, this may not improve its prose style). At all events, transhumanists and extropians alike jubilantly announce the 'end of man'.

By contrast, catastrophists like Jean-Pierre Dupuy and Francis Fukuyama (in *Our Posthuman Future*) preach the imminent likelihood of science and technology exceeding the human capacity to control them – and thereby, for many if not all catastrophists, the imminence of meltdown, apocalypse, annihilation.[17] They are the 'Cassandras of future shock', shivering with apprehension at each announcement of a new development in cloning, prostheses, genetically modified foods, androids, cyborgs, nano-materials, micro-fabrication and so on.[18] The case of the catastrophists has become increasingly hectic, not least as the list of their techno-scientific anxieties has steadily increased. For the catastrophists, the logic of the 'anthropocene' era – the period, now defined by geologists and palaeontologists as beginning more or less with the Industrial Revolution, in which humans have been the dominant influence on climate, environment, the world at large – more and more obviously presages disaster.

Techno-prophets and catastrophists, however, agree in at least one single respect: human beings as constituted up till now are comprehensively inadequate to their world. The two groups merely draw different consequences from that assumption. The catastrophists suppose that the work of humanity is pointing towards an apocalyptic conclusion, while the techno-prophets tend to exhibit the presumption of the scientist who knows what humanity wants and should be better than humanity itself. Neither group has any belief in ordinary human beings. But there are different ways of thinking about the meaning of the modern apocalypse, different ways of understanding its historical logic. In feminist accounts of it, the history of horror coincides with the history of patriarchy and the coercive grip of heterosexual norms. It is not surprising, then – and here again a form of misanthropy actually seems to spring from a contemporary progressivism – that the most interesting and best-known post-humanists have been women. Like the techno-prophets, Donna Haraway, Rosi Braidotti and N. Katherine Hayles have all given a new and unusually cheerful twist to misanthropy, turning it into a positive value. The title of Haraway's famous 'Cyborg Manifesto' partly tells the tale. For such women, the hope for the future lies in what Braidotti calls 'human enhancement', which for her means escaping the anthropocentric perspective and recognizing the kinship of human being with the 'auto-poietic' forces of an 'intelligent and self-organizing' living matter.[19] This is her 'vision of posthuman humanity for the global era'.[20] Hayles asserts that such a thought 'does not really mean the end of humanity. It signals instead the end of a certain conception of the human'.[21] Haraway reads the process of our increasing 'cyborgization' as a similar 'signal'. Nonetheless, in effect, all three women are radically rethinking the very meaning of misanthropy. After all, Haraway sees the 'genetically engineered lab critter' OncoMouse as her 'sister', and exclaims that 'the machines are so alive; whereas the humans are so inert!'.[22]

Daniel Cottom is an even more representative figure, because he links post-humanism and misanthropy very explicitly indeed. Cottom argues for a benevolent or 'strategic' misanthropy that, because it cares for what human beings might become, fiercely opposes their present *hubris*. 'The trope of misanthropy is the hope of society', he says.[23] Misanthropy is a manifestation of the unhuman in the human, and means turning away from mankind in order to fulfil one's humanity.[24] In effect, Cottom's is a singular, misanthropic version of the Benjaminian belief that we have yet to escape our prehistory – except that being human is the very condition of our prehistory. For Cottom, philosophy, literature, photography, art and sculpture are best equipped to instruct us. He incorporates and fuses the kinds of misanthropy implicit in the work of the queer pessimists, post-humanists, techno-prophets, catastrophists and techno-feminists and articulates them together, but in an aesthetics. Certain kinds of art and thought 'expose the fallacy that continuity is founded on communication'.[25] It is in art and philosophy that we glimpse the possibility of not belonging to humanity at all.

But possibly the most influential source of contemporary misanthropy – and here, since we are dealing with an apprehension about and an ensuing mistrust of ourselves that is increasingly widely shared, we start to edge our way out of the corridors of the academy – is ecology. This is particularly true of 'deep ecology', ecology in its most philosophical form. From Arne Naess onwards, so-called 'deep ecology' has been particularly inclined to eco-misanthropy. The distinguished James E. Lovelock, whose influential Gaia theory was crucial to deep ecology, suggests that by the end of the twentieth century, it seemed clear that humans were 'almost a planetary disease organism'.[26] Others have coincided or followed suit. In 2006, to give just one example, University of Texas biologist Eric Pianka, whom the Texas Academy of Science made Distinguished Texas Scientist of the Year and to whom it gave a standing ovation, described what he merely took to be a biologically likely scenario, if one encouraging no faith in human powers of rational management.[27] Human beings had proliferated (in ecological terms) dysfunctionally, like bacteria or viruses. They would continue to do so unless they somehow transcended their own witless drives, and would ultimately enjoy the fate of any flourishing microbe, which is sooner or later to reach its natural limits and be displaced by another.

It is not hard to multiply instances of eco-misanthropy, if, like that of the techno-prophets and post-humanists, it seems often to be a misanthropy of a rather new kind. Eco-critic Greg Garrard is quite rightly wary of what he calls 'disanthropy', the dream of a world finally and comprehensively rid of people. He suggests that, by now, ecological misanthropy is in large part a myth circulating in the right-wing blogosphere.[28] The misanthropic tendency was notably evident in early forms of ecology, like a budding 'Earth First!', with its 'epidemiological metaphors', its talk of the 'human pox'.[29] Certainly, some more recent developments in ecology have not seemed remotely misanthropic. Environmental sociology, for example, has been producing very different models of the relationship between nature and human culture. One can hear advanced sociologists attempting to reconcile ecology with so-called 'business ethics' and management practices, not least through the concept of 'environmental services', which urges us to pay more attention to how we may best tend the services nature offers us (as our subordinate, because we have bigger brains than anything else in it). Yet the distrust of the human vector also remains, in a misanthropy that has perhaps become more dispassionate. After all, as he exclaimed himself, Pianka was not exactly a hater of humanity, and never wanted the world purged of it.

In any case, if one cared to derive from Garrard a model merely opposing sunny managerialists and eco-progressives to scowling, benighted, retrograde eco-Timons, it would be radically insufficient. Eco-misanthropy has migrated a long way beyond the confines of ecology itself, and crops up in a wide range of discourses. Like others, Land appears to imagine the 'comprehensive ruin' ahead of us chiefly in terms of eco-apocalypse. Cottom argues that more misanthropy might actually be good for the environment. But here a particularly intriguing example is English economist and political theorist John Gray, by no means a kooky radical. Gray foresees 'an increasing devastation of the planet'. This effectively inclines him both to a kind of eco-theory in the negative – humanity is an 'exceptionally destructive species' that cannot check its own sprawling, insane, virus-like spread – and to a vision of an imminent 'era of solitude' when human beings will have so far destroyed other species and their natural habitats that they will be able to look forward to a life, not in a richly variegated world, but one in which they are the sole survivors.[30] He is not alone. Indeed, a contemporary misanthropist might feel that, since the 'anthropocene' era is one in which human activity starts to afflict the very mineral stuff of the world, it also ushers in the final prospect of Planet Earth manifesting itself as human, that is, rotten, to the core. What price any of our theologies or metaphysics, our misanthropist might ask, if that assumption is conceivably right? In general, from the vast devastation of the rainforests to the melting of the icecaps, from the changes in weather patterns worldwide to the indifferent destruction of homelands, ways of life, lives themselves, from the imminence of major species loss to the vast ruination of natural beauty, for all the official propaganda, to many, economic activity as presently constituted, and that great contemporary fetish, 'growth', do not appear to be a self-evident good. The bleak conundrum, however, is that the evidence suggests that its momentum is also irresistible, not least because of the steady increase in the world's population. The juggernaut must roll on. As Sheriff Bell says in *No Country For Old Men*, '*I know as certain as death that there aint nothing short of the second coming of Christ that can slow this train*' (NC, p. 159).

*

Here we arrive at popular misanthropy. Like McCarthy, Gray provides a particularly intriguing if an inflected example of it, if one that, strictly, is popularizing rather than popular. Gray is an original and perhaps almost uniquely English-sceptical proponent of the concept of the end of the Enlightenment, notably in *Enlightenment's Wake*. The grand narratives that emerged from the Enlightenment are at an end. Unusually, and starkly, Gray takes this concept all the way down: the death of the Enlightenment project spells the end of any belief in universals to come, whether 'grounded in a generic humanity' or a 'rational morality' or both,[31] and thus of any orientation of thought towards a moral *telos*. This disbelief holds good, not just for the grand narratives that were already disintegrating some decades ago – Hegelian, Marxist, emancipatory, humanist – but for those that have sought to replace them, notably the narratives of liberal democracy and the consciousness-raising narratives of an 'Anglo-American academic class', which for Gray is doomed to inwardness and political marginality (EW, p. 3).

This might seem to indicate a political and cultural position associated with the contemporary right. But in *False Dawn* in particular, Gray in fact turns out to be an excoriating critic of free-market ideology, neo-liberals, the supposed worldwide diffusion of the American way of life and the very concept of globalization – above all, globalization understood as the victory of a single economic principle. Globalization is not happening: witness the Asian economies. Concepts of the universal spread of free-market economics remain 'fatefully entwined' with the Enlightenment project; indeed, they are the chief and most plausible means by which the Enlightenment project has renewed and perpetuated itself. This is unsurprising, since the United States, chief source and home of neo-liberals, is in fact 'the world's last great Enlightenment regime'.[32] Thus Gray ends up as a fierce critic of almost all the extant forms of liberalism: classical, economic, Rawlsian and postmodern. For all of them discover or at least hope for a possibility of peaceful coexistence or commensurability between values where, in truth, there must always be conflict.

Such intransigent scepticism might seem to leave him with nothing to rescue from the ruins. But there is one form of liberal thought that he continued to defend. This thought – the liberal thought of *modus vivendi*, or 'agonistic liberalism' – stems from Isaiah Berlin, more distantly, from John Stuart Mill and, more distantly still, significantly, from Hobbes. It rejects the possibility of any 'universal principles' and is therefore opposed to the prevailing 'liberal ideal of toleration', which itself implies them.[33] The incommensurability of different value-systems does not point in the direction of an easy-going cultural relativism, but rather of 'value pluralism', a different matter (TF, p. 6). No 'universal toleration' underpins plural values, since values will always be at war. There is no way of ensuring that tragedy and disaster can be excluded from human affairs, and no way of putting an end to them in the future. All we can aspire to is the management of plural values through negotiation, in a state of constant alertness to the possible reappearance of conflict.

Agonistic liberals and value-pluralists imply the need for a modest, wary, limited faith, and for vigilance and patient endeavour, since the wrong decisions may easily be made, negotiations may go astray and havoc resume. The labour of reaching agreement and of circumventing conflict is a demanding if not a consuming one. The mechanisms required may be awesomely complex. Over the past decade, Gray has lost faith in them. Agonistic liberals and value-pluralists have increasingly receded from his later work. In *Straw Dogs*, *Heresies* and *The Silence of Animals* he has grown sombrely prophetic and distinctly misanthropic at once. The future will not be able to keep mayhem at bay, and this raises the most searching questions for the human trajectory itself. The twenty-first century threatens us with problems for the resolution of which no adequate structures have been conceived or are conceivable. Various factors are at stake here, but the root of the difficulty, again, is the cumulative overcrowding of the planet. This menaces us with the near-certainty of resource or scarcity wars, and the persistence of widespread political failure and disorder. (We are currently seeing this in the Middle East). Even now, says Gray, most of 'the sovereign states of the world' are inherently 'unstable' (SD, p. 13). Overcrowding also confirms the truth of eco-misanthropy and anticipates the 'era of solitude' to come. New technologies will not help: they are bound to spawn new 'ferocious crimes' (ibid.). No putatively universal or international structures can possibly be adequate to deal with this predicament. 'Controls cannot be enforced' (SD, p. 12); or rather, insofar as they can be, it will be only on the basis of gross and brutal imbalances of wealth and power, radical and founding injustices which will perpetuate violent domination on the one hand and violent retaliation on the other – in other words, a regression to general turmoil. There is nothing in our humanisms that can counter all this. Humanism is by now 'the creed of conventional people' (SD, p. 37). It underpins both our progressive thinking and our more or less surreptitious persistence with Enlightenment ideals. But, says Gray, as Schopenhauer understood, the separation of man from his world on which it depends is baseless. 'Like other animals, we are embodiments of universal Will, the struggling, suffering energy that animates everything in the world' (SD, p. 41). Since we are a peculiarly successful embodiment of the Will, this ensures both the destruction of the planet and what will be our final inability to do anything serious about it. For we neither understand nor retain control of our actions.

Here the full significance of Gray's misanthropic turn becomes clear. It has been ever more inseparable from a popular appeal. Gray shrewdly anticipated the populist turn in government policy in British higher education, but quickly started to give it a misanthropic complexion, as though assuming that not only a certain kind of style of thinking and writing but also misanthropy itself were likely to find a considerable public. The same would seem true of the controversial novelist Michel Houellebecq. Houellebecq is *par excellence* the postmodern Diogenes. In *The Map and the Territory*, the novel in which he turns himself into a character, he refers to his 'strong misanthropic tendencies', announcing that 'I feel only a faint sense of solidarity with the human species'.[34] Houellebecq has identified 'maintaining a certain critical distance with regard to humanity' as intrinsic to his project. He is mainly concerned, he writes, to ask 'whether humanity is an experiment worth pursuing'.[35] He has increasingly developed an excoriating critical perspective on the cultural domains attached to what, following Joe Brooker and Finn Fordham,[36] we might start calling total capital, 'advanced capitalism' sounding as oxymoronic as 'darkness visible', and 'late capitalism' by now looking like what in fact it has long been, a pitifully obsolete piece of wishful thinking (unless we believe in the imminence of the eco-apocalypse). Houellebecq writes of capital as going 'in step and hand in hand ... with mercantilism, publicity, the absurd and sneering cult of economic efficiency'. He takes 'the exclusive and immoderate appetite for material riches' to have spread from the domain of economics to other domains, above all, that of sexuality, eradicating 'every sentimental fiction' and increasingly measuring human value solely in terms of 'economic efficiency and sexual potential'.[37] This is Houellebecq's total capital, his 'extension of the domain of struggle' (the original French title of his first novel).

Thus contemporary adulthood '*is* [nothing but] hell' – for what, predominantly, does it have to offer? 'The reality principle, the pleasure principle, competitiveness, permanent challenges, sex and status – hardly reasons to rejoice' (HPL, p. 31). Houellebecq matches this vision of hell with an insistent evocation of the anomic urban and metropolitan cityscapes that, for him, are a concrete embodiment of the whole ethos of the contemporary scene. One crucial problem with total capital, for Houellebecq, is that it cannot begin to see itself straight. It cannot afford to recognize the endless dreariness, the boundless mediocrity, the innumerable miseries it generates, cannot begin to bring them to light nor suffer them being brought there. After all, in Theodor Adorno's well-known words, 'It is part of the mechanism of domination to forbid recognition of the suffering it produces'.[38] This is precisely where the novelist intervenes. The business of the novelist, as Houellebecq most persistently articulates it, is recording, observation, 'the most precise, the most broad description', without any attempt to go behind description and 'assemble the machine' (PE, p. 140). Here one might object: do recording and description, however broad, not always mean choices? But as Houellebecq understands matters, the novelist's choice is to record and describe that which total capital refuses to acknowledge as intrinsic to its operations. He or she works to ensure that the triumph of total capital is less than total in at least one respect, in that the novelist resists any of the totalizing mythologies by which total capital seeks to justify, sustain and obscure itself.

Houellebecq's major debts are to three French traditions: the positivists, especially Comte; the moralists of the Ancien Régime, whom he repeatedly cites, especially the misanthropic ones; and French sociology. In this context, we should note that he published his first novel in 1994, just a year after one of the major books of the nineties appeared, Pierre Bourdieu's *La Misère du Monde*, *The Misery of the World*. Bourdieu sought to turn economic neo-liberal thinking inside out, unfashionably telling a mass of real-life stories of what, in his phrase, the 'extraordinary and almost unbearable violence' of neo-liberalism was actually generating,[39] its vast and ceaseless production of social suffering. Houellebecq's misanthropic project might be thought of as picking up on Bourdieu's and transplanting it precisely to the domains into which there has been an extension of the struggle, thereby accomplishing the novelist's business, but at the same time stripping the sociological project of any and all of the political convictions that were still Bourdieu's in 1993, whatever the circumspection with which he was by then expressing them.

By transplantation of the project, I mean that Bourdieu is principally concerned with a social suffering clearly described as economically determined. Third-generation metalworkers find themselves brusquely left on the scrap heap and shut out of society. On the promise of returning to their villages as full post-persons, young women leave the countryside for Paris and sort letters on the night shift, only to find that they are indefinitely condemned to it. By contrast, Houellebecq refuses the terms of the sociologist's class analysis. More than anything else, perhaps his most obvious social concern is with the clerkly class, office workers; except that the office workers are now modestly affluent, technologically proficient, often loosely associated with 'creativity' (a word that has become deeply depressing), and take their holidays in Thailand. Here, Houellebecq in effect retorts to Bourdieu, in this huge class too, there has been an extension of the domain of struggle, and with it an extension of social misery, a production of new forms of psychic emptiness and social affliction. It is the novelist's task to document them, to bring them to the surface. If these new fields of social misery have emerged for the novelist's attention, however, in Houellebecq's terms, that is precisely because there has been, again, an extension of the domain of struggle, because it has reached spheres of life that had seemed quite separate from the sphere of economic activity and a defence against it. One might support both Bourdieu's project and Houellebecq's revision of it with the Benjamin-based case for misanthropy in Chapter 4, though of the three of them (including Benjamin), it is only Houellebecq who looks misanthropic.

Houellebecq's real subject is the radical and constitutive inadequacy of life under total capital, an inadequacy that grows ever more ubiquitous and hopeless. Lives become fearfully insubstantial. 'I've lived so little that I tend to imagine I'm not going to die', says the narrator of *Whatever*, 'it seems improbable that human existence can be reduced to so little'.[40] 'They really don't amount to much, anyway, human relationships', says Jed Martin, ruefully, in *The Map and the Territory* (MT, p. 9). It is one of Houellebecq's more misanthropic refrains, and a view of the world that he amply confirms in Martin's life-story. Here the vexed subject of Houellebecq's treatment of sexuality becomes key; but what is startling about Houellebecq is that there is little of the physical disgust for sexuality or bodies in themselves that one finds so often within the misanthropic tradition, as for example in the work of H. P. Lovecraft, a writer whom Houellebecq admires and on whom he has written. The fullness and abundance of sexual description in *Platform*, for example, might have almost been expressly designed to counter any such accusation. Nor is the point that Houellebecq's is a loveless world; one can quickly refute this. Nor is the relevant assertion that Houellebecq hates women. He doesn't: there is no loathing in his fiction, unlike, say, Swift's work, of women's organic being *per se*. It is not hard to cite passages where Houellebecq's thought about women appears to be not only affirmative, but aware of the fact that women have to struggle with a world – that of total capital – the major determinants of which have been and continue to be principally masculine.

The accusations of misogyny levelled at Houellebecq, then, are untenable, and in fact disguise another disquiet. For Houellebecq – and here he resembles Lacan, but also in some measure the women writers in Chapter 5 – refuses to convert any identification with the position of women into progressive thought. What his critics cannot abide in him is the virulent and intransigent anti-progressivism of the misanthropist. Houellebecq writes that 'the idea of progress has come to be an indisputable and almost unconscious credo' (PE, p. 115). Indeed, he reserves some of his most satirical passages for a peculiarly lightweight progressive chatter that by now is quite pervasive, and merely a matter of empty self-persuasion. 'It doesn't take long for a thinker on information technology to be transformed into a thinker on social evolution', he notes, sardonically, and of course 'his discourse will often be brilliant' (W, p. 44). We need only the promise of a dinner '*with intimate friends in their kitchens created by* Daniel Hechter *or* Primrose Bordier' to end up busily planning '*to remake the world*' (W, p. 124). Houllebecq counters this kind of progressivism degree zero with a distinctive mode of historicism, distinctive in that it doesn't produce or rely on a story. On the one hand, there is always historical change. On the other hand, it is aimless drift: 'There is no progress', he writes, 'there's no point deluding yourself, only the historical circumstances are different' (PE, p. 220). It may be that '*change* in itself' has become a value, but that does not imply the strength or durability of any progressive model of experience or history (TPI, p. 361). Here Houellebecq's understanding of historical temporality is actually rather close to that of another French sociologist, Jean Baudrillard.

Thus again, like the writers in Chapter 5, Houellebecq is not so much sceptical about feminist premises as he is about any progressive assertion to which they might become attached. Houellebecq's novels as a whole misanthropically propose that love exists, that there are beautiful bodies, that women can be affirmed ... and yet that this does nothing to diminish the weight of the wholesale social catastrophe under total capital. As Bourdieu is preoccupied with the economic casualties of neo-liberal thinking, so Houellebecq is obsessed with the sexual casualties of the libertarian revolution, which he refuses to separate from the emergence of neo-liberal attitudes, or, at least, the conditions that produced them. This has been clear from his first novel, and his portrait in it of the hapless Tisserand, sexual casualty *par excellence*. Since then, he has broadened out his treatment of sexual relations into a devastating indictment of the sexual *mœurs* of the airy permissives of the sixties and the seventies, and the consequences of those *mœurs*, not least for parenthood. Everywhere, Houllebecq finds damaged emotional and sexual lives. What has wrecked them, above all, as he tirelessly insists, is the more or less subtle, more or less oblique extension of the market, of the domain of struggle, to sexual relations themselves. In this context, Houellebecq's fanciful account of a globalized system of sex tourism, notably as developed in *Platform*, is probably best read as a hyperbolic extrapolation from the inexorable economic logic of our times to the point of monstrous parody.

Houellebecq everywhere diagnoses an ever more comprehensive extension of total capital throughout culture, coupled with an ever more imperious will within total capital to self-closure – but also an ungainsayable failure of total capital to remedy or even begin to address the problems it creates (remember Dio Chrysostom). Misanthropy is the consequence of this. Indeed, we might argue that human history even fulfils itself in total capital and contemporary misanthropy together. This proves to be the case, not least since Houellebecq takes the contemporary economic obsession to be the culmination and fulfilment of the movement in which the human organism has historically long been involved, like an unstoppable growth. 'Of all economic and social systems', says one of his characters, 'capitalism is unquestionably the most natural. This already shows that it is bound to be the worst' (W, pp. 124–5). Indeed, his characters are prone to think in terms of a kind of irremediable ontological mediocrity. 'The texture of the world is painful, inadequate, unalterable', says the narrator of *Whatever*, stating that he genuinely prefers reading to living (W, p. 12).

This misanthropic vision, however, also depends on fierce rejections. In the first instance, Houellebecq rejects the long-lived and powerful traditions of the French left. These are by now, if not discredited, defunct, irrelevant. Houellebecq is resiliently atheistic but equally indifferent to any political affirmation, claiming that he belongs with the *'absolute atheists* – not simply religious atheists but political atheists' (PE, p. 164). His disbelief in the efficacy of any oppositional politics has less to do with the memory of Stalinism or the collapse of the Communist bloc than the death of that comic piety of the post-war European left, *ouvrierisme*, its assertion of the revolutionary potential of the European working class. He very deliberately travesties terms formerly of great weight for the French left, like *la lutte*. He repeatedly asserts that he is a materialist. But his materialist thought is very precisely, even outrageously distinct from Marxist historical materialism, still more from dialectical materialism. 'Maybe ... all I have ever written', he tells us, 'are *materialist horror stories*' (PE, p. 275). Seen materially, as Lovecraft understood, the human world may possibly be just endlessly swept by monstrous forces. If materialism has become a necessary, even an incontrovertible thought, it has also become a stimulus to grand revulsion.

Revulsion also breeds an emphatic repudiation of the humanist tradition, particularly in its soft-centred, contemporary versions, or what one of his characters calls 'saccharine humanist blether' (TPI, p. 344). Houellebecq continues the great French anti-humanist tradition that runs from Beckett, Bataille and Blanchot to Foucault and Lacan to Lyotard, Badiou and Meillassoux. But he is also scathing about the idea of freedom, particularly the notion of existential freedom, because of its contemporary travesty, the free market, but also in itself. 'Theories of freedom, from Gide to Sartre', as his fictional *alter ego* puts it in *The Map and the Territory*, are just 'immoralisms thought up by irresponsible bachelors' (MT, p. 115). Beyond that, Houellebecq understands humanism, above all, in its contemporary manifestations – the discourse of human rights and other liberalisms – as, like contemporary philanthropy, a veil drawn over the brutality of total capital for the purposes of general reassurance. Indeed, in one striking passage in *The Possibility of an Island*, he appears to suggest that, as compared to liberalism, the revolutionary mindset had at least this to be said in its favour, that it was honest enough to take the full measure of the stupid brutality of things, 'responding to it with [an] increased brutality' of its own.[41] That is precisely the gauntlet a serious politics throws down. Do we want to pick it up? Houellebecq's own answer, as one would expect from a misanthropist, is a resounding no. His logic is nonetheless that of a decisive break with the humanists. 'The disappearance of humanity would be a good thing', a prelude to the possibility of 'another intelligent species, more cooperative, better adapted by its original tribal organization to ascend towards moral law' (PE, p. 169).

Convinced that progressivists, humanists and liberals have no real purchase on total capital, in his willingness to strip away the fancy dress it keeps wearing to its party, unsurprisingly, Houllebecq and his work have caused a major furore. He predicts the moment, however, 'when the reaction to my books is [recognized] to be a *symptom*' (PE, pp. 277–8). A symptom of what? It is worth noting, first, that, by and large, Houellebecq's principal antagonists have not been intellectuals, scholars or serious novelists. Had this been the case and reflected his focus, he might have attracted less opprobrium. Those who have chiefly hounded him have been journalists, the press, the media, pundits and so-called 'literary critics'. Recent photographs of him have made him look like a pathetic, hunted figure, and he writes of his relations with the media as having 'reached the point of all-out hatred' (PE, p. 188). If this is so, it is because Houellebecq contests an ideological set-up that he takes to be specious and false. His enemies hate him because he disputes the conviction they more or less consciously wish to promote, the conviction, not just that capital is the only game in town, nor merely that the triumph of total capital is logical, but that total capital can be moral, can be consistent with the good, is even the good itself, is in the process of bringing us all the necessary blessings.

With hangdog, miserable stubbornness, Houellebecq everywhere misanthropically resists the champagne screech, the whoopee culture, the euphorics of total capital. Furthermore, he does so on his enemies' terrain. For he is a popular novelist, and democratic in that he refuses to lift himself above the people he describes. It is impossible to dismiss him as either an old leftist long past his sell-by date or an intellectual elitist. Certainly, there is a wide range of cultural reference in Houellebecq's fiction. But it has no particular privilege relative to his other materials, and offers his characters no Olympian position in which security from and condescension to their milieux become possible. Hugo in *Atomized* may teach Mallarmé in school, but Mallarmé offers him no refuge at all from what Houellebecq portrays as his class's utter indifference to the poet. Houellebecq has a wide readership that overlaps with his enemies' own. For this they cannot forgive him. He opens up too glaring a set of differences with them. Indeed, writers like Houellebecq are popular because, again, they express a new misanthropy, or at least one that has only newly come into the glare of the lights: a democratic misanthropy, which is partly the people's own obscure self-hatred at not being able to do better themselves.

Houellebecq himself puts matters well: his fiction has long been drastically at odds with 'the official version' of things, which is 'that everything is fine, that things are getting better and better and that the only people who deny this are a bunch of neurotic nihilists' (PE,

p. 279). At its simplest, we might hear this as a declaration of war on the social-democratic culture of spin and *gestion*, management, though also on the culture of 'excitement' (W, p. 40), 'fantastic' innovation, infinite 'brilliance', corporate buoyancy and fake solidarity. There are some tellingly caustic representations of workplace-bonding in *Whatever*. Houellebecq everywhere arraigns the infernally upbeat mood in contemporary life. 'It's not that I feel tremendously low', says one of his characters, 'it's rather that the world around me appears high' (as indeed it may well be, W, p. 135). Take this a little further, and we might detect a profound if implicit dispute with the proselytizers for the 'good society', particularly insofar as they suppose that it can readily and even quite promptly emerge out of this one or is reconcilable with total capital.[42] Houellebecq's misanthropic novels implacably pile up the evidence against toxic positivity above all. If the Houllebecq controversy in all its ferocity is symptomatic, it may represent a moment when some at least of the discourses of toxic positivity were forced to defend themselves, as in the case of his critics, and thereby to reveal how wanting they are.

Houellebecq's work is to be read, then, not as an expression of a philosophy to be accepted or rejected but rather as a misanthropic provocation. Our culture appears to give the lie to what Chapter 1 initially established as the logic of the cultural emergence of misanthropy. If the concept of the good society ought logically to spell *finis* to misanthropic discourses, then, for all its liberal democracy and cultivation of the pleasure principle, ours cannot even begin to herald, let alone approximate to it, since it is rather spawning them. Misanthropy bubbles up insistently in our culture, perhaps especially in popular culture. From Francis Ford Coppola's *Apocalypse Now* (1979) to Martin Scorsese's *Gangs of New York* (2002) and beyond, misanthropy has been abundantly evident in popular cinema. The techno-fabulist tradition repeatedly verged on misanthropy. After all, if it is Skynet, not human beings, that threatens the world with nuclear holocaust in *The Terminator*, the film emphasizes that, in the first place, human beings have been responsible for the uncontrollable nightmare unleashed by the machines. Compare the figure of the robot- or cyborg-hero as (more or less) the sole defender of truth and good in the *Robocop* films, *Terminator 2* etc. Otherwise, in *The Terminator* itself, the general condition of humanity is summed up in the egregiously complacent psychologist who, when Kyle tells him the truth about a catastrophic future, quickly decides that he is totally insane.

So, too, in John Carpenter's *Escape from New York* (1981), the political system is monstrous, those who have offended against and been incarcerated by it quite as much so – and in between them crawl a small bunch of killers and misfits who hardly seem untainted themselves. The film's intense disgust is patent in its very texture, and leads inexorably to a conclusion in which Snake Plissken (Kurt Russell) unreels and throws away the tape that would guarantee peace and save humanity from annihilation. Neither the world of law and order nor the world outside has even slightly encouraged Carpenter's anti-hero to bother. In Jim Jarmusch's *Ghost Dog* (1999), from the beginning, with Ghost Dog (Forest Whitaker) half-dead from a beating at the hands of a gang of violent thugs, as his name suggests, his life is at an end. Saved from the gang by a mobster, he accepts that he must become the mobster's samurai and finally meet execution at his hands. In the time remaining, he chooses honourable service, a quietist way of life and withdrawal. (He prefers the company of pigeons to people). 'I seen all I need to see', he says, just before he dies. The film gives us no reason to think otherwise, and the shufflingly, ineffably sombre soundtrack (by the Wu-Tang Clan) only further authenticates the mood.

Misanthropy is also thriving in contemporary fiction. On occasions, its manifestations may be relatively highbrow, as in the work of Martin Amis, John Banville, Thomas Bernhard, Tibor Fischer, Elfriede Jelinek and W. G. Sebald (though such writers also tend to have popular appeal). But it equally appears in novelists who would probably not want to be dubbed highbrow and on occasions relish not seeming so, from, at one end of the spectrum, Bret Easton Ellis, Jamaica Kincaid, the later J. G. Ballard and Will Self to T. K. Kenyon (*Rabid*) and Christopher Moore (*Fluke*), at the other. We might also note playwright Martin Crimp's attempt to update Molière's *Le Misanthrope* to modern Britain. Though television is hardly a misanthropic medium – with its endless array of beaming talking heads, television is even in effect the objective essence of a contemporary fear of misanthropy – there are strains of misanthropy in a few popular television series, if admittedly ones of an unconventional kind, from *Blackadder* to *House* to Larry David's *Curb Your Enthusiasm* to some of David Simon's great work, notably, perhaps, his Iraq invasion mini-series, *Generation Kill*.

But let's turn briefly to two great explosions of misanthropy in pop music: punk rock and gansta rap (some of which featured on the soundtrack to *Generation Kill*). The relative innocence of the 'boy meets girl' or 'boy longs to meet girl' pop of the fifties and after, and the heady dreaminess, political idealism, hippie mysticism and weird extravagance of late sixties rock met their death quite starkly, in the Rolling Stones's Altamont concert (1969) and The Who's 'Won't Get Fooled Again' (1971). Though glam rock kept an overblown and more and more stagey tradition going for a while, and the rock grandees (and their dynastic heirs) became ever grander, as they still do, partly in reaction, from at least the New York Dolls, Johnny Thunders and the Heartbreakers and the Ramones (e.g. 'Poison Heart'), an acid and durable strain of misanthropy steadily appeared in pop music. It laced its way through Indie (think of 'The Smiths' 'Death of a Disco Dancer', 1987) to Grunge. Heavy metal has on occasions seemed partly powered by it (think of Motörhead – 'No Voices in the Sky', 1991, 'Brave New World', 2002, 'Brotherhood of Man', 2010). But like the Cynics and Houellebecq, it was punk that especially scandalized people. On occasions it even triggered off bouts of extreme violence. In the words of its historian Jon Savage, it was 'an explosion of negatives'.[43] Punk made its obscene arrival, screaming and yelling, at a time when an honourable progressive hope had failed: Britain was known as the sick man of Europe, the British economy was in crisis, the welfare state under threat and the enlightened post-war consensus collapsing. But like the Irish misanthropy in the fourth chapter, the music was an expression of classes (usually working and obscure lower middle) to whom the kindly light had never penetrated anyway, those who had remained untouched by the progressive dispensation and whom its failure prodded into gobbing profusely at the general show. Punk involved girls, too: young women's misanthropy was an important aspect of it. That Johny Rotten (John Lydon) should sing, with the grimace with which others increasingly identified him, both 'I am an antichrist' and 'I wanna destroy passer-by', in a mid-seventies song called 'Anarchy in the UK', captures much of the point.[44]

Pauline Murray (of Penetration) thought the Sex Pistols' message was very simple: the world and people were 'a load of shit'.[45] The names of the rockers themselves tell the tale: Sid Vicious, Rat Scabies. Lydon summed up his view of human society in a single sentence: 'There are those who fart, and those who inhale those farts' (punk was as scatological as Swift).[46] In 1975, Lydon was wearing a Pink Floyd T-shirt with the eyes torn out and a biro'd scrawl across it that simply if also somewhat ambiguously read 'I hate ...'.[47] The hatred was evident, as much as anything else, at the venues, where the musicians and the audience frequently all got caught up in a mood of shared aggression and insult, cursing, vomiting, spitting, smacking and even bottling each other. But the rage was not merely directed at the present. Punk happened in a dead space somewhere between an inert past – 'History is for pissing on', said the Sex Pistols' manager Malcolm McLaren[48] – and an empty prospect ('No future', sang the group itself). Nor were punks solely revolted by the self-deception and false decency of one particular phase in the growth of social democracy. They also directed their vitriol at an establishment that had not so much failed them as never noticed their existence in the first place. 'We're the flowers in your dustbin', sang the Pistols, 'we're the poison in your human machine', in 'God Save the Queen', which they released, as a supreme provocation, a ferocious counterblast to the official and public fantasy, just ten days before the royal Jubilee. Equally, like the best misanthropists, punks became the self-condemned. If 'the fascist regime' had made a punk a 'potential h-bomb' ('God Save the Queen' again), a blaster of human beings, it had also made him or her a 'moron'. Punks turned on themselves, with a terrifying, by now almost legendary, masochism. They were 'pretty vacant', 'not all there', 'out to lunch' ('Pretty Vacant'). Musically, they quite often saw themselves as, and sometimes declared themselves to be, rubbish. 'We're just trash', said Howard Devoto of the Buzzcocks, was what he got as the punk motto from the New York Dolls.[49] The audiences picked up on the rubbish theme, sometimes wearing bin-liners to gigs. In the circumstances, as 'Pretty Vacant' also proclaimed, the punks' only alternative was not to care, to turn their guns indifferently in all directions, including themselves.

In the words, then, of Derek Jarman, maker of *Jubilee* (1977), the punk film par excellence, 'Punk was an understandable and very correct disgust with everything'.[50] Rap music has been punctuated by a similar loathing. The theme can be quite blatant (X-Raided's 'Misanthropy', 'Misanthrope' by 'Caged'). But it is gangsta rap, above all, that has been richly misanthropic. Liberal academics prefer to mute the disturbing sides of subcultures, the degree to which they may actually be sour and bitter endgames,[51] and rap is no exception. When, in her expert book about it, for example, Tricia Rose cheerfully erases the 'non-progressive' elements in rap, making of it a music of affirmation and empowerment,[52] she sounds a bit like a Salvation Army worker in a brothel. The gangsta rappers are hardly Mary Poppinses of slum life. Rose's view of them does not seem borne out by many of their titles and refrains: 'Shit Don't Stop', 'Me Against the World', 'The Streetz are Deathrow' (2Pac [Tupac Shakur]); 'Welcome to the Terrordome' (Public Enemy); 'Fuck Y'all' (2Pac, 'I don't give a fuck')', 'Fuck the world' (Biggie Smalls, 'Ready to Die', 2Pac, 'Fuck the World'). The rage and despair have nothing in common with the upbeat orthodoxies of cultural studies. Nor do the fates of Biggie and 2Pac. (They carried on a feud, eventually dying in murders that were its consequence, like villains in a revenge play). Nor indeed do some of the female rappers (Li'l Kim, Foxy Brown): by the time they have indifferently trashed both the 'thug niggas' and 'gangsta bitches' (their terms), they seem scarcely more right-on than the men.

Rap emerged from the Civil Rights and Black Nationalist movements of the 1960s and 1970s, from the Zulu Nation and the Nation of Islam, and initially bore their stamp, in figures like Afrika Bambaataa. But some of the rappers – not least the Wu-Tang Clan – also identified with the misanthropic Five Percenters, a splinter group who believed that only 5 per cent of the world's population, the 'poor righteous teachers', were worth listening to.[53] More importantly, as rap continued, sections of the culture became steadily more pessimistic, sometimes savagely so, about the gulf that yawned between new promises and old realities, realities that had not only proved (and continue to prove) lasting but, given the changes in US government policies and practices in taxation, welfare, industry, education, housing and city planning in the 1970s and 1980s, were getting worse: ghettoes, extreme poverty and the extreme hopelessness that it breeds, gangs, mayhem, murder, AIDS, drugs (especially crack) and a generalized violence, including police brutality and violence against women. 'Welcome to the Killin Fields', proclaimed the Wu-Tang Clan, in 'Method Man'. In the words of Cornel West, the result of this situation was 'a numbing detachment from others and a self-destructive disposition towards the world'.[54] But the rappers were also rooted. Rose emphasizes that the 'ghetto badmen' and their posses or crews fundamentally belonged to localities, or hoods.[55] Gangsta misanthropy was an aspect of the attitude of 'slackness'.

'Slackness' meant deliberately flouting consensual norms of decent behaviour that others had pasted over the social disaster, which the rapper knew first-hand, immediately, intimately, locally and vividly.[56] Gangsta rappers were determined to keep the music real and of the streets – gangsta is sometimes known as 'reality rap'[57] – not least as an expression of disgust. People stink:

> Broken glass everywhere
> People pissing on the stairs, you know they just don't care
> I can't take the smell, can't take the noise
> Got no money to move out, guess I got no choice
>
> (Melle Mel, 'The Message')

They are also involved in a war of all against all:

> Crime visions in my blood got me locked in prison
> While we die hard people whine about religion, vision
> Blow, spin, and sin and killing what's revealing
> It's a never ending battle with no ending and beginning
>
> (Wu-Tang Clan, 'A Better Tomorrow')

It is hardly surprising, then, if some of the rappers cast themselves as horsemen of the apocalypse:

> I came to shake the frame in half
> With thoughts that bomb, shit like math.
>
> (Wu-Tang Clan, 'Protect Ya Neck')

If the black American child is born 'blind to the ways of mankind', says Grandmaster Mel, it will certainly soon get the education it needs: 'You'll grow in the ghetto living second-rate/And your eyes will sing a song of deep hate'. When quoted drily, such lyrics can sound lame. But that ignores the power that the music and the fiercely percussive voices of rap music generate as a complement to them.

*

One thing has by now become starkly clear. From the vantage point of the arguments in Chapters 1–3, contemporary culture ought *par excellence* to be describable as post-misanthropic. But this is very certainly not the case, except in particular social and cultural spheres where being post-misanthropic pays, and the arguments in Chapters 4–6 do a great deal to explain that, as we have seen here and there. Punk and gangsta rap, for example, are the objective proof of the thesis of Chapter 4: there are, there always will be, so far as we know, others who are or feel themselves to be terminally excluded, and therefore will express a loathing of humanity. Admittedly, I am citing great eruptions in popular music in the 1980s and 1990s, surely quite a long time ago, which may seem to minimize any remarkable turn for the best that the world has taken over the past fifteen years. But gangsta rap remains vital, punk is an almost grippingly vivid memory, and, in any case, in a globalizing world, misanthropy continually migrates elsewhere, to a whole world still horribly disempowered: witness the favelas of Brazil, to take just one example among many, now producing their own versions of chronic misanthropy in Brazilian rap and heavy metal (e.g. Vulcano). The music of the favelas represents and exemplifies the misanthropic sneer of vast swathes of global culture that have absolutely no stake in the privileges that underlie others' good cheer, a rictus that remains, now jeering at the 'new enlightenment' promoted by politics, business, commerce and various kinds of contemporary liberal together. But if anyone wants to find out more about misanthropy today, he or she need only go on the net. Try reading the writings of football fans.

Furthermore, as in Chapter 5, we've also seen that postmodern and liberal discourses are themselves capable of taking a misanthropic direction, as though they had been nursing a seed of misanthropy within themselves, or surreptitiously equipping themselves with some of Houellebecq's armoury. Our culture, then, fairly teems with different, more or less explicit, more or less incipient forms of misanthropy; indeed, misanthropy appears to be a major if unacknowledged theme for our times. Recognizing this may make us feel less sceptical about some of the great misanthropists of Western tradition than we possibly sounded earlier: Hobbes, for example, foreseeing that, 'when all the world is overcharged with inhabitants', the logical consequence and indeed the remedy must be total war;[58] Schopenhauer, declaring that the will feasts on itself until in time 'the human race, because it subdues all the others, regards nature as manufactured for its own use';[59] Rousseau, grasping the logic of modern squandering: 'What will [a man] think of this luxury when he finds that every region of the world has been made to contribute; that perhaps twenty million hands have worked for a long time, that it has cost the lives of perhaps thousands of men, and all this to present to him with pomp at noon what he is going to deposit in his toilet at night?';[60] or Ivy Compton-Burnett on progressives:

> 'We are in error in thinking that the old abuses are eradicated,' said Rosebery gravely.
> 'They cannot be while people have power,' said Emma. 'If they did not use it for themselves, what use would it be to them?'[61]

None of them seem remote from the predicament that exercises contemporary misanthropists.

Ours is a period that has witnessed the continuing decline of the great religious narratives that for so long underpinned our culture and others, too – above all, providential narratives. This decline is, brutally, a fact, and it was right that it should happen. But the period has also witnessed the collapse of the great secular narratives of redemption (supremely, the Marxist narrative). The many and diverse efforts to resuscitate these secular narratives, to cling to their language and tones, to produce new or modified versions of them, invariably sound hollow, redundant litanies. Modernities and progressivisms proliferate and reappear as vigorously and indomitably as convolvulus or Japanese knotweed. That hardly increases their worth; rather, the reverse, it should make us more sceptical about them. They may express nothing more than muted panic, an apprehension of the imminent and wholesale failure of any hope of advance. But the great religious and secular narratives of salvation always subscribed at some level to the value of humanity, or at least the question of that value. Without them, much more radically alienated concepts of humanity become possible. Indeed, such concepts may be, not only one of the more significant achievements of our times, but almost uniquely significant accounts of what those times have really been about. Take W. G. Sebald, for example:

> Cities phosphorescent,
> on the river bank, industry's
> glowing piles waiting
> beneath the smoke trails

like ocean giants for the siren's
blare, the twitching lights,
of rail and motorways, the murmur
of the millionfold proliferating molluscs,
wood lice and leeches… [62]

The molluscs, it would seem, are unstoppable. And they cling on for grim death.

But, though Sebald makes them seem disturbingly eerie, the molluscs are not exactly repulsive. There is no Swiftian conviction of the necessity of disgust in the passage. This brings me right back to the argument in Chapter 2. There I suggested that the most persuasive argument against misanthropy was the possibility of delight that, as organic, fleshly beings, humans always hold out. In one respect, that argument is right. But what exactly happens to it once the narratives of theological reassurance, providence and redemption have all disappeared? People remain beautiful – but then, so do certain parasites. It makes them no less destructive. Loveliness – and, in human beings, feeling for human loveliness – is part of the inward, organic logic of creatures, intrinsic to their blind self-persistence. That does not grant the creatures any certain value, particularly if, into the equation, we factor the anti-anthropocentric case, Rorty's critique, now shared by many, of the 'natural cut', 'the bad old metaphysical notion' that the world is made up of two kinds of species, human and non-human.[63] If we return to Gray's imminent 'era of solitude' on the assumption that the idea of the 'cut' is no longer tenable, the question of whether, if they could communicate a view, other species could conceivably have much to say for man is not as inane as it might seem to some. Is it self-evident that the morality we might derive from the imagined vantage point of a species virtually extinct because of human activity is negligible alongside a human one? An impracticable and impotent morality, perhaps – but wrong?

'To what serves mortal beauty – dangerous', wrote Gerard Manley Hopkins.[64] It is a memorable sentiment, articulating what may conceivably be a truth other than and beyond the one Hopkins intended. (He was a devout Catholic, and deeply troubled by his homosexuality). It may also supply a logic for misanthropy in the end more plausible than Swiftian disgust. That logic can only be countered by a convincing progress narrative of the kind we have now lost. Otherwise, nothing can quite dispel the fear that human beings can survive and flourish only by implacably destroying themselves, each other and their world. Equally, however, no case for misanthropy is provable. Astronomer Royal and former President of the Royal Society Lord Rees thinks that the twenty-first century may very well be our last.[65] The Future of Humanity Institute at Oxford – no bunch of fools – has recently said more or less the same.[66] Distinguished Japanese philosopher Kojin Karatani argues that, without the emergence of a world republic – and what chance that – there will be more devastating world wars, to the point of annihilation.[67] But Juvenal was similarly gloom-laden – a very long time ago. As Frank Kermode elegantly demonstrated some decades previously, the epochs repeatedly dream their own apocalypse.[68] The Cold War era, in particular, seemed like the perfect occasion for Armageddon; never before had human beings had a better opportunity to bring it about. Instead, the very forces that might have led to catastrophe actually cancelled each other out. But in any case, even if some or all of the pessimists turned out to be right, and humanity faded from the scene, would that serve as an objective proof of misanthropy? It would merely mean that a phenomenon (in the neutral, scientific sense) was at an end, like the practically innumerable phenomena that scientists observe. In this respect, the question of misanthropy seems to leave us in absolute doubt. The most piquant irony of all is that it is only within the context of theological, providential or redemptive narratives, or logics of meaning that take us beyond what is immediately to hand, that the question of misanthropy really makes sense at all.

So we finally arrive at an aporia, it seems (an aporia that partly returns us to the premise from which we started, the incoherence or incompleteness of misanthropy). Intellectuals and scholars tend to like aporias. But if the question is the worth and indeed the future of the human project, should we just meekly subside into indecision? The misanthropic case cannot be proved; but it would be no bad thing right now if it were widely taken a little more seriously. What might be the ends of contemporary misanthropy? This chapter has tentatively broached the notion of approaching such questions from another angle. Intermittently, at least, it is just faintly possible, though one couldn't have known it, that misanthropy has long been what Karl Wilhelm Goettling called cynicism and what I earlier called a democratic misanthropy, 'the [actual, true] philosophy of the … people'.[69] With the new forms of democracy that have recently appeared, might this by now be steadily emerging, articulating itself as such? This is not entirely impossible to credit, if what contemporary misanthropy betokens is a fitful bubbling over of a radical if commonly repressed dissatisfaction among ordinary people with what continues to be, as it always has been, their comprehensive economic, political and cultural disempowerment, the impotence of the majority, democratic or not (here I am at one with Land). Indeed, given, for example, the immense outpouring of loyalty that a basically quite humane, reputedly kind and generous if unrepentantly dissolute contemporary pop misanthropist like Ian Kilminster (Lemmy of Motörhead) generated before his recent death,[70] one may wonder whether the people cannot be trusted to know themselves far better than do left-liberal or postmodern academics, Pelagians almost to a woman and man. (The Pelagianism of course may not necessarily go very far beneath the surface, but that is not the immediate point). Academics left, right and centre now more or less explicitly preach the people's virtues, preen themselves on their solidarity with the people, self-defeatingly and unthinkingly identify with popular culture, sometimes in all its forms. Alas, they repeatedly fail to hear the people's snarl, not least because it is directed as much at their kind as the powerful. Contemporary misanthropy, then, is perhaps most significant as a self-dissatisfaction within the people, and therefore, possibly, just possibly, an end to *complaisance*. That would make of it a first, very faint, tiny flicker of something that might, indeed, plausibly be called progress. If the flicker were ever to become a flame, it would necessarily take radical issue with toxic positivity, the notion of the imminence of the good society and their publicists, mules and vendors. It might dump them in the Sex Pistols' dustbin, instead of the punks. Who knows, it might even represent the beginning of a historical dialectic.

NOTES

Introduction

1 See A. Macc Armstrong, 'Timon of Athens: A Legendary Figure?', *Greece & Rome*, 2nd series, vol. 34, no. 1 (April 1987), pp. 7–11.

2 William Shakespeare, *Timon of Athens*, ed. H.J. Oliver (London: Arden, 1959), hereafter cited in the text as TA; III.iv 82, p. 68.

3 *Specimens of the Table Talk of the late Samuel Taylor Coleridge* (2 vols, London: John Murray, 1835), vol. 2, p. 301.

4 Molière, *Le misanthrope*, ed. Jacques Chupeau (Paris: Gallimard, 2000), hereafter cited in the text as LM; I.i 96, p. 51.

5 Jean-Jacques Rousseau, *Les Confessions*, ed. Bernard Gangebin and Marcel Raymond, pref. J.-B. Pontalis, notes by Catherine Kœnig (Paris: Gallimard, 1973), pp. 448, 450.

6 Louis-Ferdinand Céline, *Voyage au bout de la nuit* (Paris: Gallimard, 1988), p. 30.

7 Thomas Middleton, *The Revenger's Tragedy*, hereafter cited in the text as RT, in *Five Revenge Tragedies: Kyd, Shakespeare, Marston, Chettle, Middleton*, ed. with introd. Emma Smith (London: Penguin, 2012), V.iii 157, p. 415.

8 Thomas Kyd, *The Spanish Tragedy*, ed. J. R. Mulryne (London: Ernest Benn, 1970), hereafter cited in the text as ST; III.ii 3–4, 9–10, p. 53.

9 Middleton and William Rowley, *The Changeling*, ed. Patricia Thomson (London: Ernest Benn, 1970), hereafter cited in the text as TC; V.iii 163, 168–9, pp. 90–1.

10 See John Webster, *The White Devil*, ed. Elizabeth M. Brennan (London: Ernest Benn, 1970), hereafter cited in the text as WD; V.i–ii, pp. 99–106.

11 Middleton, *Women Beware Women*, in *Selected Plays*, ed. David L. Frost (Cambridge: Cambridge University Press, 1978), I.ii 19–20, p. 198.

12 John Marston, *The Malcontent*, ed. Bernard Harris (London: Ernest Benn, 1967), hereafter cited in the text as TM; I.iv 4–5, p. 24, I.vii 53, p. 37.

13 Shakespeare, *Macbeth*, ed. Kenneth Muir (London: Arden, 1979), V.v 49–50, p. 155.

14 Webster, *The Duchess of Malfi*, ed. Elizabeth M. Brennan (London: Ernest Benn, 1977), hereafter cited in the text as DM; I.i 23–8, pp. 7–8.

15 Plato, *Dialogues*, trans. Benjamin Jowett (5 vols, Oxford: Oxford University Press, 1953), vol. 1, pp. 445–6.

16 Jonathan Swift, letter to Alexander Pope, 29 September 1725, *Correspondence*, ed. Harold Williams (5 vols, Oxford: Clarendon, 1963–5), vol. 3, p. 103.

17 Erasmus, *Apothegmes*, trans. Antoine Macault (Paris: J. Dupins, 1556), 305a.

18 Arsenius, *Violetum*, quoted *Diogenes the Cynic: Sayings and Anecdotes, with Other Popular Moralists*, trans. with an introd. and notes by Robin Hard (Oxford: Oxford University Press, 2012), p. 209.

19 *The Cynic Philosophers from Diogenes to Julian*, ed. and trans. Robert Dobbin (London: Penguin, 2012), hereafter cited in the text as CP; p. 69. 'Supposed' because the letters were probably written in Rome in the first century AD. However, they would have been the product of the faithful and a means of transmitting the tradition, and would therefore have been true *'to the spirit of the original Cynics'* (p. 56; Dobbin's comment).

20 Quoted Derek Krueger, 'The Bawdy and Society: The Shamelessness of Diogenes in Roman Imperial Culture', in *The Cynics: The Cynic Movement in Antiquity and Its Legacy*, ed. R. Bracht Branham and Marie-Odile Goulet-Cazé (Berkeley and London: University of California Press, 1996), pp. 222–39, p. 232. Krueger has 'appearance' not 'opinion'. Both are at stake.

21 George Orwell, 'Charles Dickens', in *Essays, Journalism and Letters, Vol. 1: An Age Like This, 1920-1940*, ed. Sonia Orwell and Ian Angus (Boston: Nonpareil, 2000), pp. 413–60, p. 460. I have substituted 'forever' for Orwell's 'now'.

22 See Bracht Branham and Goulet-Cazé, 'Introduction', *Cynics*, pp. 1–27, p. 19. My account of the Cynics is heavily indebted to this admirably scholarly volume.

23 Mikhail Bakhtin, *The Dialogical Imagination*, trans. C. Emerson and M. Holquist (Austin: University of Texas Press, 1983), p. 39.

24 Diogenes Laertius, *The Lives of Eminent Philosophers*, trans. R. D. Hicks (2 vols, London: Heinemann, 1925), 6.22, vol. 2, p. 25.

25 See Laertius, *Lives*, 6.20-81, vol. 2, pp. 23–85, passim.

26 Krueger, 'Bawdy', p. 239.

27 Ibid., p. 236.

28 A. A. Long, 'The Socratic Tradition: Diogenes, Crates and Hellenistic Ethics', in Bracht Branham and Goulet-Cazé (eds), *Cynics*, pp. 28–46, p. 42.

29 See Bracht Branham and Goulet-Cazé, 'Introduction', *Cynics*, p. 5.

30 Laertius, *Lives*, 6.64, vol. 2, p. 67.

31 Ibid., 6.49, vol. 2, p. 51.

32 Aelian, *Historical Miscellany*, quoted *Diogenes the Cynic*, p. 9.

33 Bracht Branham and Goulet-Cazé (eds), 'Introduction', p. 13.

34 But the poet was nonetheless prudently hedging his bets. In Satire XIII, he has earlier refused to be 'lined up with the Cynics'. See Juvenal, *The Sixteen Satires*, trans. with an introd. and notes by Peter Green (rev. edn, London: Penguin, 2004), hereafter cited in the text as SS; xiii, 120–1, p. 100. Cf. xiv, 308–14, p. 114.

35 Edward Gibbon, *The History of the Decline and Fall of the Roman Empire*, ed. David Womersley (3 vols, London: Penguin, 1994), vol. 1, p. 104.

36 See for example Edward Champlin, *Nero* (Cambridge, MA: Harvard University Press, 2003); and Brian W. Jones, *The Emperor Domitian* (London: Routledge, 1993).

37 W. H. Auden, 'September 1, 1939', in *Selected Poems*, ed. Edward Mendelson (New York: Vintage, 1979), p. 87.

38 Gibbon, *History*, vol. 1, p. 104.

39 William J. Dominik and William T. Wehrle (eds), *Roman Verse Satire – Lucilius to Juvenal: A Selection with an Introduction, Text, Translation and Notes* (Mundelein, IL: Bolchazy-Carducci, 2000), pp. 16, 17, 19.

40 Horace, *Satires and Epistles*, and Persius, *Satires*, trans. with an introd. and notes by Niall Rudd (rev. edn, London: Penguin, 2005), hereafter cited in the text as S; i, 114–15, p. 141.

41 See for example Susanna Morton Braund, *The Roman Satirists and Their Masks* (Bristol: Bristol Classical Press, 2007), passim. This seems like an eminently postmodern response to a literature not obviously available to one, seeing aesthetic detachment and an abstracted cleverness as at a premium even in Imperial Rome, while doubting the power and searing intensity of both the moral imperative and the satirical vision. Such readings beg the question as to why Juvenal should have bothered at all, especially in so problematic an environment. For a very persuasive view similar to mine, see Peter Green, 'Introduction', Juvenal, SS, pp. lxvi–xvii and passim. See also Green's notes, passim.

42 G. Highet, *Juvenal the Satirist* (Oxford: Oxford University Press, 1954), p. 58.

43 Green, notes, Juvenal, SS, p. 130.

44 See Green, Juvenal, SS, introd. and notes, p. xliii and passim.

45 See Harold Hagendahl, *Augustine and the Latin Classics* (2 vols, Studia Graeca et Latina Gotoburgensia, Gothenburg: Elanders, 1967), vol. 2, pp. 470–8.

46 Cf. Saint Augustine, *Confessions*, trans. with introd. and notes by Henry Chadwick (Oxford: Oxford University Press, 2008), hereafter cited in the text as C; p. 15. I have taken the liberty (and it is one) of usually substituting quotations from the King James Bible for Chadwick's translations of quotations from Augustine's Latin Bible, in the interests of expressiveness.

47 See Augustine, *Against the Academicians*, trans. with an introd. Sister Mary Patricia Garvey (Milwaukee: Marquette University Press, 2000), p. 81; and G. R. Evans, *Augustine on Evil* (Cambridge: Cambridge University Press, 1982), p. 30.

48 For an excellent collection, see Augustine, *Anti-Pelagian Writings*, ed. and trans. Peter Holmes and Robert Ernest Wallis, rev. and introd. by Benjamin B. Warfield (Whitefish: Kessinger, 2004).

49 See for example Augustine, *Treatise against Two Letters of the Pelagians*, I.iii 7, in *Anti-Pelagian Writings*, pp. 373–434.

50 Augustine, *The Soliloquies, Being the Secret Discourses and Conferences of his Soul with God* (Dublin: John Lamb, 1747), pp. 19–20 and passim.

51 Bertrand Russell, *A History of Western Philosophy* (London: Allen & Unwin, 1967), p. 362.

52 Evans, *Augustine on Evil*, p. 184.

53 Ibid., p. 130.

54 Steven Pinker, *The Better Angels of Our Nature: A History of Violence and Humanity* (London: Penguin, 2012).

Chapter 1

1 Nancy Mitford, *The Sun King: Louis XIV at Versailles*, introd. Stella Tillyard (1966; London: Vintage, 2011), p. 174.

2 Jean de la Bruyère, *Les Caractères de Thèophraste* (Paris: Hochereau, 1765), hereafter cited in the text as CT; p. 307.

3 Madame de Sévigné, *Letters*, 6 May 1671; quoted Thomas Pike Lathy, *Memoirs of the Court of Louis XIV, Comprising Biography and Anecdotes of the Most Celebrated Characters of that Period* (London: Matthew Iley, 1819), p. 361.

4 Emmanuel Le Roy Ladurie, *The Ancien Régime: A History of France, 1610-1774*, trans. Mark Greengrass (Oxford: Blackwell, 1996), p. 31.

5 See R. J. Knecht, *The Fronde* (London: Historical Association, 1975), pp. 11–12.

6 See ibid., p. 26.

7 'Préface', La Rochefoucauld, *Refléxions ou sentences et maximes morales*, ed. Jean Lafond (Paris: Gallimard, 1976), hereafter cited in the text as R; p. 8.

8 See Alain Mazère, *La Rochefoucauld: Le duc rebelle*, pref. Jean Mesnard (Paris: Le Croît vif, 2007), pp. 73–91.

9 Quoted Morris Bishop, *The Life and Adventures of La Rochefoucauld* (Ithaca, New York: Cornell University Press, 1953), p. 144.

10 Quoted Mazère, *La Rochefoucauld*, p. 76; and p. 119; Bishop, *Life and Adventures*, p. 100.

11 Quoted Bishop, *Life and Adventures*, p. 241.

12 Quoted ibid., p. 144; and p. 245.

13 Lafond, 'Préface', La Rochefoucauld, *Refléxions*, p. 9.

14 See for instance W. G. Moore, *La Rochefoucauld: His Mind and Art* (Oxford: Clarendon, 1969), passim.

15 Quoted Ladurie, *Ancien Régime*, p. 210.

16 *Relazioni degli ambasciatori Veneziani nel secolo XVII*, III, 47; quoted Arthur Tilley, *The Decline of the Age of Louis XIV, or, French Literature 1687-1715* (Cambridge: Cambridge University Press, 1929), p. 5.

17 See Lathy, *Memoirs*, pp. 163–4.

18 Madame de Sévigné, *Letters*, 24 April 1871; quoted Lathy, *Memoirs*, p. 355.

19 Lathy, *Memoirs*, p. 23.

20 Ladurie, *Ancien Régime*, p. 258.

21 Quoted Mitford, *Sun King*, p. 69.

22 See ibid. Mitford's source, as for other of the details I have used, is Georges Mongrédien, *La Vie quotidienne sous Louis XIV* (Paris: Hachette, 1948).

23 See Lathy, *Memoirs*, p. 185.

24 Quoted Emmanuel Le Roy Ladurie, with Jean-François Fitou, *Saint-Simon and the Court of Louis XIV*, trans. Arthur Goldhammer (Chicago and London: University of Chicago Press, 2001), p. 122.

25 Ladurie, *Saint-Simon*, p. 189. See also passim.

26 See ibid., p. 12.

27 Ibid., p. 301.

28 Mitford, *Sun King*, p. 126.

29 Quoted Ladurie, *Saint-Simon*, p. 332.

30 Louis de Rouvroy, duc de Saint-Simon, *Mémoires*, ed. Yves Coirault (8 vols., Paris: Gallimard/Pléiade, 1983–88), vol. 4, p. 1009.

31 Though this had also been a neo-Stoic emphasis, as in Justus Lipsius's *De Constantia*, which, in the immediately preceding era of the Wars of Religion, had argued for solitary retirement as a response to a dangerous and frightening world. I am grateful to Anthony Ossa-Richardson for this point.

32 William Doyle, *Jansenism* (Basingstoke: Macmillan, 2000), p. 4.

33 Quoted ibid., p. 39.

34 Quoted ibid., p. 30.

35 Quoted Bishop, *Life and Adventures*, p. 231; cf. Lafond, 'Préface', p. 10.

36 See Bishop, *Life and Adventures*, p. 245.

37 Blaise Pascal, *Pensées*, ed. Gérard Ferreyrolles (Paris: Livres de Poche, 2000), hereafter cited in the text as P; p. 55.

38 A version of Isa. 41.24.

39 George Herbert, *The Temple: Sacred Poems and Private Ejaculations* (Cambridge: T. Buck and R. Daniel, 1635), p. 120.

40 Bernard le Bovier de Fontenelle, *Nouveaux dialogues des morts*, ed. with introd. and notes Jean Dagen (Paris: Marcel Didier, 1971), p. 276.

41 François de La Mothe Le Vayer, *Œuvres* (Paris: L. Billaine, 1699), vol. ix, p. 270.

42 Nicolas Boileau, *Satires, épitres, art poétique*, ed. with notes Jean-Pierre Collinet (Paris: Gallimard, 1985), pp. 97–105.

43 Quoted Jean Delvolvé, *Religion, critique et philosophie positive chez Pierre Bayle* (Paris: F. Alcan, 1906), p. 285.

44 François de Salignac de La Mothe Fénelon, Letter LXXXVII, *Œuvres complètes* (Paris, 1810), vol. 5, *Lettres Spirituelles*, p. 22.

45 Quoted Ladurie, *Saint-Simon*, p. 199.

46 Ibid., p. 232.

47 Ibid., p. 207.

48 Colin Jones, *The Great Nation: France from Louis XV to Napoleon* (London: Penguin, 2002), p. 205.

49 La Fontaine, *Fables et épitres*, introd. Émile Faguet (Paris: Nelson, 1914), p. 380.

50 See Jones, *Great Nation*, p. 75.

51 Quoted K. Baker, *Inventing the French Revolution: Essays on French Political Culture in the Eighteenth Century* (Cambridge: Cambridge University Press, 1990), p. 214.

52 Jones, *Great Nation*, p. 128.

53 Ibid., p. 70.

54 Ibid., p. 96.

55 Ibid., p. 144.

56 J. S. Spink, *French Free-Thought from Gassendi to Voltaire* (London: Athlone, 1960), p. 4.

57 Françoise Charles-Daubert, *Les Libertins érudits en France au XVIIe Siècle* (Paris: Presses Universitaires de France, 1998), p. 6.

58 See Bernadette Hoeffer, 'Penser la mélancolie: La Mothe le Vayer et Molière', in *Libertinism and Literature in Seventeenth-Century France*, ed. Richard G. Hodgson (Tübingen: Gunter Narr Verlag, 2009), pp. 129–42, p. 131.

59 Quoted Spink, *French Free-Thought*, p. 39.

60 Cyrano de Bergerac, *Œuvres libertines*, ed. F. Lachèvre (Paris: Champion, 1921), p. 61.

61 La Mothe le Vayer, *Les États et empires du soleil*, quoted Jean-Charles Darmon, 'Ironie libertine et analytique de l'imposture', in *Libertinism and Literature in Seventeenth-Century France*, ed. Richard G. Hodgson (Tübingen: Gunter Narr Verlag, 2009), pp. 9–36, p. 24.

62 *Le Parnasse satyrique du Sieur Théophile, avec le receuil des plus excellens vers satyriques de ce temps* (2 vols., Paris: Gand, 1861), vol. 1, pp. 50–3.

63 See Marc André Bernier, *Libertinage et figures de savoir: Rhétorique et roman libertin dans la France des Lumières* (Saint-Nicolas: Presses de l'Université Laval, 2001), p. 8 and passim.

64 'Avertissement de l'éditeur', Choderlos de Laclos, *Les Liaisons dangereuses*, pref. André Malraux (Paris: Gallimard, 1972), p. 26.

65 Laclos, *Liaisons dangereuses*, pp. 471–2.

66 See for instance the introduction and foreword to Donatien Alphonse François, Marquis de Sade, *The Complete Marquis de Sade*, trans. with a foreword Paul J. Gillette, introd. John S. Yankowski (2 vols., Los Angeles: Holloway House, 1966), vol. 1, pp. 11–23, 27–41.

67 For a contrary argument, see for instance Angela Carter, *The Sadeian Woman and the Ideology of Pornography* (London: Penguin, 2001), passim. I am grateful to Vicki Mahaffey for pointing this out to me.

68 Daniel Cottom, *Unhuman Culture* (Philadelphia: University of Pennsylvania Press, 2006), p. 5.

69 Sébastien-Roch Nicolas Chamfort, *Maximes, pensées, caractères et anecdotes*, with 'Une Notice sur sa vie' by Pierre-Louis Ginguené (Paris and London: J. Deboffe, 1796), hereafter cited in the text as MP; p. 21.

70 See ibid., p. 87.

71 Quoted Ginguené, 'Notice', p. lii.

72 Quoted ibid., p. xlv.

73 'Manfred: A Dramatic Poem', in George Gordon, Lord Byron, *Poetical Works*, ed. Frederick Page and John Jump (Oxford: Oxford University Press, 1970), pp. 390–406, 1.1. 154, 2.2. 57.

74 'Cain: A Mystery', in Byron, *Poetical Works*, pp. 520–44, 1.1. 138–9, 2.1. 67, 3.1. 184.

75 See Rémi Rizzo, *Byron et le misanthropie* (Paris: Pensée Universelle, 1985), p. 55.

76 Giacomo Leopardi, *Poems*, trans. with introd. Arturo Vivante (Wellfleet: Delphinium, 1988), pp. 57, 61.

77 Ladurie, *Saint-Simon*, p. 40.

78 Pascal, *Pensées*, p. 80.

79 See Saint-Simon, *Mémoires*, vol. 7, p. 706, 1491.

80 See Lathy, *Memoirs*, p. 202.

81 Quoted Mitford, *Sun King*, p. 104.

Chapter 2

1 Quoted Alexandr Solzhenitsyn, *The Gulag Archipelago 1918-56*, trans. Harry T. Willetts (New York: Random House, 2011), p. 446.

2 I am grateful to Anthony Ossa-Richardson for making almost exactly this point to me.

3 Blaise Pascal, *Pensées*, ed. Gérard Ferreyrolles (Paris: Livres de Poche, 2000), pp. 88, 235.

4 Louis de Rouvroy, duc de Saint-Simon, *Mémoires* (18 vols., Paris: Editions Ramsay, 1977), vol. 9, p. 47.

5 Saint-Simon, *Mémoires*, ed. Arthur Michel de Boislisle, Léon Lecestre and Jean de Boislisle (43 vols, Paris: Hachette, 1879–1930), vol. 31, p. 16.

6 Samuel Johnson, *A Journey to the Western Islands of Scotland*, ed. R.W. Chapman (Oxford: Oxford University Press, 1974), p. 8.

7 James Boswell, *Life of Johnson*, ed. R. W. Chapman (Oxford: Oxford University Press, 1976), hereafter cited in the text as LJ; p. 130.

8 Johnson, *The Rambler*, ed. W. J. Bate and Albrecht B. Strauss, *The Yale Edition of the Works of Samuel Johnson* (23 vols, New Haven and

London: Yale University Press, 1958–2010), vols. iii–v, hereafter cited in the text as R; 175, vol. v, p. 160. Johnson is quoting Diogenes Laertius, *The Lives of Eminent Philosophers*, 1.5.

9 Quoted Peter Martin, *Samuel Johnson: A Biography* (London: Weidenfeld and Nicholson, 2008), p. 15.

10 Johnson, 'Irene', *Poems*, ed. E. L. McAdam Jr. with George Milne, *Works*, vol. vi, pp. 109–218, p. 155.

11 Johnson, 'The Vision of Theodore, The Hermit of Teneriffe, Found in his Cell', *Rasselas and Other Tales*, ed. Gwin J. Kolb, *Works*, vol. xvi, pp. 195–212, pp. 195, 198.

12 Johnson, 'London: A Poem in Imitation of the Third Satire of Juvenal', *Poems*, pp. 47–61.

13 *Dr Johnson by Mrs Thrale: The 'Anecdotes' of Mrs Piozzi, in their Original Form*, ed. with introd. Richard Ingrams (London: Chatto and Windus, 1984), p. 36.

14 Samuel Beckett, *Letters, Vol. 1: 1929-1940*, ed. Martha Dow Felsenfeld and Lois More Overbeck (Cambridge: Cambridge University Press, 2009), p. 529.

15 See Thomas R. Preston, *Not in Timon's Manner: Feeling, Misanthropy and Satire in Eighteenth Century England* (Tuscaloosa: University of Alabama Press, 1975), pp. 121–43.

16 Johnson, *The History of Rasselas, Prince of Abyssinia* (Oxford: Oxford University Press, 1977), p. 1.

17 Johnson, 'The Young Author', *Poems*, p. 72.

18 Ecclesiastes, 1.14.

19 Quoted Martin, *Johnson*, p. 203.

20 Cf. ibid., p. 342.

21 Quoted ibid., p. 247.

22 Cf. Lacan's well-known assertion that 'there is no sexual relation'; for which see *On Feminine Sexuality: The Limits of Love and Knowledge, 1972-1973: Encore, The Seminar of Jacques Lacan, Book XX*, trans. Bruce Fink (London and New York: W.W. Norton and Co., 1975), for instance at p. 58.

23 Boswell, *Journal of a Tour to the Hebrides*, ed. R.W. Chapman (Oxford: Oxford University Press, 1974), p. 302.

24 Martin, *Johnson*, p. 458.

25 An early biographer, quoted Boswell, LJ, p. 1121.

26 Martin, *Johnson*, p. 113.

27 Quoted Boswell, LJ, p. 105.

28 Tobias Smollett, 'Preface', in *Roderick Random*, introd. H. W. Hodges (London: J.M. Dent and Sons, 1973), hereafter cited in the text as RR; p. xx.

29 See Smollett, *Travels Through France and Italy*, ed. Frank Felsenstein (Oxford: Oxford University Press, 1979), hereafter cited in the text as TFI; p. 40.

30 Preston, *Not in Timon's Manner*, pp. 73–4.

31 Quoted Jeremy Lewis, *Tobias Smollett* (London: Pimlico, 2004), p. 144.

32 See Smollett, *The Expedition of Humphry Clinker*, ed. with an introd. Angus Ross (Harmondsworth: Penguin, 1977), hereafter cited in the text as HC; p. 234.

33 Lewis, *Smollett*, p. 113.

34 See ibid., p. 109.

35 Ibid., p. 35.

36 Smollett, *The History and Adventures of an Atom*, ed. O. M. Brack Jr., introd. and notes Robert Adams Day (Athens and London: University of Georgia Press, 1989), p. 7.

37 Quoted Lewis, *Smollett*, p. 174.

38 Quoted Rev R. Wyse Jackson, 'The Secret Religion of Jonathan Swift', *Churchman*, vol. 52, no. 3 (April–June 1939), pp. 148–51, p. 150.

39 Jonathan Swift, *An Argument Against Abolishing Christianity*, in *Satires and Personal Writings*, ed. with introd. and notes William Alfred Eddy (London: Oxford University Press, 1967), pp. 1–18, pp. 3–4.

40 Swift, *A Modest Proposal for Preventing the Children of Ireland from Being a Burden to Their Parents or Country*, hereafter cited in the text as MP, in *Satires and Personal Writings*, pp. 19–31, p. 23.

41 David Nokes, *Jonathan Swift: A Hypocrite Reversed* (Oxford: Oxford University Press, 1985).

42 Swift, *Correspondence*, ed. Harold Williams (5 vols, Oxford: Oxford University Press, 1963–5), vol. iii, p. 118.

43 Swift, *Gulliver's Travels*, ed. with introd. and notes Robert Demaria Jr. (London: Penguin, 2003), hereafter cited in the text as GT; p. 47.

44 Swift, *A Tale of a Tub*, to which is added *The Battle of the Books* and *The Mechanical Operation of the Spirit*, ed. with introd. and notes R. C. Guthkelch and D. Nichol Smith (Oxford: Clarendon, 1958), hereafter cited in the text as TT; p. 167.

45 See Nokes, *Swift*, p. 183.

46 Swift, 'When I Come to be Old', in *Prose Works*, ed. Herbert Davis et al. (14 vols, Oxford: Oxford University Press, 1939–68), vol. 1, p. xxxvii.

47 Ibid.

48 Swift, *Poems*, ed. Harold Williams (3 vols, Oxford: Clarendon, 1958), vol. 2, pp. 525–30, p. 527.

49 Ibid., p. 529.

Chapter 3

1 Friedrich Nietzsche, *Twilight of the Idols, or How to Philosophize with a Hammer*, trans. Duncan Large (Oxford: Oxford University Press, 2009); and *The Will to Power*, trans. Walter Kaufmann and R. J. Hollingdale, ed. Walter Kaufmann (New York: Vintage, 1968), p. 7.

2 Ken Gemes and Christopher Janaway, 'Life-Denial versus Life-Affirmation: Schopenhauer and Nietzsche on Pessimism and Asceticism', in *A Companion to Schopenhauer*, ed. Bart Vandenabeele (Blackwell: New York, 2012), pp. 280–99, p. 289.

3 Alain Badiou, *Circonstances 1: Kosovo, 11 Septembre, Chirac/Le Pen* (Lignes: Éditions Léo Scherer, 2003), p. 8.

4 Guy Lardreau, *La Véracité: Essai d'une philosophie negative* (Lagrasse: Verdier, 1993), p. 166, 170.

5 Christian Jambet and Guy Lardreau, *Le Monde: Réponse à la question, qu'est-ce-que les droits de l'homme?* (Paris: Grasset, 1978), p. 13.

6 Karl Marx, *The Eighteenth Brumaire of Louis Bonaparte* (London: Lawrence and Wishart, 1984), p. 65.

7 Plato, *Theaetetus*, in *The Dialogues of Plato*, trans. with analysis and introd. Benjamin Jowett (5 vols, Oxford: Clarendon, 1892), 155d, vol. 4, p. 210; and Aristotle, *Metaphysics*, trans. Hugh Tredennick (2 vols, London: Heinemann, 1933), 1.2.982b12-14, vol. 1, p. 13.

8 Arthur Schopenhauer, *The World as Will and Representation*, trans. E. F. J. Payne (2 vols, New York: Dover, 1969), hereafter cited in the text as WW1 and 2; vol. 1, p. 81.

9 Jacques Rancière, *The Philosopher and his Poor*, trans. Andrew Parker (Durham: Duke University Press, 2004), p. 98.

10 Thomas Hobbes, *Leviathan, or, the Matter, Forme and Power of a Commonwealth Ecclesiastical and Civil*, ed. Michael Oakeshott, introd. Richard S. Peters (New York: Collier, 1978), hereafter cited in the text as L; p. 115, 186.

11 Quoted in A. P. Martinich, *Hobbes: A Biography* (Cambridge: Cambridge University Press, 1999), p. 2.

12 Hobbes, *On the Citizen*, ed. and trans. Richard Tuck and Michael Silverthorne, introd. Richard Tuck (Cambridge: Cambridge University Press, 1997), hereafter cited in the text as OC; p. 37.

13 Quoted Peters, 'Introduction', L, p. 12.

14 Bertrand Russell, *A History of Western Philosophy* (London: George Allen and Unwin, 1961), p. 541.

15 I owe my awareness of this term to friend and Hobbes scholar Martin Dzelzainis.

16 See Jules Steinberg, *The Obsession of Thomas Hobbes: The English Civil War in Hobbes's Political Philosophy* (New York: Peter Lang, 1988), p. 4.

17 See in particular the work of Quentin Skinner, as in *Hobbes and Republican Liberty* (Cambridge: Cambridge University Press, 2008), and *Reason and Rhetoric in the Philosophy of Hobbes* (Cambridge: Cambridge University Press, 1996).

18 See Martinich, *Hobbes*, pp. 38–9, 53–7, 93.

19 See Noel Malcolm, *Reason of State, Propaganda and the Thirty Years' War: An Unknown Translation by Thomas Hobbes* (Oxford: Clarendon, 2007), passim.

20 Hobbes, *Behemoth, or, an Epitome of the Civil Wars of England, from 1640 to 1660* (London, 1679), p. 1.

21 Ibid., pp. 2, 142, 144.

22 The original runs thus: 'Even in this short space of life, no man is so blessed by fortune that he would not many times desire to die rather than cling on to life'. Herodotus, *Histories*, Books VII–IX, trans. G Woudrouffe Harris (London: Swan Sonnenschein & Co, 1907), 7.6.46, p. 19.

23 Peter Oliver Loew, *Danzig: Biographie einer Stadt* (München: Verlag C.H.Beck oHG, 2011), pp. 11, 47, 143.

24 See ibid., p. 143.

25 Quoted David E. Cartwright, *Schopenhauer: A Biography* (Cambridge: Cambridge University Press, 2010), p. 1.

26 Christopher Clark, *Iron Kingdom: The Rise and Fall of Prussia 1600-1947* (London: Allen Lane, 2006), p. 354.

27 See Adam Zamoyski, *1812: Napoleon's Fatal March on Moscow* (London: Harper, 2005), pp. 93–4.

28 Quoted ibid., p. 497. I take all details in this paragraph from this excellent book.

29 See for example Clark, *Iron Kingdom*, p. 357; another superb book.

30 See ibid., pp. 356–7.

31 Cartwright, *Schopenhauer*, p. 239.

5

32 Ibid., p. 180.

33 See Christopher Janaway, *Schopenhauer: A Very Short Introduction* (Oxford: Oxford University Press), pp. 16–27.

34 Jean-Jacques Rousseau, *Emile ou de l'éducation*, *Œuvres complètes*, vol. IV, ed. Bernard Gagnebin and Marcel Raymond, with the collaboration of Pierre Burgelin, Henri Gouhier, John S. Spink, Roger de Vilmorin and Charles Wirz (Paris: Gallimard, 1969), hereafter cited in the text as E; p. 470.

35 See in particular Rousseau, *Les Rêveries du promeneur solitaire*, *Œuvres complètes*, vol. I, ed. Bernard Gagnebin, Marcel Raymond and Robert Osmont (Paris: Gallimard, 1959), hereafter cited in the text as RPS; p. 1066.

36 Rousseau, *Les Confessions*, ed. Bernard Gangebin and Marcel Raymond, pref. J.-B. Pontalis, notes by Catherine Kœnig (Paris: Gallimard, 1973), hereafter cited in the text as CO; p. 75.

37 Rousseau, *Du Contrat social ou principes du droit politique*, *Œuvres complètes*, vol. III, ed. Bernard Gagnebin, Marcel Raymond, with the collaboration of François Bouchardy, Jean-Daniel Candaux, Robert Derathé, Jean Fabre, Jean Starobinski and Sven Stelling-Michaud (Paris: Gallimard, 1964), hereafter cited in the text as CS; p. 351.

38 Joseph Conrad, *Victory* (Harmondsworth: Penguin, 1984), p. 169.

39 Rousseau, *Julie, ou la nouvelle Héloise*, ed. with introd., chronology and notes by René Pomeau (Paris: Bordas, 1988), hereafter cited in the text as J; p. 738.

40 See Isaiah Berlin, 'Rousseau', in *Freedom and Its Betrayal: Six Enemies*, ed. Henry Hardy (London: Pimlico, 2003), pp. 27–49, esp. pp. 47–9.

41 For an excellent account of Rousseau's relationship with Geneva, subtle beyond my scope here, see Helena Rosenblatt, *Rousseau and Geneva: From the 'First Discourse' to 'The Social Contract' 1749-62* (Cambridge: Cambridge University Press, 1997).

42 Maurice Cranston, *Jean-Jacques: The Early Life and Work of Jean-Jacques Rousseau, 1712-1754* (Harmondsworth: Penguin, 1987), p. 14.

43 Nicolas Bouvier, 'Geneva', in *Geneva, Zurich, Basel: History, Culture and National Identity*, ed. Nicolas Bouvier, Gordon A. Craig and Lionel Gossman, introd. Carl E. Schorske (Princeton: Princeton University Press, 1994), pp. 17–38, pp. 28–9.

44 Rousseau, letter to Mme. d'Houdentot, 5 January 1758; in *Correspondance complète*, ed. R. A. Leigh (51 vols, Geneva: Institut et Musée Voltaire, 1965–91), vol. 5, p. 7.

45 Quoted Cranston, *Jean-Jacques*, p. 228.

46 Quoted ibid., p. 309.

47 Leo Damrosch, *Jean-Jacques Rousseau: Restless Genius* (New York: Houghton Mifflin, 2007), p. 376.

48 Quoted Roderick Graham, *The Great Infidel: A Life of David Hume* (Edinburgh: John Donald, 2004), p. 312.

Chapter 4

1 Arthur Koestler, *Darkness at Noon*, trans. Daphne Hardy (Harmondsworth: Penguin, 1946), p. 229.

2 Jane Austen, *Northanger Abbey* (Harmondsworth: Penguin, 1972), p. 202.

3 Quoted Tim Pat Coogan, *Wherever Green is Worn* (London: Hutchinson, 2000), p. 63.

4 Ruth Dudley Edwards, *Ireland in the Age of the Tudors: The Destruction of Hiberno-Norman Civilization* (London: Croom Helm, 1977), pp. 23, 26.

5 James Joyce, *Occasional, Critical and Political Writing*, ed. with an introd. and notes by Kevin Barry, with translations from the Italian by Conor Deane (Oxford: Oxford University Press, 2000), p. 119.

6 Quoted David Edwards, Pádraig Lenihan and Clodagh Tait, 'Early Modern Ireland: A History of Violence', in *Age of Atrocity: Violence and Political Conflict in Early Modern Ireland*, ed. Edwards, Lenihan and Tait (Dublin: Four Courts, 2007), pp. 9–33, p. 26. I get much of the material in this passage from this excellent essay.

7 See Edwards, 'The Escalation of Violence in Sixteenth-Century Ireland', in *Age of Atrocity*, ed. Edwards, Lenihan and Tait, pp. 34–78, p. 69.

8 Edwards, Lenihan and Tait, 'Early Modern Ireland', pp. 23–4.

9 See Kenneth Nicholls, 'The Other Massacre: English Killings of Irish 1641-2', in *Age of Atrocity*, ed. Edwards, Lenihan and Tait, pp. 176–91, p. 190.

10 John Childs, 'The Laws of War in Seventeenth Century Europe and their Application during the Jacobite War in Ireland', in *Age of Atrocity*, ed. Edwards, Lenihan and Tait, pp. 283–300, p. 298.

11 See Ian McBride, *Eighteenth-Century Ireland: The Isle of Slaves* (Dublin: Gill & Macmillan, 2009), p. 34.

12 Anon., *The Mantle Thrown Off: Or, The Irish-Man Dissected* (London: for Richard Baldwin, 1689), p. 9.

13 Edmund Burke, *A Letter from the Right Hon. Edmund Burke, M.P., in the Kingdom of Great Britain, to Sir Hercules Langrishe* (London: J. Debrett, 1792), p. 87.

14 Michael McConville, *Ascendancy to Oblivion: The Story of the Anglo-Irish* (London: Quartet, 1986), p. 125.

15 Joyce, *A Portrait of the Artist as a Young Man*, ed. with introd. and notes by Seamus Deane (London: Penguin, 1992), p. 195.

16 See Deane, notes, Joyce, *A Portrait*, p. 309.

17 See Hugh Kenner, *A Colder Eye: The Modern Irish Writers* (Baltimore: Johns Hopkins University Press, 1989).

18 See Nicholls, 'The Other Massacre', p. 183.

19 Richard McCabe, *Spenser's Monstrous Regiment: Elizabethan Ireland and the Poetics of Difference* (Cambridge: Cambridge University Press, 2005), p. 86. This is one of three excellent accounts of Spenser in an Irish context. See also Willy Maley, *Salvaging Spenser: Colonialism, Culture and Identity* (Basingstoke: Macmillan, 1997); and Andrew Hadfield, *Spenser's Irish Experience: Wilde Fruit and Salvage Soyl* (Cambridge: Cambridge University Press, 1997).

20 Joyce, *Occasional, Critical and Political Writing*, p. 119.

21 McCabe, *Spenser's Monstrous Regiment*, p. 92.

22 See R. F. Foster, *Modern Ireland 1600-1972* (London: Penguin, 1989), p. 328.

23 For an account of a specific aspect of this, see my *The Strong Spirit: History, Politics and Aesthetics in the Writings of James Joyce 1898-1915* (Oxford: Oxford University Press, 2013), pp. 96–100.

24 Joyce, *Occasional, Critical and Political Writing*, p. 119.

25 See for instance Foster, *Modern Ireland*, pp. 38–42.

26 Joyce, *Occasional, Critical and Political Writing*, p. 58.

27 *An Duanaire: 1600-1900: Poems of the Dispossessed*, trans. Thomas Kinsella (Portlaoise: Dolmen Press, 1981), p. 115.

28 See Máirtín Ó Briain, 'Satire in Seventeenth- and Eighteenth-Century Gaelic Poetry', in *Memory and the Modern in Celtic Literatures*, ed. Joseph Falaky Nagy (Dublin: Four Courts Press, 2006), pp. 118–42, p. 126.

29 Quoted James Hardiman (ed.), 'Notes', in *Irish Minstrelsy or Bardic Remains of Ireland, with English Poetical Translations*, introd. Máire Mhac an tSaoi (2 vols, Shannon: Irish University Press, 1971), vol. 1, p. 183.

30 Seamus Deane, Andrew Carpenter and Jonathan Williams (eds), *Field Day Anthology* (2 vols, Derry: Field Day Publications, 1991), vol. 1, p. 287.

31 Ibid., vol. 1, p. 294.

32 *An Duanaire*, p. 141; and Edwards, 'The Escalation of Violence', p. 58.

33 Brian Mac Cuarta, 'Religious Violence against Settlers in South Ulster, 1641-2', in *Age of Atrocity*, ed. Edwards, Lenihan and Tait, pp. 145–75, p. 154.

34 In Deane, Carpenter and Williams (eds), *Field Day Anthology*, vol. 1, p. 287.

35 Quoted Alan Bliss, 'The English Language in Early Modern Ireland', in *A New History of Ireland, vol. III: Early Modern Ireland 1534-1691*, ed. T. W. Moody, F. X. Martin and F. J. Byrne (Oxford: Oxford University Press, 2009), pp. 546–60, p. 555. The word 'tory' was originally used to describe an Irish rebel or outlaw. Its mutation is piquant, and profoundly instructive.

36 In Deane, Carpenter and Williams (eds), *Field Day Anthology*, vol. 1, p. 297.

37 Brian Ó Cuív, 'The Irish Language in the Early Modern Period', in *A New History of Ireland*, ed. Moody, Martin and Byrne, vol. III, pp. 509–42, p. 510.

38 Ibid.

39 In Deane, Carpenter and Williams (eds), *Field Day Anthology*, vol. 1, p. 286.

40 *An Duanaire*, p. 169.

41 See Alan Harrison, 'Literature in Irish 1600-1800', in *Field Day Anthology*, ed. Deane, Carpenter and Williams, vol. 1, pp. 274–8, p. 277.

42 *An Duanaire*, p. 125.

43 Ibid., p. 157.

44 Ibid., pp. 195, 197.

45 See Ó Cuív, 'The Irish Language', pp. 541–2.

46 Cecile O'Rahilly, *Five Seventeenth-Century Political Poems* (Dublin: Dublin Institute for Advanced Studies, 1952), pp. 17, 146.

47 Anon., *Aphorismical Discovery of Treasonable Faction, 1641-52*, with an appendix of original letters and documents, ed. John T. Gilbert (3 vols, Dublin: Irish Archaeological and Celtic Society, 1879–80), vol. 1, p. 40.

48 Ibid., vol. 1, p. 75, vol. 2, p. 78.

49 Ibid., vol. 1, p. 85.

50 Ibid., vol. 1, p. 43.

51 See Harrison, 'Literature in Irish 1600-1800', p. 274.

52 *An Duanaire*, p. 153.

53 See Murray G. H. Pittock, *Poetry and Jacobite Politics in Eighteenth-Century Ireland* (Cambridge: Cambridge University Press, 1994), p. 194.

54 Hardiman (ed.), *Irish Minstrelsy*, p. 9.

55 Joyce, *Occasional, Critical and Political Writing*, p. 55.

56 Anthony Cronin, *No Laughing Matter: The Life and Times of Flann O'Brien* (London: Grafton, 1989), p. 73.

57 Ibid., p. 130.

58 Quoted Darcy O'Brien, *Patrick Kavanagh* (London: Associated University Presses, 1975), pp. 23, 31.

59 Lung cancer turned him into a pantheist and a contented dreamer. I am grateful to Joe Brooker for alerting me to this.

60 See Cronin, *No Laughing Matter*, p. 192.

61 Ibid. The question for doubters is whether Cronin does not read back too freely from the explicit Manichaeanism of *The Dalkey Archive*.

62 Quoted ibid., p. 105.

63 Mhac an tSaoi, 'Introduction', in *Irish Minstrelsy*, ed. Hardiman, vol. 1, pp. v–xii, p. v.

64 Oliver Goldsmith, *The Vicar of Wakefield: A Tale* (London: H.D. Symons, 1793), p. 46.

65 Goldsmith, *The Citizen of the World: Letters from a Chinese Philosopher, Residing in London, to his Friends in the East*, with notes by J. W. M. Gibbs (London: George Bell & Sons, 1894).

66 Ibid., p. 48.

67 Ibid., p. 300.

68 Ibid., p. 39.

69 Samuel Beckett, *How It Is* (London: John Calder, 1964), hereafter cited in the text as HII; p. 70.

70 Beckett, letters to Alan Schneider; quoted Anthony Cronin, *Samuel Beckett: The Last Modernist* (London: Harper Collins, 1996), pp. 459, 462.

71 Jonathan Swift, *Gulliver's Travels* (London: Penguin, 2003), p. 242.

72 Alexander Somerville, *Letters from Ireland During the Famine of 1847*, ed. and introd. K. D. M. Snell (Dublin: Irish Academic Press, 1994), p. 108.

73 In this respect, he can sound, *mutatis mutandis*, like a travesty of Anglo-Irish revivalists (W. B. Yeats, AE [George Russell]), and his discourse like a Beckettian parody of Revivalism.

Chapter 5

1 Emmeline Pankhurst, *My Own Story* (London: Everleigh Nash, 1914), p. 294.

2 See Sandra Stanley Holton, *Feminism and Democracy: Women's Suffrage and Reform Politics in Britain 1900-1918* (Cambridge: Cambridge University Press, 1986).

3 In 'A Plea for Women', quoted Patricia Hollis, *Women in Public: The Women's Movement 1850-1900* (London: Allen & Unwin, 1979), p. 293.

4 Pankhurst, *My Own Story*, pp. 281–2.

5 Pankhurst, quoted Jane Marcus (ed.), *Suffrage and the Pankhursts* (London: Kegan Paul, 1987), pp. 153–62, p. 157.

6 Pankhurst, *My Own Story*, pp. 295, 323.

7 Angela K. Smith, *Suffrage Discourse in Britain During the First World War* (Aldershot: Ashgate, 2005), p. 13.

8 'Introduction', in *The Case for Women's Suffrage*, ed. Brougham Villiers (London: Fisher and Unwin, 1907), p. 18.

9 Liz McQuiston, *Suffragettes to She-Devils: Women's Liberation and Beyond*, foreword Germaine Greer (London: Phaidon, 1997), p. 18.

10 Julia Bush, *Women Against the Vote: Female Anti-Suffragism in Britain* (Oxford: Oxford University Press, 2007), p. 75.

11 Bush, *Women*, pp. 78, 88.

12 Mrs Humphry Ward, *Delia Blanchflower* (London: Ward, Lock & co., 1917), p. 340.

13 See Christabel Pankhurst, 'The Great Scourge, and How to End It' (London: E. Pankhurst, 1913); and Cicely Hamilton, *Marriage as a Trade* (London: Chapman and Hall, 1909).

14 Bush, *Women*, p. 106.

15 Holton, *Feminism and Democracy*, p. 152.

16 See Hilary Spurling, *Ivy: The Life of I. Compton-Burnett* (London: Richard Cohen, 1995).

17 See Robert Green, *Edith Sitwell: Avant-Garde Poet, English Genius* (London: Virago, 2011), pp. 123, 175, 182–3, 276, 319.

18 See Green, *Edith Sitwell*, pp. 35–41.

19 See Lilian Pizzichini, *The Blue Hour: A Portrait of Jean Rhys* (London: Bloomsbury, 2009), p. 61.

20 Ibid., p. 71.

21 'Lady Rogue Singleton', Stevie Smith, *Collected Poems*, ed. with pref. James MacGibbon (London: Penguin, 1977), p. 194.

22 Edith Sitwell, *I Live Under a Black Sky*, with a memoir by Reresby Sitwell (London: Peter Owen, 2007), hereafter cited in the text as BS; p. 102.

23 Ivy Compton-Burnett, *Pastors and Masters*, with a foreword by Sue Townsend (London: Hesperus, 2009), hereafter cited in the text as PM; p. 90.

24 Compton-Burnett, *A Family and its Fortune* (Harmondsworth: Penguin, 1983), hereafter cited in the text as FF; p. 30.

25 Compton-Burnett, *A Heritage and its History* (London: Gollancz, 1959), pp. 5–6.

26 'Introduction', in *Woman's Work and Woman's Culture*, ed. Josephine E. Butler (London: Macmillan, 1869), pp. vii–lxiv, p. xviii.

27 Henry James, *Letters to A.C. Benson and Auguste Monod*, ed. E. C. Benson (London: Elkins Mathews and Marrot, 1930), p. 35.

28 Joseph Baines, 'Ivy Compton Burnett', in *New Makers of Modern Culture*, ed. Justin Wintle (2 vols, London: Routledge, 2007), vol. 1, pp. 319–20, at p. 320.

29 Compton-Burnett, *Elders and Betters* (London: Gollancz, 1944), hereafter cited in the text as EB; p. 146.

30 Compton-Burnett, *Men and Wives* (London: Bloomsbury, 2012), hereafter cited in the text as MW; p. 75.

31 Compton-Burnett, *Mother and Son* (London: Gollancz, 1955), hereafter cited in the text as MS; p. 63.

32 Quoted in Charles Burkhart (ed.), *The Art of I. Compton-Burnett* (London: Gollancz, 1972), p. 55.

33 Jean Rhys, *Good Morning, Midnight*, introd. A. L. Kennedy (Penguin: London, 2000), hereafter cited in the text as GMM; p. 6.

34 Pizzichini, *Blue Hour*, p. 116.

35 Ibid., p. 31.

36 Ibid.

37 See ibid., p. 67.

38 Rhys, *Quartet*, introd. Katie Owen (London: Penguin, 2000), hereafter cited in the text as Q; p. 12.

39 Rhys, *Wide Sargasso Sea*, ed. Francis Wyndham (London: Penguin, 1993), hereafter cited in the text as WSS; p. 48.

40 Clément Rosset, *Le Réel: Traité de l'Idiotie* (Paris: Éditions de Minuit, 1977), p. 41.

41 Pizzichini, *Blue Hour*, pp. 19–20.

42 Nathalie Sarraute, 'L'Ère du soupçon', hereafter cited in the text as ES , in *Œuvres Complètes*, ed. Jean-Yves Tadié et al. (Paris: Gallimard, 1996), p. 1584.

43 Sarraute, 'Preface', hereafter cited in the text as PR, in *Tropisms, and The Age of Suspicion*, trans. Maria Jolas (London: John Calder, 1963), pp. 7–11, at pp. 7–8.

44 Sarraute, *Le Planétarium* (Paris: Gallimard, 1972), hereafter cited in the text as LP; p. 157.

45 Sarraute, *Martereau* (Paris: Gallimard, 1953), hereafter cited in the text as M; p. 177.

46 Roger McLure, *Le Planétarium* (London: Grant & Cutler, 1987), p. 26.

47 See Sarraute, *Portrait d'un homme inconnu* (Paris: Gallimard, 1956), hereafter cited in the text as PHI; pp. 32, 35.

48 *Tropismes*, hereafter cited in the text as T; in *Œuvres complètes*, p. 17.

49 See Hermione Lee, *Virginia Woolf* (London: Chatto & Windus, 1996). I am indebted to her book in this paragraph.

50 Virginia Woolf, *Jacob's Room* (London: Triad Panther Books, 1977), p. 93.

51 Leonard Woolf, *Downhill all the Way* (London: Hogarth Press, 1975), p. 250.

52 Virginia Woolf, Letter to Ethel Smythe, 26 November 1935, in *The Letters of Virginia Woolf*, ed. Nigel Nicolson and Joanne Trautmann (6 vols, London: Hogarth Press, 1975–80), vol. 5, p. 446.

53 Virginia Woolf, Letter to Sibyl Colefax, 6 May 1936, *Letters*, vol. 6, p. 36.

54 Virginia Woolf, *Diaries*, ed. Anne Oliver Bell and Andrew McNeillie (5 vols, London: Hogarth, 1977–84), vol. 5, p. 234.

55 Ibid.

56 See Lee, *Woolf*, p. 737.

57 Julia Briggs, *Virginia Woolf: An Inner Life* (London: Allen Lane, 2005), p. 398.

58 See for example Jacques Lacan, 'The Meaning of the Phallus', trans. Jacqueline Rose, *Feminine Sexuality: Jacques Lacan and the École Freudienne*, ed. Juliet Mitchell and Jacqueline Rose (London: Macmillan, 1982), pp. 74–85; and Joan Riviere, 'Womanliness as a Masquerade', *International Journal of Psychoanalysis*, vol. 10 (1929), pp. 303–13.

59 Emily Dickinson, *Poems*, ed. R. W. Franklin (3 vols, Cambridge, MA: Harvard University Press, 1998), hereafter cited in the text as EDP with poem, volume and page number; Poem 527, 2.535.

60 Sylvia Plath, *Collected Poems*, ed. Ted Hughes (London: Faber and Faber, 1989), hereafter cited in the text as PCP; p. 245.

61 *The Journals of Sylvia Plath*, ed. Ted Hughes and Frances McCullough (New York: Random House, 1982), p. 227.

62 Jacqueline Rose, *The Haunting of Sylvia Plath* (London: Virago, 1991), p. 6.

63 Sylvia Plath, *Letters Home: Correspondence 1950-1963*, ed. with a commentary Aurelia Schober Plath (London: Faber & Faber, 1975), p. 473.

64 See Ruth Ann Halicks, 'Interview with Nathalie Sarraute', at http://artfuldodge.sites.wooster.edu/content/conversation-nathalie-sarraute (accessed 22 December 2013).

Chapter 6

1 Quoted in Christopher Clark, *The Sleepwalkers: How Europe Went to War in 1914* (London: Penguin, 2012), p. 361. The second phrase is Clark's. Though it is not Clark's concern to say so, few if any of the human beings concerned come out of his superb book very well.

2 Michel Foucault, *Le Courage de la verité* (Paris: Seuil/Gallimard), 2009.

3 See Colin Wells, *The Devil and Doctor Dwight: Satire and Theology in the Early American Republic* (Chapel Hill: University of North Carolina Press, 2002), p. 36 and passim.

4 See Anthony Cronin, *Samuel Beckett: The Last Modernist* (London: HarperCollins, 1996), p. 591.

5 Sinclair Lewis, *Babbitt* (New York: Dover Books, 2003), hereafter cited in the text as B; p. 144.

6 For which see http://en.wikipedia.org/wiki/Prosperity_theology (accessed 1 October 2014).

7 David Yount, *America's Spiritual Utopias: The Quest for Heaven on Earth* (Westport: Praeger, 2008), p. xiii.

8 John Winthrop, 'A Model of Christian Charity', quoted Amy S. Greenberg, *Manifest Destiny and American Territorial Expansion: A Brief History with Documents* (Boston and New York: Bedford and St Martin's, 2012), p. 43.

9 See Thomas O. Beebee, *Millennial Literatures of the Americas 1492-2002* (Oxford: Oxford University Press, 2008), pp. 24–45.

10 See Lawrence R. Samuel, *The American Dream: A Cultural History* (Syracuse: Syracuse University Press, 2012), p. 6. Much of this paragraph derives from Samuel's book.

11 Ibid.

12 I take 'harrowing' from J. E. Chamberlin, *The Harrowing of Eden: White Attitudes Towards Native Americans* (New York: Seabury, 1975), to which this paragraph is indebted.

13 Perry Miller and Thomas H. Johnson, *The Puritans* (2 vols, New York and London: Harper and Row, 1963), vol. 1, p. 1. All references are to this volume.

14 Samuel Willard, 'The Character of a Good Ruler', in Miller and Johnson, *Puritans*, p. 251.

15 Thomas Hooker, 'A True Sight of Sin', in Miller and Johnson, *Puritans*, p. 295.

16 John Cotton, *A Briefe Exposition with Practicall Observations upon the Whole Book of Ecclesiastes* (London: T.C. for Ralph Smith, 1654), p. 131.

17 See Miller and Johnson, *Puritans*, p. 191.

18 Ibid., p. 58.

19 Cotton, *Briefe Exposition*, p. 160.

20 See Willard, 'Degenerating New England', Miller and Johnson, *Puritans*, p. 375.

21 Cotton, 'Limitation of Government', in Miller and Johnson, *Puritans*, p. 213.

22 Hooker, 'True Sight' and 'Meditation', in Miller and Johnson, *Puritans*, pp. 293, 303.

23 Hooker, 'Wandering Thoughts', in Miller and Johnson, *Puritans*, p. 307.

24 Winthrop, 'Speech to the General Court', 3 July 1645, in Miller and Johnson, *Puritans*, p. 246.

25 Increase Mather, 'Sleeping At Sermons', in Miller and Johnson, *Puritans*, pp. 348–9.

26 Nathaniel Hawthorne, *The Blithedale Romance, The Centenary Edition of the Works of Nathaniel Hawthorne*, vol. 3, ed. Fredson Bowers et al. (Columbus: Ohio State University Press, 1971), p. 37.

27 Letter to Hawthorne, 16? April? 1851, in Herman Melville, *Moby Dick*, ed. with introd. Tony Tanner (Oxford: Oxford University Press, 1988), hereafter cited in the text as MD; p. 597.

28 See G. R. Thompson and Virgil L. Locke, *Ruined Eden of the Present: Hawthorne, Melville and Poe* (West Lafayette: Purdue University Press, 1981).

29 See Julius Pratt, 'The Origin of "Manifest Destiny"', *American Historical Review*, vol. 32, no. 4 (1927), pp. 795–8.

30 Herman Melville, *Typee*, with an afterword by Harrison Hayford (New York: Signet, 1964), hereafter cited in the text as T; p. 33.

31 Melville, *Redburn*, ed. with introd. Harold Beaver (Penguin: Harmondsworth, 1977), hereafter cited in the text as R; p. 54.

32 The point is clear, the Howard referred to a mystery so far as I know.

33 Letter to Hawthorne, 1? June 1851, in MD, p. 598.

34 Melville, 'Benito Cereno', hereafter cited in the text as BC, in *Billy Budd, Sailor and Selected Tales* (Oxford: Oxford University Press, 1997), p. 164.

35 W. H. Auden, 'September 1, 1939', in *Another Time* (New York: Random House, 1949), p. 112.

36 Melville, 'Bartleby', hereafter cited in the text as BA, in *Billy Budd*, pp. 21, 23.

37 Lawrence Thompson, *Melville's Quarrel With God* (Princeton: Princeton University Press, 1952), p. 425.

38 Henry David Thoreau, *Walden*, ed. J. Lyndon Shanley (Princeton: Princeton University Press, 1971), hereafter cited in the text as W; p. 135.

39 Thoreau, 'A Winter Walk', *The Major Essays*, ed. Richard Dillman (Albany, NY: Whitston, 2001), pp. 146–60, p. 149.

40 Thoreau, 'The Natural History of Massachusetts', hereafter cited in the text as NHM, *The Major Essays*, pp. 192–211, p. 193.

41 Thoreau, 'Civil Disobedience', hereafter cited in the text as CD, *Political Writings*, ed. Nancy L. Rosenblum (Cambridge: Cambridge University Press, 1996), pp. 1–22, p. 3.

42 Thoreau, 'The Maine Woods', in *A Week on the Concord and Merrimack Rivers, Walden, The Maine Woods, Cape Cod*, with notes by Robert F. Sayer (New York: Library of America, 1985), pp. 589–845, p. 596.

43 Thoreau, 'Life Without Principle', hereafter cited in the text as LWP, *Political Writings*, pp. 103–22, pp. 118–19.

44 Robert Lowell, 'Waking in the Blue', in *Collected Poems*, ed. Frank Bidart and David Gewanter (London: Faber and Faber, 2003), p. 184.

45 Dorothy Parker, *Complete Stories*, ed. Colleen Breese, introd. Regina Barreca (Harmondsworth: Penguin, 1995), hereafter cited in the text as CS; p. 35.

46 See for instance Parker, CS, p. 204.

47 So, too, of course, have historians and literary critics, but more drily and unmisanthropically. For an instructive early example, see Frederick L. Paxson, *The Last American Frontier* (New York: Macmillan, 1910). Among numerous later instances, see Sharon Block, *Rape and Sexual Power in Early America* (Chapel Hill: University of North Carolina Press, 2006); and Deborah L. Madsen, 'Discourses of Frontier Violence and the Trauma of National Emergence in Larry McMurtry's *Lonesome Dove* Quartet', *Canadian Review of American Studies*, vol. 39, no. 2 (2009), pp. 185–204.

48 Mark Twain, *The Prince and the Pauper* (New York: Signet, 1964), p. 167.

49 Twain, *Life on the Mississippi* (New York: Signet, 1961), hereafter cited in the text as LM; pp. 21–2.

50 Twain, *The Adventures of Tom Sawyer* and *The Adventures of Huckleberry Finn*, introd. Andrew Sinclair, notes by Michael Lerner (London: Pan, 1972), hereafter cited in the text as HF; p. 272.

51 Twain, 'The Man Who Corrupted Hadleyburg', in *The Mysterious Stranger and Other Stories* (New York: Dover, 1992), hereafter cited in the text as MS; pp. 46–7.

52 Twain, 'The Mysterious Stranger', in MS, p. 78, 83.

53 Twain, *A Connecticut Yankee at King Arthur's Court*, introd. Justin Kaplan (Harmondsworth: Penguin, 1977), hereafter cited in the text as CY; p. 144.

54 Twain, *The Tragedy of Pudd'nhead Wilson* (New York: Perennial, 1965), hereafter cited in the text as PW; p. 136.

55 Robert A. Jelliffe, *Faulkner at Nagano* (Tokyo: Kenkyusha, 1956), p. 88.

56 William Faulkner, *Absalom, Absalom!* (Harmondsworth: Penguin, 1970), hereafter cited in the text as AA; p. 103.

57 Faulkner, *Sanctuary* (Harmondsworth: Penguin, 1970), hereafter cited in the text as S; p. 147.

58 Edmund Wilson, 'William Faulkner's Reply to the Civil-Rights Program', in *William Faulkner: Critical Assessments*, ed. Henry Claridge (4 vols, East Sussex: Helm Information, 1999), vol. iv, pp. 347–53, p. 353.

59 Faulkner, *Snopes: The Hamlet, The Town, The Mansion*, ed. George Garrett (New York: Modern Library, 1994), hereafter cited in the text as H, T and M; T, p. 372.

60 Faulkner, 'Speech of Acceptance upon the Award of the Nobel Prize for Literature' (New York: Spiral, 1951).

61 Berkeley Carolyn Porter, *William Faulkner: Lives and Legacies* (Oxford: Oxford University Press, 2007), p. 167.

62 Cormac McCarthy, *No Country for Old Men* (London: Picador, 2006), hereafter cited in the text as NC; p. 4.

63 McCarthy, *The Crossing*, hereafter cited in the text as TC, *The Border Trilogy* (London: Picador, 1998), p. 457.

64 McCarthy, *All The Pretty Horses*, *The Border Trilogy*, p. 241.

65 McCarthy, *Blood Meridian: The Evening Redness in the West* (London: Picador, 1990), pp. 43, 83.

66 McCarthy, *The Road* (London: Picador, 2007), p. 79.

67 Hooker, 'Meditation', in Miller and Johnson, *Puritans*, p. 305.

Conclusion

1 For which see Simon Critchley, *Faith of the Faithless: Experiments in Political Theology* (London: Verso, 2012); and *Infinitely Demanding: Ethics of Commitment, Politics of Resistance* (London: Verso, 2013).

2 See Howard Hotson, 'Big Business at the Heart of the System: Understanding the Global University Crisis', at http://www.srhe.ac.uk/conference2012/; and the home page of the World Economic Forum at http://www.weforum.org/ (both accessed 30 November 2014).

3 See Steve Fuller, 'Dark Ecology as the Higher Misanthropy', http://slowlorisblog. wordpress.com /2014/05/20/ dark-ecology-as-the-higher-misanthropy/ (accessed 7 November 2014).

4 See Nick Land, *The Dark Enlightenment*, http://www.thedarkenlightenment.com/the-dark-enlightenment-by-nick-land/ (accessed 7 November 2014).

5 Graham Harman, *Towards Speculative Realism: Essays and Lectures* (Winchester and Washington: Zero Books, 2010), pp. 94–5, 101.

6 Ray Brassier, *Nihil Unbound: Enlightenment and Extinction* (London: Palgrave Macmillan, 2010), p. 58.

7 Quentin Meillassoux, *Après la finitude: Essai sur la nécessité de la contingence*, pref. Alain Badiou (Paris: Seuil, 2006), p. 31.

8 Brassier, *Nihil Unbound*, p. 49.

9 Iain Hamilton Grant, *Philosophies of Nature After Schelling* (London: Continuum, 2008), p. 127.

10 Brassier, *Nihil Unbound*, p. 52.

11 Judith Halberstam, *The Queer Art of Failure* (Durham and London: Duke University Press, 2011), hereafter cited in the text as QA; pp. 110–11.

12 Irving Welch, *Trainspotting* (London: Norton, 1996), p. 187; quoted Halberstam, QA, p. 90.

13 Lee Edelman, *No Future: Queer Theory and the Death Drive* (Durham: Duke University Press, 2004), hereafter cited in the text as NF; p. 2.

14 On the evidence Stefan Herbrechter provides. See his *Posthumanism: A Critical Analysis* (London: Bloomsbury, 2013).

15 See for instance Raymond Kurzweil, *The Age of Spiritual Machines* (New York: Viking, 1999); Hans Moravec, *Robot: Mere Machine to Transcendent Mind* (Oxford: Oxford University Press, 2000); and Marvin Minsky, *The Emotion Machine: Commonsense Thinking, Artificial Intelligence, and the Future of the Human Mind* (New York: Simon & Schuster, 2007).

16 See their Wikipedia entry at http://en.wikipedia.org/wiki/Extropianism (accessed 6 November 2014).

17 See Jean-Pierre Dupuy, *Pour un catastrophisme éclairé: Quand l'impossible est certain* (Paris: Seuil, 2004); and Francis Fukuyama, *Our Posthuman Future: Consequences of the Biotechnology Revolution* (New York: St Martin's Press, 2003). For a detailed account of this contemporary nightmare and those who subscribe to it, see Sasha

Lilley, David McNally, Eddie Yuen and James Davis, *Catastrophism: The Apocalyptic Politics of Death and Rebirth*, foreword Doug Henwood (Oakland: PM Press/Spectre, 2012).

18 Ihab Hassan, 'Prometheus as Performer: Towards a Posthumanist Culture? A University Masque in Five Scenes', *The Georgia Review*, vol. 21, no. 4 (1977), pp. 830–50, at p. 848; quoted Herbrechter, p. 35.

19 Rosi Braidotti, *The Posthuman* (Cambridge: Polity, 2013), pp. 3, 35.

20 Braidotti, *Posthuman*, p. 11.

21 N. Katherine Hayles, *How We Became Posthuman: Virtual Bodies in Cybernetics, Literature and Informatics* (Chicago: University of Chicago Press, 1999), p. 286.

22 Donna Haraway, *When Species Meet* (London and Minneapolis: University of Minnesota Press, 2008), p. 76. The second quotation is Braidotti's paraphrase of Haraway, *Posthuman*, p. 58.

23 Daniel Cottom, *Unhuman Culture* (Philadelphia: University of Pennsylvania Press, 2006), p. 150.

24 Ibid., p. 152.

25 Ibid.

26 James E. Lovelock, *The Vanishing Face of Gaia: A Final Warning* (London: Penguin, 2009), p. 38.

27 Greg Garrard is wistful for such faith, but can give no indication of a feasible political programme that would make the 'voluntary global One Child Policy' he espouses a reality (as I write, China has just reneged on such a programme). Almost all contemporary liberal, social-democratic and 'resistant' optimisms run up against the same problem: trying to provide answers to immensely serious questions in an era that has given up on any serious politics.

28 See http://news.heartland.org/newspaper-article/2006/08/01/eco-misanthropes-want-better-living-through-mass-death (accessed 6 November 2014). Scandalously, Pianka was alleged to be a big fan of Ebola.

29 Greg Garrard, 'Worlds Without Us: Some Types of Disanthropy', http://www. academia. edu/257407/ (accessed 7 November 2014). Cf. for instance Terre Satterfield, who shows how adept loggers have been in exploiting the negative connotations of eco-misanthropy in their struggle with their opponents. See *Anatomy of a Conflict: Identity, Knowledge, and Emotion in Old-Growth Forests* (Vancouver: UBC Press, 2002), pp. 121ff.

30 John Gray, *Straw Dogs: Thoughts on Humans and Other Animals* (London: Granta, 2003), hereafter cited in the text as SD; p. 13.

31 Gray, *Enlightenment's Wake: Politics and Culture at the Close of the Modern Age* (London: Routledge, 1995), hereafter cited in the text as EW; p. 2.

32 Gray, *False Dawn: The Delusions of Global Capitalism* (London: Granta, 1998), pp. 2–3.

33 Gray, *Two Faces of Liberalism* (Cambridge: Polity, 2000), hereafter cited in the text as TF; p. 2.

34 Michel Houellebecq, *The Map and the Territory*, trans. Gavin Bowd (London: Heinemann, 2011), hereafter cited in the text as MT; p. 81, 113.

35 Houellebecq and Bernard Henri-Lévy, *Public Enemies*, trans. Frank Wynne and Miriam Frendo (London: Atlantic, 2011), hereafter cited in the text as PE; p. 172.

36 Friends and colleagues, in conversation.

37 Houellebecq, *H.P. Lovecraft: Against the World, Against Life*, trans. Dorna Khazeni, introd. Stephen King (London: Gollancz, 2008), hereafter cited in the text as HPL; p. 116.

38 Theodor Adorno, *Minima Moralia: Reflections from Damaged Life*, trans. E. F. N. Jephcott (New York: Verso, 1997), p. 63.

39 Pierre Bourdieu, interview with Günter Grass, https://www.youtube.com/watch?v=SZNt1-Ncojs (accessed 7 November 2014).

40 Houellebecq, *Whatever*, trans. Paul Hammond, introd. Toby Litt (London: Serpent's Tail, 2011), hereafter cited in the text as W; p. 46.

41 Houellebecq, *The Possibility of an Island*, trans. Gavin Bowd (London: Phoenix, 2006), hereafter cited in the text as TPI; p. 133.

42 See in particular Robert J. Schiller, *Finance and the Good Society* (Princeton: Princeton University Press, 2012); and John Kenneth Galbraith, *The Good Society: The Humane Agenda* (New York: Houghton Mifflin, 1996); also some of the work of Anthony Giddens.

43 Jon Savage, *England's Dreaming: Sex Pistols and Punk Rock* (London: Faber and Faber, 1991), p. 195.

44 See http://www.azlyrics.com/lyrics/sexpistols/anarchyintheuk.html (accessed 7 November 2014). I quote all punk and rap lyrics from the excellent *azlyrics* archive.

45 Quoted John Robb, *Punk Rock: An Oral History*, ed. Oliver Craske, foreword Michael Bracewell (London: Ebury Press, 2006), p. 163.

46 Quoted ibid., p. 246.

47 Savage, *England's Dreaming*, p. 114.

48 Quoted Robb, *Punk Rock*, p. xi.

49 Ibid., p. 78.

50   Quoted Savage, *England's Dreaming*, p. 377.

51   One obvious example would be the account of punk in that classic point of reference, Dick Hebdige's *Subculture: The Meaning of Style* (London: Routledge, 1979).

52   Tricia Rose, *Black Noise: Rap Music and Black Culture in Contemporary America* (Middletown, CT: Wesleyan University Press, 1994), pp. xvi, 154 and passim.

53   Cheryl L. Keyes, *Rap Music and Street Consciousness* (Urbana and Chicago: University of Illinois Press, 2004), p. 161.

54   Cornel West, *Race Matters* (New York: Vintage, 1994), pp. 22–5.

55   Rose, *Black Noise*, pp. 9–10 and passim.

56   See Carolyn Cooper, *Noises in the Blood: Orality, Gender and the 'Vulgar' Body of Jamaican Culture* (Durham: Duke University Press, 1995), p. 143.

57   Keyes, *Rap Music*, p. 90.

58   Thomas Hobbes, *Leviathan: Of the Matter, Forme and Power of a Commonwealth Ecclesiasticall and Civil*, ed. Michael Oakeshott, introd. Richard S. Peters (New York: Collier, 1978), p. 255.

59   Arthur Schopenhauer, *The World as Will and Representation*, trans. E. F. J. Payne (2 vols, New York: Dover, 1969), vol. 1, p. 147.

60   Jean-Jacques Rousseau, *Emile ou de l'éducation*, *Œuvres complètes*, vol. IV, ed. Bernard Gagnebin and Marcel Raymond, with the collaboration of Pierre Burgelin, Henri Gouhier, John S. Spink, Roger de Vilmorin and Charles Wirz (Paris: Gallimard, 1969), p. 190.

61   Ivy Compton-Burnett, *Mother and Son* (London: Gollancz, 1955), p. 205.

62   W. G. Sebald, *After Nature*, trans. Michael Hamburger (London: Penguin, 2004), p. 118.

63   Richard Rorty, *Contingency, Irony and Solidarity* (Cambridge: Cambridge University Press, 1989), p. 192; *Philosophy and the Mirror of Nature* (Oxford: Blackwell, 1980), p. 351.

64   Gerard Manley Hopkins, *Major Works*, ed. Catherine Phillips (Oxford: World's Classics, 2009), p. 167.

65   Quoted Herbrechter, *Posthumanism*, p. 29.

66   See for instance http://www.bbc.co.uk/news/business-22002530 (accessed 7 November 2014), for details.

67   Kojin Karatani, *The Structure of World History: From Modes of Production to Modes of Exchange*, trans. Michael K. Bourdaghs (Durham and London: Duke University Press, 2014), pp. 297–8, 307.

68   See Frank Kermode, *The Sense of an Ending: Studies in the Theory of Fiction* (Oxford: Oxford University Press, 1967).

69 Karl Wilhelm Goettling, *Gesammelte Abhandlung aus dem Classischen Alterthume* (Munich: Friedrich Bruckmann, 1863), p. 251. Goettling's term is actually 'proletariat', but 'people' is what he means: the real people, not their ideal reconstruction.

70 Kilminster died on 28 December 2015. The character of the tributes that have poured out since has been intriguing.

INDEX